Slap Shot Original
The Man, the Foil, and the Legend

Dave Hanson
with Ross Bernstein

TRIUMPH
B O O K S

This book is available in quantity at special discounts for your group or organization. For further information, contact:

Triumph Books LLC
814 North Franklin Street
Chicago, Illinois 60610
(312) 337-0747
www.triumphbooks.com

Printed in U.S.A.
ISBN: 978-1-60078-875-8
Design by Sue Knopf
Photos courtesy Dave Hanson unless otherwise indicated

Contents

This book is dedicated to some very exceptional people in my life, four of whom I miss dearly every day: my mom, whose precious love always made me feel special; my brother, whose smile and dimples will never fade from memory; and Gram and Pap, who were two incredible blessings in my life.

To my wife Sue, who has endured, supported, challenged, guided, and loved me during our roller-coaster life together. To my beautiful children, Erin, Sarah, and Christian, who are evidence that God's miracles still happen on earth.

To my dad and sisters, Bud, Joni, and Joyce, who are more precious to me than they'll ever know.

To my Lord Jesus Christ, who has provided me with a guardian angel that continues to work overtime.

To God, who has truly blessed me.

Preface

I T ALL STARTED HARMLESSLY ENOUGH BACK IN 2006 WHEN I called up Dave "Killer" Hanson out of the blue to introduce myself and tell him that I wanted to interview him for a new book I was writing about the honor code in professional hockey. Being a hockey player from Minnesota, I had known of Dave and been a huge fan of the movie *Slap Shot*. In these parts, the Hanson Brothers are like hockey royalty. I knew that Dave had a reputation for being a tough-as-nails warrior who had fought many battles on the ice over the years. I wanted to talk to him about *The Code,* and to get his thoughts on everything from good old-fashioned fisticuffs to the art of intimidation to his take on the legacy of the greatest sports movie ever made. What I found was that in addition to being incredibly poignant, thoughtful, and insightful, this man was also extremely funny and down to earth.

I was fascinated to learn about his adventures while navigating through the murky underbelly of hockey's minor leagues. I was enthralled to hear about how he was able to rack up more than 2,000 career penalty minutes, most of them with his bare knuckles. And I was left wide-eyed and aching from listening to all of his hilarious stories. I wanted to know more. There was the one about the time he actually tore the toupee off the great Bobby Hull during the middle of a fracas; and there was another one about the time his old teammate in Birmingham, Frankie "Never" Beaton, came flying out of the locker room buck naked to take part in an all-out melee up in Winnipeg. As the author of more than 40 sports books, trust me when I tell you—you just can't make this stuff up.

Dave called me several months later to tell me that he really enjoyed my book and that he appreciated the fact that I had written about his role as an enforcer in an honorable light. He was grateful that I didn't just refer to him as a goon, and that I talked at great length about the respect guys like him had for this great game. He liked how I was able to convey the message that without players like Dave Hanson doing the dirty work, there probably wouldn't be players like Wayne Gretzky or Sydney Crosby dishing out picture-perfect passes and scoring breathtaking goals. He was glad that I was celebrating the virtues of honor, courage, and respect—the cornerstones behind every heavyweight enforcer—and spoke of the sacrifices that those players made for their teammates.

From those humble beginnings that afternoon, Dave and I really hit it off, and today I am proud to call him my friend. From there we immediately began discussing how I could help him write his life story. That is the genesis of this incredible saga. I immediately called my publisher in Chicago and pitched them the idea. They liked it, but they wanted to hear more. I asked them if they were aware of the fact that *Slap Shot* was actually the number two rented video of all time, behind only *Animal House* and just ahead of *Caddyshack*? They had no idea. I then explained to them how the cultlike popularity of the movie, with all of its classic one-liners, was legendary within hockey circles. I even told them that they would be hard-pressed to find a men's league across North America where there wasn't at least one team donning "Charlestown Chiefs" jerseys and talking about "Puttin' on the foil" and about how the "F*cking machine took my quarter!" Close, but they still wanted a little more.

So I enlightened them about how an obscure comedy made more than three decades ago starring Paul Newman, which was based on the hilarious and outrageous real-life antics of a tough-as-hell minor league hockey team in Johnstown, Pennsylvania, called the Jets was able to achieve "classic" status thanks to Dave Hanson and the notorious Carlson brothers. The parody focuses on a fictitious "Federal League" team called the "Charlestown Chiefs," a perennial loser due to be folded at season's end because of the mill closing in town. In a last-ditch desperation move to win the championship, the team's veteran player-coach Reggie Dunlop (played by Newman), goes out on a limb and acquires the Hanson Brothers, happy-go-lucky bespectacled goons played by Dave Hanson and Jeff and Steve Carlson, who beat the hell out of anything and everything in their path. Their overly aggressive and homicidal style of play inspires their team-mates and is eaten up by the fans, who come out in droves to see them in action. They, of course, go on to terrorize the league and win the title, providing an absolutely hilarious and satirical look at what professional hockey was really like back in the early '70s. I explained to them how the movie was much deeper than just cheap laughs, though, and about how it was really a case of art imitating life. They were sold.

Welcome to *Slap Shot Original,* a book that aims to both entertain and enlighten you. In it, Dave Hanson provides an amazing firsthand look as to what really went on behind the scenes of this iconic movie and shares much of that wisdom with us. He also takes us on a journey from the frozen ponds of St. Paul to the University of Minnesota to just about everywhere in between on his quest to make it in the National Hockey League. Like Doc Moonlight Graham of *Field of Dreams* lore, who magically gets his wish granted to play in one professional baseball game, so too Dave briefly makes it to the "show," where he scores one career NHL goal. This amazing odyssey of Dave chasing his dream across North America is worth the price of admission. The punches, politics, and partying along the way are never ending and far reaching. It is not just a funny book about hockey, though. It is much deeper than that. Dave shares his most intimate and vulnerable life experiences with us and brings us along for the ride. It is a story of inspiration and hope as well as vulgarity and hilarity. Once you get to know the real Dave, however, and get past his gruff and stitched-up exterior, you will find a teddy bear of a father and husband who truly loves his family. That, more than anything, will be his lasting legacy. Cheers!

—*Ross Bernstein*

Acknowledgments

If I were to list all of the people I'd like to recognize for giving me a story to tell and helping me with its telling, it would take an entire chapter of its own. Since I can't do that, I'll acknowledge a few of the many with thanks for helping to make this book possible.

To my brothers Steve and Jeff Carlson who continue to give me side-splitting laughs and an enjoyable way to escape the daily grind by putting on the foil and the glasses for our adoring fans.

To my fellow *loogan* friend Paul Newman for that fateful knock on my apartment door in 1976 and for his willingness to write my book's foreword before an unfortunate setback prevented him from sharing his thoughts with us.

To Patti Jackson, our Universal champion who continues to believe and fight for our cause.

To Bob Costas and Gordie Howe for their friendship and awesome forewords.

To Ross Bernstein who first interviewed me for his book *The Code* and through casual conversation felt that I might have a story of interest to tell.

To Mitch Rogatz and Tom Bast of Triumph Books who took a leap into the unknown by agreeing to publish it.

I'd also like to extend my sincere appreciation to Matt Polk, Chuck Mamula, and sports editor Chip Minemyer of the

Johnstown Tribune-Democrat newspaper as well Brody Wheeler for providing some unique and cool photos.

Plus, to my buddies Charlie "Chaz" Hallman, Doug "Wooger" Woog, Paul "Homer" Holmgren, Brian "Burkie" Burke, Coach McDonough, Jerry "Killer" Houser, Allan "F*cking Chrysler Plant Here I Come" Nichols, Paul "Dr. Hook" D'Amato, Yvon "The Hair In The Place Make Me Sick" Barrette, Guido "Pretty Boy" Tenesi, John "Broph" Brophy, Glen "Cy" Sonmor, Frank "Beater" Beaton, Jack "Big Bird" Carlson, Jim "One-Punch" Boo, Roy Mlakar, Gilles Leger, Rob "Rammer" Ramage, Barry "Bubba" Melrose, Paul "Stewie" Stewart, Ron "Doc" Docken, Will "Woody" Espey, and John "Bud" Hanson for taking the time to express their thoughts of our treasured time together.

This has been an incredible journey for me and I truly appreciate everyone that I've had a chance to share it with.

Foreword

By Bob Costas

ON THE SURFACE, DAVE HANSON AND I MAY APPEAR TO HAVE little in common. Ah, but that impression turns out to be false. Here's what Dave and I share: a personal history in the "you had to be there to believe it" world of minor league hockey. In fact, we were part of the same league. The old (and legendary) Eastern Hockey League, renamed the North American Hockey League, where in the early '70s I broadcast the games of the Syracuse Blazers. Soon after, Dave skated for the archrival Johnstown Jets. Dozens of players whose exploits and antics fill these pages skated under my gaze as I fired off play-by-play on WSYR in Syracuse. At thirty dollars a game (and five dollars a day meal money on the road), I thought I'd made it big. And if big laughs, great memories, and lasting friendships are the measure, then I had.

So when *Slap Shot* was released, I was among those who knew firsthand that this portrait of hockey life in hard-scrabble minor league outposts wasn't all that exaggerated. I mean, I knew Ogie Ogelthorpe, it's just that his real name was (and is) Bill Goldthorpe. Goldie skated for the Blazers. I assume he did so because league rules stated you had to skate in order to fight. Goldie and I are friends now. Then, not so much.

Ned Dowd, Reg Krezanski, Blake Ball (*Slap Shot*'s Gilmore Tuttle), Gary Sittler, Rod Bloomfield—I knew 'em all. Plus Ron Ingram, Jamie Kennedy, Ted Ouimet, Claude Charte, Carlo

Ugolini, John Brophy, Herman Karp, Nick (the king) Fotiu, and others too numerous to mention, but no less memorable.

With that rich tableau to draw upon (and Paul Newman as its star) *Slap Shot* became a hit. And soon enough, a cult classic, which it remains today. As a result, the Hanson Brothers got a second hockey life. They took their show on the road and they're still out there—popping up in puck venues large and small. Beloved heroes of hockey hijinks from Montreal to Medicine Hat, from Pittsburgh to Podunk. It's been a long stretch of ice time, and between shifts Dave Hanson has managed to produce a loving and laugh-filled remembrance. Pretty good, eh? And if you can't decipher it all, I'll tell you the same thing I told Goldie Goldthorpe that day on the Blazer bus as he ripped my copy of the *New York Times* to shreds: "Don't be jealous, I'll teach you to read." Although, come to think of it, if you made it this far, you can read! And now, as Dave takes over, read on and enjoy.

—*Bob Costas*

Foreword

By Gordie Howe

I HAVE ALWAYS ENJOYED MY TIME WITH DAVE OVER THE YEARS. HE is a good man and a man of character. As a player, Dave was honest and he was tough. He always stood up for what he believed in and I always respected that about him. Players knew that if they tried to disrespect him or his teammates, he was going to be there to hold them accountable for their actions. Opposing players really had to keep their heads up when Dave was out there; he made them play the game honest. I really appreciated guys like Dave because they were in the trenches doing the dirty work so that their teammates could score goals. This is a team game and you won't get very far without guys like Dave, protecting your top players and going into the corners. The thing I admired most about Dave, though, was how he always had a smile on his face when the game got rough. Dave has a real passion for the game and I am happy that he is able to celebrate that passion in his new book.

As for the movie, I really enjoyed it. It was a lot of fun and it always brings back great memories of what hockey was like back in the '70s. What people don't realize about it, though, is just how much truth was in it. That was how hockey used to be in those days and the movie captured the spirit of that very well. Sure, it was a parody, a comedy, but there were many things about it that were dead-on. The language, the bus trips, the brawls, it was all a part of the game. I know it is hard for non-hockey fans to understand sometimes just how we could get into fights with one another out on the ice and then go out and have a beer together afterward. Those things on the ice weren't personal, just business. I took great pride in defending myself as well as my teammates, no matter the cost. If that meant spilling some blood, then so be it. This is a tough game played by tough men and nobody wanted to be disrespected out there.

You know, I can't help but think about my relationship with my two sons, Mark and Marty, in the same way that the Hanson Brothers took care of each other. In the movie you got a sense of just what those guys would do for each other, to protect one another. I was the same way with my sons. We were fortunate enough to play together for several seasons as teammates and it was one of the most enjoyable times in my career. I brought those two into the world and was sure not going to let anybody take liberties with them. If an opposing player wanted to touch them, then I was going to touch him. That's the way it is in hockey and I believe that there is a lot of honor in that. My fatherly instinct might have gotten the best of me at times, but those were some good times nonetheless.

Beyond that, I can't say enough good things about all of the wonderful charity work that the Hanson Brothers do and have done over the years. They are always giving back to the communities that have embraced them and that is just marvelous. That is what it is all about, giving back to causes and to kids, to teach them about this great game. It is nice to see that they have been able to stay in the game, too, after all of these years, and still bring joy to people's lives. When they perform and do their shows, it is just pure fun. I have been to many signings and events with them over the years and they are always the most popular figures there. And yes, I did appreciate and enjoy their "elbow tribute" to me in *Slap Shot Part II*. The Hanson Brothers really are a big part of our hockey history, and that is wonderful to see.

— *Gordie Howe*

Introduction

By Jeff and Steve Carlson

IN THE FALL OF 1973, WE LEFT MOM'S HOME COOKING IN Virginia, Minnesota, to go to the Twin Cities to pursue our dreams. Instead of getting stuck mining taconite on the Iron Range like many of the locals did once they got out of high school, we drove to St. Paul to attend one of the open tryouts the WHA Minnesota Fighting Saints were having. Little did we know that our desire to play together as a line would someday be the base for creating the most famous brother trio in hockey lore.

While Steve was still in high school, the Flin Flon Bombers of the Western Canadian Hockey League drafted him. He turned them down, though, and decided to stay with his two big brothers Jack and Jeff so that we could try our hands at making pro. We thought that by going to the Saints tryouts we would have the best chance of staying together and getting paid to play, even though our primary objective was just to keep playing. At our first tryout camp, a bystander who attended every session told us that we had about 50 shifts and scored 30 goals. Steve played center between Jeff at right wing and Jack at left wing. We wore our black-rimmed glasses, which raised a few eyebrows when we took the ice. After playing pretty well during the tryouts, the Saint's general manager Glen Sonmor and coach Harry Neale said they were impressed, but we needed more experience.

We went to Waterloo, Iowa, to try out for the Blackhawks who were a semipro team in the United States Hockey League.

We thought we had a real good tryout there also, but they only wanted to sign Steve, not all three of us. So, we decided to leave Waterloo and try our luck on the Upper Peninsula of Michigan with the Marquette Iron Rangers. We thought with a name like that and where we were from, the Iron Range, that we would have some good luck. We packed all of our stinky hockey gear and our dirty underwear and drove north. Jeff and Jack banged and fought while assisting Steve in putting the puck in the net. When it was over, Coach Oakie Brumm said, "Boys, welcome to the team." We were thrilled to sign our first pro contract and have a place to play. We were paid $35 a game, and if we won we would get an extra $10 per goal and $5 per assist.

Never in our wildest dreams did we imagine that what we were doing would morph into legendary status and be instrumental in creating one of the most popular sports movies of all time. We had some small-town fame in Virginia from our high school sports, but we never imagined that we would be the inspiration for some of the most quoted, recognized, and enjoyed characters in cinematic history. To think that it all started when our coach put a bounty on the head of one of the Green Bay Bobcats' defensemen. Coach Brumm said he would give $50 to the first guy who dropped Ernie Dupont and Jack beat Jeff to the punch to collect the bounty. That's where it started and it continued in Johnstown, Pennsylvania, after we met our teammate, Dave "Killer" Hanson.

We remember Johnny Mitchell, the Johnstown Jets GM, driving us from Niagara Falls, Ontario, to Johnstown, Pennsylvania. We had no idea where we were going or what we were about to get ourselves into, but during the ride with Mitch, we listened like three little schoolboys and giggled every time he started a new sentence. He would say, "Son..." We even passed the time by betting on how many times he'd say "Son," but we lost track by the time we got there. What a character he was.

Before Jack got called up to Minnesota during our first season with the Jets, we and Dave established ourselves as a wrecking crew in the NAHL and played a brand of hockey that Commissioner Jack Timmins had hoped to be rid of when he changed the name of the league from the Eastern Hockey

League to the North American Hockey League. We not only caused havoc throughout the league, we showed the commissioner some things that we're sure he thought could only be possible in a Hollywood movie. We all grew up in Minnesota and even though Dave was from the "Cities" (Twin Cities), we had a lot in common with him. We loved to play hockey, loved to fight, and loved to party. Well, Steve liked to play hockey and party, while the rest of us fought. Our living together, riding the bus together, hanging out together, and playing hockey together made us, at times, almost look and act like we could've all been related.

By the time the making of *Slap Shot* rolled around and Jack was unable to be our brother in the Hanson Brothers role (he had been called up to the WHA), Dave was the only logical and worthy choice to take his place. At first we were a bit concerned that he was too ugly and too much of a cement–head to be cast as our brother, but once he put the glasses on, he was perfect. Also, by this time we had spent two full hockey seasons together and shared more wacky things than most brothers could or should experience in a lifetime. He may not have been a brother in blood, but he certainly was a brother in arms, spirit, and insanity.

Shooting *Slap Shot* was fun, but oftentimes it was very boring while waiting for something to happen. To bide the time we drank, sang, pulled pranks, and made many new friends. Paul Newman, Strother Martin, and George Roy Hill were some of the exceptional ones, but most of the other actors and many of the behind-the-scenes crew became such good pals that it made the filming a wonderful experience. After the movie was wrapped up, we all went our separate ways in our hockey careers. We would occasionally cross paths out on the ice rink or during the summer, but we always stayed in touch. As for the movie, we really never knew the magnitude of its popularity and of the Hanson Brothers until we were all retired from playing. Jeff was working as an electrician in Muskegon, Dave was the general manager of a minor league hockey team in upstate New York, and Steve was the head coach of a team in the south when he pulled us all together for an impromptu appearance at one of his games. We sold out the hockey arena and got swamped by autograph seekers. Who knew?

Since then, the Hanson Brothers have appeared together to play in countless charity hockey games, sign autographs, take photos, shoot commercials, do interviews, make more movies—*Slap Shot II* and *III*—and shake the hands of millions of fans from around the world. At the same time we've proudly contributed to raising millions of dollars for charitable causes. Besides getting into the rare sibling squabble over who gets to sit in the front or who has to sit in the middle, one of the many benefits we've reaped over the years has been putting smiles on hundreds of thousands, if not millions, of people we've met. Plus, the greatest spinoff of all is that we've been able to grow in our brotherhood and love for each other...but don't tell Dave.

We consider Dave a true brother, even though we tell everyone that he's our cousin. We know that he would give the shirt off his back for us if either one of us needed it. We would do the same for him, but he can keep his underwear no matter how badly we might need a pair. To share so much of our lives with each other over the years because of the Hanson Brothers has been great. The day we retire from going on the road with our race car set to spread the Hanson Brothers' joy will be a sad day in many ways. The least of which will be not being able to get together and share stories of the Carlson Brothers and Killer Hanson. But until that time comes, we will keep raising an elbow together in unison and giving our battle cry, *"Gordie!"*

— Jeff and Steve Carlson

Chapter I

Growing Up Tough

O N MAY 7, 1953, MARILYN "PEACHES" PATRAW MARRIED JOHN "Bud" Hanson in Beach Haven, New Jersey. On April 12, 1954, Seaman First Class Hanson was stationed with a US Naval Reserve Fleet in Portsmouth, Virginia, while his pregnant wife was staying with her mother, Diamond Lil, and her stepfather, Dewey Ogren, at their single-story home, the Staples Lake Tavern in Barron County, Wisconsin. Very early on a Monday morning, Marilyn woke her mom and Dewey to announce that it was time to go to the hospital. Everyone, including the family dog, Penny, piled into the old blue Studebaker that Dewey had from his days on the Ogren family farm. Together they all made the 11-mile dirt-road trip to Island City, also known as Cumberland. The town's hospital was a simple two-story clapboard house with a front screen porch that sat on the shore of the backwaters of Beaver Dam Lake.

Marilyn gave birth at 7:47 AM that day, and around 12:00 PM Bud received a call while aboard the USS *Xanthus*, an auxiliary repair ship, and was told that he was a proud papa of a seven-pound baby boy. Never in their wildest dreams did these new parents think that this little bundle of joy would grow up to earn the nickname "Killer" or voluntarily wear black-rimmed coke-bottle glasses, long hair, and tinfoil on his knuckles; or be accused by his player-coach of being too dumb to play with himself; or be referred to by a play-by-play radio announcer as the

1

"Terror of the Federal League." It never crossed their minds that "Little Davy Crockett" would play a small role in a worldwide movie and be a big reason why a movie—labeled as the "Best Guy Movie of All Time" (*Maxim* magazine) and one of the "Top 10 Best Sports Movies of All Time" (*Sports Illustrated*)—would become a classic, or that he would constantly be written about, promoted in local, regional, national, and worldwide publications, featured in all different fashions in the electronic media, and requested by hundreds of thousands of people to appear with his "brothers." From starring in national and international television and radio commercials to the front page of the *Wall Street Journal* and featured on the cover of *Sports Illustrated* magazine, this little curly "towheaded boy," who came from humble beginnings, has etched out a small piece of immortality.

• • •

Shortly after I was born, my dad returned from his second tour of duty as a naval officer. He had grown up in Cumberland and left as a teenager to enlist in the US Navy in 1949, serving on the USS *Pawcatuck* in Norfolk, Virginia, and was released in 1950. He got recalled in 1952 during the Korean War, and while he was in the service, he married the former Rutabaga Queen of Cumberland's annual Rutabaga Fest.

When my dad was honorably discharged for a second time, he took Mom and me from Wisconsin to Troutdale, Oregon, where we lived in an old rented house just down the hill from his mom and stepdad, Ruth and Carl Hayes. He took a job working for a freightliner trucking company, while mom stayed home to take care of our pet dog, Lassie, and me. While living there, my brother Durk was born in a Portland hospital (he would be called Baby Durk by almost everyone until he reached the age of 14). Shortly after Durk was born, we packed up the 1955 Pontiac and moved to Redondo Beach, California, where Dad worked as a bartender in a tavern called Swede's Bar, which my mom's biological father and his wife, Harold and Eileen Patraw, owned. We stayed long enough for Durk to be baptized and then we headed back to the Midwest again. There, we stayed at the Staples Lake Tavern with Grandma Lil and Grandpa Dewey for a few months until Dad got a job at GTC (General Trading Company) on Prior Avenue in St. Paul, Minnesota. He worked as a foreman at this auto-parts company from 1957 to around 1981, when he left to work a small bar that he and Mom bought in Comstock, Wisconsin.

When we moved to St. Paul from Wisconsin, we rented a duplex on St. Anthony Street, which was near Merriam Park. There, I would have my first introduction to ice skating. We stayed on St. Anthony Street for about two years, just long enough for my two sisters, Joni and Joyce, to be born in the new Cumberland hospital. When Mom was pregnant with each girl, she'd take Durk and me to stay in a little house overlooking Staples Lake. It was a very simple house with no indoor plumbing and one bedroom. The bathroom was an outhouse (crapper) up in the woods behind the house, and a dirt road was our front yard, separating the house from the lake. This house was a short walk from the bar and next to family friends. Mom would move back to Staples Lake in order to get some extra help in taking care of her boys and herself during the pregnancies.

Our house on St. Anthony Street was adjacent to the railroad tracks and near an area called Midway, which was considered a tough inner-city section of St. Paul. The Chapmans, a family of six, lived upstairs and we lived downstairs. I remember drinking powdered milk that Mom mixed up and eating raw green beans I plucked from the vine that grew naturally along the fence between our dirt backyard and the alley. I remember sleeping in bunk beds with my little brother Durk on the bottom bunk and me on the top. One time, during the middle of the night while we were sleeping, the top bunk bed broke and I fell straight down—mattress, pillow, and all—landing directly on top of Durk. He never moved; I thought I killed him. He just slept right through it, and although I was screaming, he never opened an eye or twitched a limb. That was Durk, tough and quiet. The next morning, he woke up without a bruise on his body and like nothing had happened.

My brother and I spent a lot of time together as young kids. He seemed to always be on the receiving end of many unfortunate things that his big brother would do to him. Baby Durk was the cutest little boy on earth. He had dark hair and dark eyes, with the smile of the Cheshire Cat, the plump cheeks of the Coca-Cola Santa Claus, and dimples that would rival little Shirley Temple's. He also had this hole in his chest. Well, it really wasn't a hole, but more like an indentation. We all acted like it was a hole because that sounded cooler than just calling it a dent. Whenever I wanted to show anyone, I'd say, "Hey, you want to see the hole in Durk's chest?" I made money by charging people to watch Durk pop his belly out and stack quarters on top of it and in the hole. I really thought it was quite an amazing act at the time. I was so impressed by Durk's ability that one time, as we were walking past the freak shows at the Minnesota State Fair, I suggested to my mom and dad that they put Durk in the show so we could make some extra money. They told me to be quiet and eat my corn dog.

His chest and stomach were the target for some childish abuse I would give him. We spent many a summer at Staples Lake and freely ran around like little barefooted orphans, mostly getting into harmless mischief. Well, at least harmless for me. We would go out on the lake in the rowboat, hunt down mud turtles sitting on the reeds, catch them, and bring them back to shore to play with. One time, I was holding a turtle in front of Durk's chest, showing him and everyone how friendly he was, when suddenly it stuck its head out, clamped onto the skin of Durk's chest, and wouldn't let go. Durk was screaming and running around with this turtle's mouth locked onto him while I was running next to him, holding the turtle and trying not to pull it away from Durk's chest in fear of ripping his skin off. We eventually yanked it off, but Durk's bloody turtle wound did not go over well with Grandma and Grandpa. I caught hell for that one.

Once Baby Durk and I were riding in the front seat of a car with our Uncle David driving. My Uncle Dave pretended to push the cigarette lighter in and then stick it on my stomach, acting like he was going to burn me. The lighter was never hot, so I never got burned, but we sure thought it was funny. When Uncle Dave stopped at the gas station, I thought I would pull the same funny stunt on Durk. I pushed the lighter in, pulled it out, and stuck it right onto Durk's little potbelly. The bright red-hot lighter burned him. It made a cigarette-lighter-coil scar on his tummy that he had for the rest of his life.

This was not the last that his little body would take from me, though. Another time we were playing Cowboys and Indians in the basement of our house on Sydney Street in St. Paul. He was the Cowboy and I was the Indian. He had his cowboy hat on with two shiny six-shooters strapped on his hips. I had my little feathered Indian headdress and moccasins on, and I had a bow and arrow. As I ran around the big furnace screaming my war cry, he started yelling, "Bang-bang!" I pulled my bow and let my arrow fly. It nailed him right in the chest. The arrow caused a little bloody mark that turned into another scar to add to the turtle and lighter scars. I guess I shouldn't have removed the sissy rubber suction cup from the end of my arrow.

We were best friends as little kids, playing together all summer long at Staples Lake. We loved the "run-up tree" in the woods of the old Butrick's farm; rolling down the hill by Chain Lake; discus throwing of dried cow pies in the pasture; following the cows up to the barn as they walked in single file to get fed and milked; and looking for agate rocks on the dirt roads. We also got into some mischief, like the time we lit the pack of Black Cat firecrackers in old Andy Anderson's back pocket while he was sleeping in the front lawn chair.

We loved to ride along with Grandpa Dewey in his old Studebaker on the country dirt roads. Whenever Grandpa saw a snapping turtle slowly crossing the road, he'd stop the car, open the trunk, get an old ax handle out, and stick it in front of the turtle's mouth. The turtle would snap onto the handle, and Grandpa would pick the turtle up by the tail, throw it into the trunk, and drive home. Once we got back, he'd take the turtle out back and put him on a tree stump. He would tell me to grab the turtle's tail with both hands while he and Durk grabbed each end of the ax handle. They would both then pull on the ax handle while I was holding on to the tail. The turtle would not let go of the ax handle so his neck would get stretched out over the tree stump. At point Grandpa would chop the turtle's head off with the ax. Later, Grandpa would cut off the shell and carve up the turtle meat for Grandma to fry. We'd then eat fried snapping turtle for dinner and from what I can remember, it tasted like chicken.

Durk and I always laughed about an incident that happened one summer up at the lake. When it was time to move an outhouse to a freshly dug hole, it became a bit of a community event. It took a group of people to lift the wood outhouse off the old hole and carry it to the new hole. Then everyone would go back to the old hole to fill it up and cover it with the dirt from the new hole. Well, one summer day we started the project of moving our neighbor Bill Schlitsky's outhouse. As the group was lifting the shed and starting to move it away from the old hole, Bill slipped, lost his footing, and fell head over heels into the old, stinky, full-of-crap hole. We all dropped the outhouse, threw him a rope, and pulled him out. I don't think anyone wanted to reach in to help him out for fear of being pulled in or just touching his yucky hands. He was gurgling and gagging while we laughed hysterically. Once he got out of the hole, he sprinted down the hill and jumped into the lake. It was one of the funniest and grossest things we ever saw. Bill, who did not know how to swim, didn't care. He dove into the lake and started scrubbing.

Baby Durk and I had some great times growing up together at Staples Lake—stuff that would give Norman Rockwell endless ideas of things to paint and Samuel Clemens endless stories of stuff to write.

• • •

My first recollection of putting on ice skates was when my dad took me to Merriam Park, a local neighborhood playground close to our house on St. Anthony Street. One winter day, my dad took me over to the park and into the little trailer that was set on the side of the pond as a warming hut for the skaters. Inside it were benches to sit on and if you needed skates there was a box full of used mismatched skates of all sizes, brands, and conditions to select from. Dad found two skates that looked like they would fit, put them on me, helped me through the snowbank that surrounded the ice rink, and said, "Have fun, son, I'll be back in a couple of hours." For the next couple of hours I looked like Bambi on ice, but I had fun. From that point on, I was hooked on skating and kept having dad bring me back all winter long.

We eventually moved to a bigger house in St. Paul on the corner of LaFond and Fairview Avenues that was in a nicer neighborhood, but still not too far from the Midway or from Merriam Park. It was another duplex that was closer to my dad's work and within walking distance of the elementary school, where I went to kindergarten and first grade with Mrs. Magilicuddy as my teacher. This is also where I experienced my first fight—well, sort of.

There was a bully in our kindergarten class that picked on everyone. One day as we got out of school, the bully started picking on me. Out of fear for my life, I punched her in the stomach, ran home as fast as I could, and hid under my bed. I was sure that she would chase me down or the police would come to take me to jail. To my surprise, there never was a rock crashing through my bedroom window or sirens howling down the street. I learned a very valuable lesson later that day when my dad got home from work. He coaxed me out from my room and I spilled my guts to him about what I did. My dad calmly told me the rules about protecting myself and, more important, he drove home to me the message that only cowards hit girls. The next day when I went to school, I apologized to the girl and from that day forward I vowed to never hit a girl again and proudly never have.

While we lived on LaFond Avenue, I went to Merriam Park to ice skate almost every day. I still had to use the skates from the used skate box in the warming hut and often they were not the same skates or matching sizes. It wasn't until around second grade that I would finally pick up a hockey stick and start to try to play hockey. That was when we moved across town to the West Side of St. Paul.

I remember the day we moved into our little house on 789 Ohio Street, a small two-story house that we got to live in by ourselves. Here I made friends who introduced me to Baker

Playground, where I would spend hours playing hockey, football, and baseball.

Baker Playground had an old two-story brownstone building, where the top level was a small hardwood floor gymnasium that was used for teeny-bop dances and a variety of other neighborhood activities. Around the seventh grade I played in a neighborhood band called "Little Caesar and the Romans" and we played at a couple of the small dances at Baker. Our band consisted of Tom Kirk on lead guitar, Rich Munoz on organ, Lindsay Baptist on drums, Peter Estrada as our lead singer, and me playing bass on a six-string guitar. I think we knew five songs. In the summertime the bottom floor had ping-pong tables and in the winter it was a warming room for ice skating and sledding. The building was built into the side of a hill. When you came out of the bottom floor you were in the middle of the hill. In order to get to the hockey rink, you had to either walk down a ramp or skate down an ice bank. You had to skate up the ice bank to get back into the building. Skating up and down that hill really helped to develop my skating stride and balance at an early age.

The playground was operated by the City of St. Paul Parks and Recreation Department. The main caretaker at Baker was old Bill Cutty. Bill seemed like he was always on the fields lining, raking, cutting, or standing all by himself on cold winter nights holding a fire hose and flooding the fields to make ice. We seemed to always have lots of snow. Old Bill would have the city plow trucks drive up and down the fields, clearing them off and pushing the snow out to build up snowbanks around the skating rink. Once that was done, he'd spend days flooding the fields to make a huge iced covered area for everyone to skate on.

I can still clearly picture old Bill standing in the middle of the big field in below-zero temperatures wearing this big hooded canvas parka with insulated baggy snow pants, rubber fireman's boots, huge chopper mittens, and frosty steam floating out of his mouth. He always seemed to have icicles hanging from his bushy eyebrows and snot running from his nose. He'd stand there for hours and days, holding onto this long fire hose that was spraying gallons of water over the grounds so the neighborhood kids had a place to skate. I truly believe that if Old Bill hadn't done this year after year, I would not have skated as much as I did and I possibly may not even have played hockey. This enormous skating pond that Bill created winter after winter was always packed with the neighborhood kids. We would play tag, whip, and all kinds of other games that kept us zigzagging around the big rink. Then, when he got the hockey rink built, we played pick-up shinny hockey for hour after hour, nearly every day.

It was incredible how everyone who showed up to play hockey found a way to pick teams and just play with kids of all ages and ability. No one ever seemed to get left out. Getting ready for these daily games, which were usually played after 6:00 PM during the school week and all day on weekends, I would take Mom's Montgomery Wards' catalogs and tape them to my shins with my dad's black electrical tape so I had shin pads for protection from pucks and sticks. I usually wore a pair of blue jeans over the "Monkey Wards" catalogs, so no one would see and laugh at what I had on for shin guards.

I'd walk to the playground wearing a stocking hat on my head and choppers on my hands (leather mittens with wool inserts), while carrying my taped-up used Christian Brothers hockey stick and skates over my shoulders. Unlike Merriam Park, Baker did not have a box of used skates to pull from, so my dad got me my own pair of slightly worn Bobby Hull Black Panther skates. Boy, did I think that was cool. I really put them to use. I would skate at Baker whenever I could and once Old Bill got the hockey rink built and had the lights put up, I'd skate there at night.

Parents never seemed to worry about us being at the playground or walking home after we were done. Unlike parents today, ours did not feel that they had to come along to monitor or get involved in any of the playground recreational activities. They seemed to realize that if we had a problem with other kids, we learned how to handle it between ourselves and usually we did, even if it meant getting into a scuffle. Nowadays, it seems most parents think they have to be involved in everything and don't allow kids to figure it out or work it out among themselves. I think that most problems between kids today are not so much between the kids as much as they are between the parents. Most of the time, I bet if the parents just stayed away and encouraged their kids to work it out themselves, the kids would and everything would be fine for the most part. But now parents stick their noses into everything with the result usually being a bigger mess. Then the domino effect happens: kids don't learn good coping skills and continue to have problems dealing with confrontation or challenges in their daily lives.

Frost-nipped fingers, toes, ears, and noses were frequent occurrences in Minnesota winters for outdoor hockey players. Because we loved to play so much, we would stay out until we couldn't feel our extremities any longer. We'd then go into the warming hut only long enough to thaw out, and then we'd head back out to skate again. Even though winters in Minnesota were long, snowy, and cold, we still enjoyed the four seasons with the traditional three sports played throughout the year: ice hockey was in the winter, baseball in the spring and summer, and football in the fall. I played all three and Baker Playground was the place where I played most of it during my pre–high school years. The majority of it was just pick-up, like shinny hockey or sandlot baseball, but as I got a bit older, like around fifth grade, I started to play on organized teams. Even though I ended up playing more hockey than any other sport, baseball and football were my favorite sports to play during those early years.

Around eighth grade, my friend Rich Munoz's dad convinced a group of us who hung around together at Baker to go to the lower West Side to sign up and try out for a football team at the Neighborhood House. The lower West Side had a large contingency of Mexican families living in its neighborhoods and it was considered a real tough area with a reputation for knives, guns, fights, and bad guys. There was this one man living on the lower West Side who worked at the Neighborhood House and was highly respected by all West Siders; his name was Harry Gaston and he coached the midget football team. He was a former outstanding athlete during his school days at Humboldt High School and his contributions as an adult mentor to the kids in the community were endless. Mr. Munoz was taking us, a group of young Mexican and white boys from the upper West Side, to the lower West Side to learn how to play football, and I believe to toughen us up a bit under the watchful eye of its master.

Mr. Munoz drove us all down in his station wagon and pulled up in front of a tattered-looking yellow house with a dirt lot next to it that had some swings, big rubber tractor tires, and some other tired-looking playground equipment. When we got out of the car, he led us into the house where we all first met Harry. Harry was a stocky-built black man with a big welcoming smile, a vise-grip handshake, a booming voice, and a mouth full of an endless supply of sunflower seeds. After he shook hands with each of us, he issued us our Neighborhood House football uniforms, a pair of worn canvas yellow football pants, a beat-up pair of shoulder pads, and a battered blue helmet with a double facemask bar across the front. From that point on, we practiced on the dirt grounds of the Tot Lot or on the rock-hard grass-patched fields of Belvedere Playground.

Our team was a mixed bag of upper West Siders, like me, Rich Munoz, Tom Kirk, John Stuhlman, Pete Rangel, and Tex Ruiz, along with some lower West Siders, like Jesse Adamez, Immanuel Franco, and Joe Lucio. We were a group of young boys with different backgrounds. Harry, along with his assistant coach Chatto Reyes, worked us hard to pull us together and made us into one terrific football team. Every day we practiced and every weekend we traveled to other playgrounds through-out the city to play opposing football teams. At the end of the season we were the St. Paul City Midget Football Champions. Harry was the big reason for that.

During that season, Harry really helped me to understand the importance of respect, hard work, fair play, and accountability to my teammates, my family, and myself. Harry passed away in 2006, while still living on the West Side and still holding the respect of thousands. His contributions to helping young kids, young adults, and the West Side community as a whole are countless and worthy of endless praise. I am only one of thou-sands who were fortunate and blessed to have Harry Gaston as a coach, a mentor, and a friend.

Chapter 2

Cutting My Teeth
with the Humboldt Indians

AFTER PLAYING LITTLE LEAGUE BASEBALL FOR THE WEST SIDE Tigers, youth hockey for the West Side Merchants, and football for the Neighborhood House, I finally made it to the ninth grade and started to play sports for Humboldt High School. The Humboldt Indians had a great tradition and rich history of competitive sports going back to the late 1800s, and especially excelled in wrestling, baseball, and football. After participating in track and field, wrestling, football, baseball, and hockey during my early years in high school, I settled down to just three sports by my sophomore year: football, hockey, and baseball.

I played for Coach Bob Ryan on the Humboldt junior varsity football team, better known as the B-Squad. During my sophomore year we went undefeated and were co-champions in the St. Paul City Conference with Harding. Harding went undefeated because we never got to play them that year. Most of the guys I played with at the Neighborhood House were members of the Humboldt B-Squad team with me. I was a halfback on offense as well as a linebacker and defensive back on defense. We ran the single wing formation on offense, which was the formation that the great teams of the Green Bay Packers used under the leadership of Coach Vince Lombardi.

After finishing my sophomore year, I graduated to the varsity A-Squad team that was under the rule of Coach Ken Mauer.

Every one of us who moved up from the B-Squad to the varsity was excited about the prospect of playing for Coach Mauer. We really thought we had a chance to win the undisputed City Conference championship under his leadership. We had a tough and determined team, but Harding High School, which went undefeated like we did on the B-Squad the year before, had a school district much larger than the west side. They always had a big, formidable squad, both in size and numbers. Even back to our Neighborhood House football days, the East Side area always seemed to have three times more players on their team than we did. Harding had so many good players that it was uncommon for one of their players to play both offense and defense. At Humboldt, almost every player played both ways plus special teams.

One of the players that Harding had was a human freight train named Ollie Bakken. He was a man among boys, a talented athlete who not only played football and baseball, but also played hockey as a goalie. In football, Ollie went on to play at the University of Minnesota and later got drafted by the NFL's Minnesota Vikings. At Harding, he was a running back who would not try to go around you, but would purposely try to plow right over you. When we played against Harding during my junior year, Ollie would have had a touchdown if he hadn't tried to run through my teammate Rich Munoz. Rich was our quarterback and linebacker and he was as tough as nails, but he stood about 5'9" and weighed maybe a whopping 160 pounds at the time. On this unforgettable play, Ollie broke through the line carrying the football and started to sprint into open territory. Only Rich stood between Ollie and the goal line.

I don't believe Rich had time to think about getting out of the way, nor do I think he would have, had he had time. Rich just stood there like a deer caught in the headlights and waited for Ollie to run into him. Ollie slammed into Rich like a charging longhorn mountain ram, knocking Rich flat on his back. Ollie then stepped on Rich's helmet and tripped over Rich's face. Rich's big head made a saving tackle by preventing Ollie from reaching the goal line. Rich's teammates and I picked him up to help him off the field. When we turned him over to Coach

Mauer on the sidelines, Coach patted Rich on the fanny and gave him a big "Attaboy!" Then he sent him back in the next play and told him to knock down that big fullback again. Rich and I still laugh about how his big melon brought down the great Ollie Bakken.

The Humboldt Indians had a great tradition in sports, but hockey was not really one of them. Humboldt had a hockey team for many years, but the West Side just didn't seem to put together any great teams. It produced a few very good hockey players every once in a while, though, such as Ken Yackel. Ken was a three-sport star athlete at Humboldt in the late 1940s and went on to become a three-sport star at the University of Minnesota as well, earning NCAA All-American honors along the way as a star with the Golden Gopher hockey team. He was also a member of the U.S. Olympic Team that captured a silver medal in 1952. He continued his hockey career by playing pro hockey from 1955 to 1964 and holds the distinction of being one of two American-developed players in the NHL during the 1950s, playing for the Boston Bruins in 1959. I spoke with Ken a few times before he passed away about the benefits of being a multi-sport athlete while growing up. When the West Side built a small community indoor ice arena they named it after him. I later made sure the Hanson Brothers appeared there to help raise money for the West Side Youth Hockey Association.

While hockey was not as successful as some of the other sports at Humboldt, it gave me many fond memories. I never skated on an indoor rink until I was a junior in high school. During my freshman and sophomore years on the B-Squad, every practice and every game was played outside. During my junior and senior years on the varsity, we'd have most of our practices outside and then get to play our games inside. It was truly a test of will and love for hockey to go through what we did to be on the Humboldt hockey team. There are few kids today who would do what we did then to play hockey. We even built our own rink every winter at Michelson Field. The school would put up temporary lights, but the hockey players would have to put up the boards, flood the rink, and maintain the ice throughout the winter.

We had a warming hut that was about 60 yards away from the rink where we put our skates on and stored the fire hose and snow scrapers that we used to build and maintain the rink. We would change into our hockey gear in the locker room at the school, walk about three blocks to Michelson Field, change into our skates in the warming hut, and skate out to the rink on an ice path.

Many times we would be out in the early mornings before school and late in the evenings after school, pulling the hose out of the hut, and flooding the rink to make ice. Then we'd pull the hose back into the hut and roll it up on the big wheel. We'd walk back to the school's locker room, hit the showers, and head home with our hockey bags slung over our shoulders and our hair freezing in the winter air. Once the ice was skateable, we continued to shovel and flood it after most practices to keep it built up and fresh. We used long-handled snow scrapers to shovel the snow off the rink from any snowfalls or snow build-up from our skate shavings. Pushing the snow scraper up and down the ice everyday with skates on was great for conditioning and training for the team. Today, players hire professional power skating coaches to instruct them on how to improve their strides to increase speed, strength, efficiency, and agility. Back in my day, the Humboldt Indians hockey players were getting power-skating practice by pushing snow scrapers up and down the ice, plus pulling a fire hose in and out of a warming hut with our skates on.

During the hockey season, our players' benches were snow-banks built up on the outside of the dasher boards. The snow-banks piled up from throwing snow over the boards when we cleared the ice and they would eventually get higher than the boards. When we changed shifts during the game, the players going off the ice would have to jump over the boards and climb up the snowbanks while the players going on to the ice would slide down the snowbanks on their fannies.

I got good at nailing an opponent just as he was landing on the ice. I'd watch for the kid sliding down the snowbank and just as he was about to land on his skates, I would clock him. There were times when it was so cold that during the games some of the guys on the team would wait in the warming hut until there was a whistle to stop play. Then the players who were on the ice would skate down the ice path to the warming hut and change places with the guys who were waiting in there.

Through it all, our coach, Mr. Ralph McDonough, would always stay outdoors. He was a strict and intimidating disciplinarian at times, but we were in respectful awe of him. He would stay outside as long as any of his players were out there, no matter how cold it was.

Mr. McDonough had a huge influence on my life as an athlete as well as in the development of my character. At the time, next to my parents, there was no one I respected more than Mr. McDonough. I had Mr. McDonough teaching or instructing me in some capacity throughout all four years at Humboldt. He served as my classroom teacher and my hockey, baseball, and football coach. He was full of integrity, care, compassion, and passion. He could and would bark like an army drill sergeant and make you shake in your boots, while at the same time, send a message that he really cared about you and the team.

Once we were playing at the St. Paul Auditorium and we came off the ice after getting spanked by SPA (St. Paul Academy). While we were getting undressed, Mr. McDonough came storming into the room and had the look of steam coming out of his ears. With clenched fists propped on his hips, he stared laser beams at Orville Thumpke. Orville was a large boy who played defense for us and had trouble preventing the SPA players from skating around him uncontested. Mr. McDonough barked at Orville, "You know what fat boy? I had a dream about you last night. I dreamt that you and I were fighting over a Snickers candy bar. You fought like hell, and you know what fat boy? You won!" Orville was petrified, and so were the rest of us, but it was Mr. McDonough's subliminal way of trying to encourage and motivate Orville to lose weight. Unfortunately, I don't think it worked because Orville quit the team shortly after that. But it sure worked for me. I've never had a Snickers bar since then, and I continue to hold so much respect and regard for Mr. McDonough that I still can't bring myself to call him by his first name.

I loved to score goals, but I also loved to hit people. I think that is why I enjoyed football so much. Smash-mouth football, even as a running back, was my style. I ran the ball more like a Larry Czonka than a Gale Sayers, and I was the same way on the ice. I loved slamming the opposition into the boards and nailing guys with open ice body checks.

However, because I liked to do this so much, I ended up spending a lot of time in the penalty box, which meant that my team spent a lot of time playing shorthanded. Mr. McDonough tried to send a message to me once on how my time in the box was affecting our team. In a game against Sibley High School, he sat me on the bench for one entire period while the other team was clobbering us. After the first period, he told me that this is what it was like for our team to play without me because I spent so much time in the penalty box. I got the message and did my best to keep my elbows down, but I didn't have much luck. A sports columnist for the St. Paul *Pioneer Press* newspaper, Charley Hallman, once wrote in his column, "When Dave Hanson, a center for the Humboldt Indians, goes into a corner with an opposing player, it's like venturing into the back alley with 'Murder Incorporated.' Hanson hits like a Peterbilt truck, leaving his opponent splattered like a bug on a windshield."

As much as I respected Mr. McDonough and tried to do everything he instructed me to do, backing off on the physical play was the one thing that I had difficulty with. In retrospect, I am kind of glad I did. I may never have had the hockey career I had after high school or gained the notoriety that I have today if I did everything he advised.

Mr. McDonough played a major role in helping to prevent me from continuing down a road that probably would have landed me in prison or maybe even an early grave. Even though I was playing many sports from a young age and had some great coaches and teachers, as well as very caring parents, I briefly detoured one summer when I started running with the wrong crowd. I was doing things that my parents and many of my neighborhood friends had no idea about. I started hanging with a bunch of juvenile delinquents from the lower West Side and joined them in drinking alcohol, stealing cars, getting into street fights, and other bad stuff that I am not proud of.

One night I stole a car and drove it to a guy's house to show off. Just as I was pulling up, I sideswiped a couple of cars that were parked on the street. In the adjacent yard were the owners of the cars, a group of guys around 18 to 21 years old, and they were not happy. I sped off and they started chasing me. I raced through the streets with them closing in on my tail as I tried to make a sharp turn at a high speed. Instead of negotiating it cleanly, I ran head on into a fire hydrant, crashing the car to a sudden stop. I immediately jumped out of the smashed car and ran away before they could catch me. I never told anyone about it. I was very fortunate that the owners of the cars that I hit didn't catch me, that the police didn't catch me, and that I didn't get someone else or myself killed.

That same summer, I attended a house party and got into a fistfight with a Mexican kid. I beat him up pretty good, but as I went to leave, he ran into the kitchen and came at me with a sharp knife. He backed me into a corner and he lunged at me. I caught his knife hand but during the struggle I nearly sliced his thumb off with the knife. I let go of his hand, he stabbed me in the stomach, and he quickly ran out of the house. I had a deep gash next to my belly button and I proceeded to walk to the hospital that was just a few blocks away. I immediately got admitted and had to spend a few days in the hospital. When my dad came to see me, I told him I was goofing around at a friend's house, did a belly flop on his couch and there was a knife on the couch that stuck me in the stomach. I told him the truth finally and he said he figured all along that the couch story was pretty fishy.

Mr. McDonough helped me realize that I had some special athletic ability. He stressed repeatedly to me that if I wanted to be a part of his team and develop into a top athlete, that I had to focus on school and dedicate myself to athletics. I heeded his advice and by the time I graduated, I achieved several accomplishments that I was very proud of, including: becoming a member of the National Honor Society; earning a full academic scholarship to the University of Minnesota; serving as the captain of my high school football, baseball, and hockey teams; earning Team MVP, All-City and All-

State honors; earning homecoming king accolades, and even acting and singing in the school play as Perchik in the *Fiddler on the Roof.*

An award that means a lot to me was when I was honored as a "Top Athlete of the City Conference." It came in 1998 when I was invited to attend the St. Paul Centennial Celebration. The purpose of the event was to celebrate the first 100 years of the St. Paul City Conference and recognize its top 100 athletes from 1898 to 1998. I was chosen as one of those athletes along with many notable and accomplished athletes such as Ollie Bakken, Dave Winfield, Ken Yackel, and Jack Morris. Printed in the program under my picture as a Hanson Brother, it read:

> This three-sport star played for Humboldt in the early 1970s. On the baseball diamond, Dave would play two years, making the All-City team in his senior year. He would play two years in the Indian backfield, leading the team in scoring both years and finishing in the top three in conference scoring. As a junior he would tally both touchdowns in Humboldt's 16–8 win over Monroe. He would run for a touchdown and throw for another as Humboldt would score 34 against Highland Park. Unfortunately the Scotsmen would score 35 in one of the wildest games ever played in the conference. Against Central, he would score two touchdowns in the first quarter, and another two in the second, en route to a 24-point game in the Indians 24–14 win. In his final game in his senior year, the All-City back would score the winning two-point conversion run in Humboldt's 14–12 win over Washington. Hanson would play three years for hockey coach Ralph McDonough. He is remembered for not only his ability to score, but to throw hard checks (he led the conference in penalty minutes his senior year). That year the Humboldt captain would tally two unassisted third period goals in Humboldt's 2–2 tie with Murray. He was named to the All-City team. He was a Blue Line Club Award recipient as well as being named District 15 Athlete of the Year. He would go on to attend the University of Minnesota.

My high school years were memorable, but they were just a precursor of things to come.

About Dave from His High School Coach

"I coached Dave back in the early '70s in hockey, football, and baseball at Humboldt High School in St. Paul. He was a tremendous athlete, one of the best we ever had… A coach is lucky if he gets a guy like Dave once in his career, and I was lucky enough to have him for three years. He was a straight shooter, honest, always gave his best effort, and always worked hard to make himself better. He was a team player and always put the team first.

"He was just a great leader. And he was so tough, too. He was afraid of nothing. If there was ever a problem or a situation that came up, he was always the first guy in there to clean it up and to take care of his teammates. Dave never really had to fight in high school, though, because his reputation preceded him and nobody in their right mind wanted to mess with him. He was very disciplined about that stuff because he knew that if he fought that he would get ejected for that game plus the next one, so he knew how to intimidate guys without getting tossed out of the game.

"I only had to discipline Dave one time and I will never forget it. You see, we were a small school and didn't always have the best facilities. We were practicing outdoors at the time and it was the players' responsibility to shovel and flood the rinks after every practice every night so that we could have fresh ice the next day. I would have the kids rotate every third or fourth day, so they didn't have to do it all the time. But it was necessary that they all showed up to do it. Well, one Friday I got word that Dave didn't show up to help shovel and flood the ice. He felt that he had something more important to do. So, that following Monday I came down to practice and all of the kids were dressed and ready to hit the ice. I walked over to Dave and told him that because he didn't help out his teammates that he wouldn't be able to practice with us. He then got undressed and went home very disappointed. He came back the next day and apologized to me. He told me he was sorry that he let the team down and that it would never happen again. And it never did. He learned a valuable lesson that day and it had an effect on him. He hated

21

to let anybody down and when he saw that I was disappointed in him, it really bothered him. I think he has carried that lesson with him all these years because I know he was always known as someone who would always do whatever it took to take care of his teammates and never let them down.

"Dave is a much different person than the guy you saw in *Slap Shot*. Sure, his character was a lot of fun, but the real Dave is a man of great character. I know that I speak for all of us here in St. Paul when I say that we respect him as a gentleman, as a player, as a student, and as a person who has made a significant contribution to his community."

—Ralph McDonough, former high school coach

Chapter 3

From the Gophers to the Baptism by Fire

AS MUCH AS COACHES GASTON, RYAN, MAUER, AND MCDONOUGH were positive influences during my teenage years, a sportswriter for the St. Paul *Pioneer Press* newspaper by the name of Charley Hallman would prove to be extremely instrumental with my life after high school.

Charley's looks and mannerisms reminded me of a mix between Detective Colombo, Poindexter, and Maynard G. Krebs. He was an honored Vietnam vet who was very intelligent and had an offbeat personality. He always had a frumpy appearance about him and chain-smoked Camel cigarettes, but man, did he know hockey. He was a highly respected sportswriter and he used his stature and expertise to help support and promote me. Charley not only covered the high school hockey scene, but he also covered junior hockey, the University of Minnesota, and the NHL's Minnesota North Stars. He even did some scouting on the side.

Charley was good friends with Herbie Brooks, who was serving as an assistant coach for the U of M at the time, and convinced him to come out and watch a couple of my high school games during my senior year. As luck would have it, Herbie became the head coach of the Gophers that next season and he offered me a spot on his team. It was an amazing feeling.

During my last year of high school, colleges and universities from around the country were recruiting me to play hockey and football for them. I gave up a scholarship offer to play hockey for the University of Wisconsin and an offer to play football for the University of New Mexico so I could stay home to be a Gopher. Like every young Minnesota hockey player, I too grew up hoping to one day wear the Maroon and Gold, so it really was a dream come true for me.

Just prior to heading off to school, I was selected to play on newly formed U.S. National Junior team. It was an elite team of under-18-year-old kids who would be playing the other top kids from around the world. We were going to play all over Europe and Scandinavia, and I was really excited about it. Then, just a few days before we were supposed to leave and after we took the team picture, I got a call from my coach informing me that I had been the last guy cut from the team. I am still in the team photo, even though I never got to play with them. I wasn't too upset about it—after all, I was about to become a Gopher.

I enrolled in classes and set off on my journey at the "U." Once I started to attend hockey practice, however, things did not turn out as I had planned or hoped for. Even though I was a very good skater and a strong kid for my age, I was a relatively young teenager who was coming from a small city school, where I was basically a big fish in a small pond. I did not have the polish or developed skill at that time to immediately play for the Gophers' varsity team my first year.

I practiced hard for Herbie, running the football stadium steps with a weighted jacket on, doing the full ice "Herbies" (a notorious conditioning drill), and practicing regularly with all of the other players on the varsity team. But when it came game time, I was not in the lineup. Instead, I found myself a member of the Gophers' junior varsity team. It became extremely frustrating and discouraging for me. I simply did not have the foresight or maturity to hang in there and continue to bide my time as I trained, practiced, and learned the game from Herbie Brooks, the genius who would go on to become the architect of the fabled U.S. Olympic "Miracle on Ice" team that won gold in 1980.

After spending most of my first season on the Gophers' JV squad, I decided to leave the team in order to play junior hockey instead. Junior hockey was a sort of proving ground for college-aged kids who were either hoping to get a scholarship or earn a spot on a minor league team. The kids who chose this route had to be tough, because there was a lot of fighting and physical play in junior hockey in those days. Charley Hallman was really involved in the local junior hockey scene and convinced me that this would be a good career move for me. He knew that a lot of scouts would see me at those games and that eventually I would get an opportunity to get drafted by a professional team. When I told Herbie that I was going to leave the team he encouraged me to stick it out even though I wasn't quite ready to play on the varsity. We were both stubborn and set in our ways, so I made the decision to leave—hoping that I would be able to fulfill my dream of one day playing in the National Hockey League.

I stayed in school at the U for the rest of my freshman year while I played with the Minnesota Junior Stars. The team was coached by Doug Woog, who would later become the head coach of the Gophers. He was a really good teacher and I learned a lot from him. I enrolled in classes for my sophomore year, but eventually decided to drop out to concentrate on hockey. That was a tough decision for me, but I knew that I wanted to be a professional hockey player, and that I needed to be able to give that all of my attention.

That next season the Junior Stars were sold and renamed the St. Paul Vulcans. The Vulcans played a Canadian brand of hockey, which really suited my style of physical play. Before long I had developed a reputation for being not only an explosive body checker, but also a really good fighter. Hockey was fun again.

The Junior Stars and the Vulcans had good teams both of the years I was with them. The year I played with the Junior Stars we played in the Can/Am League that was made up of teams in the United States and Canada. This is where I first encountered two the three Carlson brothers, Jeff and Jack. Steve was still in high school in Virginia, Minnesota. Jeff and Jack played on the Minneapolis Junior Bruins, a team based in Golden Valley,

Minnesota, and they were leaders of a very rugged team. Both guys had long hair, wore black-rimmed glasses, and played with a bunch of guys that attacked you like a pack of starving wolves on the hunt.

Another tough team in the league was Thunder Bay, Ontario, which was led by Bill "Goldie" Goldthorpe and Willie Trognitz. Both players were known for their wild behavior on and off the ice, but most of the tales were about Goldie. I was told that Goldthorpe was not allowed to come to the States and was only allowed to play in the games at Thunder Bay under a police escort because he was in jail for robbing graves. They said the cops would bring him from jail under tight security before the game and would have to watch him intently during the game to make sure he didn't try to escape. My teammates gave me a colorful description of Goldie as a guy who had a big blond Afro hairdo, a leather face with several missing teeth, and eyes as black as coal that sunk into his head. They warned me not to look him straight in his eyes but to make sure I didn't turn my back on him. Otherwise, he would jump on me like a rabid cat, bite my nose off, and scratch my eyes out, something they said he'd done to other players before.

Needless to say, my first trip to the dingy barn of a rink in Thunder Bay to play against Goldie and his teammates was one that I did—and did not—look forward to. When I got on the ice with Goldie and Willie, I was wired and ready to fight for my life. But once the game got under way and I got my first body check in, I had no fear and played as though they were just a couple of regular players. Both teams had their share of fights against each other, but nothing really outrageous happened. I think it was because even though they had Goldie, Willie, and a couple of other tough guys, we had a couple of tough players of our own who played hard, honest hockey. It was during this time that I learned about fighting as a tactic in hockey, and about how important fear and intimidation were in the overall success of your team. You had to have guys who would fight and protect the skill players, otherwise teams would run you right out of the rink.

We had a pretty good team my first year of Junior and actually wound up winning the national championship. We then went on to play in the Centennial Cup Championship, an annual tournament to determine the best Tier II juvenile team in Canada. There, we advanced all the way to the semifinals, where we squared off against the Central Junior A Hockey League (CJAHL) champions, the Pembroke, Ontario, Lumber Kings.

It was a best-of-seven series with Games 1 and 2 being played at our home rink, Wakota Arena, in South St. Paul. They had a talented team, with several future pro players including Tim Young and Rod Schutt, who both went on to have distinguished NHL careers. They also had a handful of tough guys, many of whom seemed to have an attitude of "Why are we wasting our time playing these wimpy Americans?" We took offense to that and set out to prove to them that we were anything but wimpy. I was comfortable with throwing my weight around and dropping my gloves against anyone at any time.

Plus, we had Buzzy Parrish, a tall lanky defenseman, who was a good player and could fight like a wild man. During the first game with Pembroke they tried to intimidate us, but we not only stood our ground, we played solid hockey. We came up just short and lost, but we made a statement that we weren't going to be pushed around. Game 2 was fast and physical and nearly got out of hand when an ugly incident took place midway through the game.

As Buzzy Parrish squared off with a Pembroke player, another Pembroke player grabbed Buzzy from behind and jerked him backward, causing Buzzy to fall back onto the ice. As he hit the ice, his skates flew up. The Pembroke player then went to jump on Buzzy, but wound up catching Buzzy's skate blade in the face. The blade sliced the player's face from his chin to his forehead and blood quickly poured out of the wound. The player was rushed off the ice and to the hospital where we were told that surgeons stitched him up with more than 400 stitches. He had to spend about a week in the hospital but he eventually recovered. We wound up losing that game, and then headed up to Canada for Games 3 and 4. Luckily, Buzzy had gotten suspended for the rest of the series and didn't make the trip, which I believe was a blessing for him and us all.

By the time we got to Pembroke, the news of the incident had made headlines in the local paper. The fans were primed to string up every one of us. We figured it was going to be a bloodbath, but it turned out that we had earned their respect. The Pembroke players decided to play a hard, honest game against us and, in return, we showed them how well we could compete. We ended up narrowly losing both games and getting swept.

Afterward, to our amazement, the Pembroke players shook our hands and even complimented us on a good playoff series. The fans also applauded our team and effort. Tim Young and I would later become teammates as members of the NHL's Minnesota North Stars, and we reminisced often about that series and how scary it was for all of us.

The 1973–74 Junior Stars were renamed the St. Paul Vulcans. The Can/Am League also went belly-up, so we became a part of the upstart Midwest Junior Hockey League (MJHL). The Minneapolis Junior Bruins also folded, so many of their players came over to join us as Vulcans. With a few former Bruins, some returning Junior Stars, and a few new recruits, the Vulcans had a better team than the one from the previous year. As a result, we not only won another national championship, but we became the first American Junior team ever to beat a Canadian Tier I team, the New Westminster Bruins. The game took place in Bismarck, North Dakota, where we beat them 4–2. It was a huge win for us, considering the fact that seven of their top players would go on to play in the NHL the next season, including future All-Star defensemen Ron Greschner. (Incidentally, the Bruins would later go on to win consecutive Memorial Cup Championships and earn the title of Canada's top Major Junior A Tier I team.)

It was during my second season of Junior hockey that I got labeled "Killer," a nickname that stuck with me throughout my entire hockey career. We had a tough hockey team and I was no exception. While it was primarily myself and Buzzy Parrish who dropped the gloves the year before, this year we had a bunch of new guys that could mix it up. The toughest of the bunch was none other than Paul Holmgren, who would go on to become a legendary enforcer with the NHL's Philadelphia Flyers and currently serves as their general manager. We also had Jim Boo, Craig Hamner, and Jimmy Cunningham, who could all throw punches with the best of them. One time we were playing the Minneapolis Junior Stars, our crosstown rivals, when a bench-clearing brawl broke out. By the time order was restored, Craig Hamner had punched the goalie, split his facemask, and knocked him out. Jim Boo put a player in la-la land with one punch. Paul and I pummeled the guys we squared off with, and Jimmy Cunningham knocked the snot out of his unfortunate foe. At the next Vulcans home game, our fans had big signs made up that read: "Look Out for Killer Hanson and One-Punch Boo—They May Be Delivering Your Next Lunch!" From that point on, Killer stuck with me and I just embraced it.

Jim and I became best friends during those days. We not only made for a pretty intimidating pair on the ice, but we also had our share of fisticuffs together off the ice. We even took karate classes together for a couple of years and the stuff we learned came in pretty handy for us. We competed in a karate tournament as members of our club team. During the tournament, the object was to outscore your opponent by hitting or kicking him cleanly to the body, but never to the head. However, you were supposed to pull your punches and kicks just short of full contact. I was in a match with a guy who was not abiding by the rules. While I was pulling my punches, he would occasionally nail me flush with a full contact punch or kick. The referee would just give a verbal warning and tell us to continue. After a few minutes of this, I had enough of this guy. I attacked him with a spinning back kick and nailed him flush on the jaw with my heel. He went down like a sack of potatoes and didn't move. I knocked him out cold and got suspended from the tournament. Jim saw me do this, so he floored his guy in his match and got suspended as well.

Jim and I were quite the pair. We even worked together as well. He would tend bar at the local saloon in his hometown, Mahtomedi, and I would be his bouncer. A couple of times we had to remove a few rowdy patrons from the establishment with our fists and feet. One time we even made a house call for Jim's younger sister, who was a student at the U of M. She was apparently having some boyfriend problems, so we both went to the guy's dorm to pay him a visit. There, we let the guy know in no uncertain terms that he was to stay clear of Jim's sister or else he would feel the wrath of "One Punch and Killer." Needless to say, she never heard from the guy again.

Chapter 4

Turning Pro

FOLLOWING THAT SECOND SEASON WITH THE VULCANS, I SPENT the summer playing softball and working at my dad's job. I spent very little time thinking about what I was going to do with the rest of my life, let alone the next hockey season. As fate would have it, I wound up running into my old buddy Charley Hallman, who then became my unofficial sports agent. He helped set into motion what I would be doing for the next 10 years of my life.

Mickey Keating was a scout for the New York Rangers and watched me regularly when I played with the Vulcans. He told me that he was going to recommend to the Rangers that they draft me, but Charley convinced Glen Sonmor, the general manager of the WHA's Minnesota Fighting Saints to draft and sign me instead. I will never forget Charley sitting with me in Glen's office when I negotiated and signed my first professional contract with the Saints. I got a two-year deal for $25,000 a season, plus a $1,000 signing bonus. My contract included some incentive bonuses, too, one of which was an extra $1,000 bucks if I led the team in penalty minutes. I was about to play big time hockey, but I first had to show what I could do against the big boys at the Saints training camp. Things were about to get interesting.

I was now 20 years old and didn't have an inkling what I was in for, but I soon found out that the nickname of the Fighting Saints was more than just a cool moniker. My first professional training camp, which was held at the St. Paul Civic Center, was a wild one with some very colorful players. There were outstanding veterans at the camp, including: Mike "Shaky" Walton, Fran Huck, Ted Hampson, Danny O'Shea, Rick Smith, Mike McHahon, Jim Johnson, and Mike Antonovich, among others. Then there were a handful of rookies, including Jack, Steve, and Jeff Carlson. The Carlson brothers had all played together the year before with the Marquette Iron Rangers in the United States Hockey League. This was a typical low-level minor pro league that the brothers decided to play in. They all wanted to play together, so they decided to play in Marquette, Michigan, where they terrorized the league.

The Carlsons made their presence immediately known at the Saints training camp. They arrived, donning the black-rimmed safety glasses, ready to mix it up with anybody and everybody. Jack was a left winger who stood 6'3" and weighed 205 pounds. He was one of the best fighters I ever saw during my career and since. He had long arms that would just throw hammers for punches and not stop until his opponent either dropped or the linesmen broke it up. Jeff stood 6'3" and weighed 210 pounds. He played right wing and was as tough as an iron crowbar. He didn't throw as many punches or throw them as fast as Jack, because he had to only hit you once with one of his big meat hooks to smash your face in. Steve was their centerman at 6'3" and 180 pounds. Even though all three were good hockey players, Steve was the best and played the game with more finesse than the other two.

There were many tough players at the Saints training camp. Glen Sonmor and head coach Harry Neale not only wanted a talented team, but a tough team. Players like Gord "Machine Gun" Gallant, Curt Brackenbury, Pat Westrum, Ron Busniuk, John Arbor, Bill "Goldie" Goldthorpe, and others known for their fighting abilities and physical play were there and made for some very entertaining times.

We played an exhibition game against the Indianapolis Racers during camp and both benches cleared. Indy had a scrappy team with a couple of tough guys like Kim "Clacker" Clackson and Ted "Iron Man" Scharf. Jeff Carlson got into a fight with Clackson and, as they were going toe-to-toe, Jeff's fingers got in Clackson's mouth. As Clackson bit down on Jeff's fingers, Jeff yanked his fingers out of Clackson's mouth and pulled Clackson's front tooth with them. When the fight broke up, Clackson looked around for his tooth, found it on the ice and stuck it back into his mouth. Goldie Goldthorpe was in this game as well and got into a fight. He was so riled up by the time it broke up that when he got sent to the penalty box he tried to go through the door with his stick crossways. The stick stopped him and he fell backward. He tried again, and it happened again. Finally, after the second time, he figured it out, turned his stick straight up and went in the box.

During an exhibition game at Mankato State University, in Mankato, Minnesota, the coaching staff divided up the players into two teams to play each other. One team was made up of a group of veterans and skilled players, led by the team's star Mike Walton. On the other squad was the Carlson brothers, Bill Butters, me, and a few other players of less experience and talent. We played in front of a full arena and I was so pumped up that I forgot I take off my skate guards before I went onto the ice. Needless to say, I was embarrassed when I fell on my butt the moment I hit the ice. I tried to get up and skate again, only to fall again before Bill Butters skated by, laughed and pointed to my skates to inform me that I might do better without the guards on. By the time the game was over, Jack Carlson broke Mike Walton's nose, and Jeff Carlson, Bill Butters, me, and a few others had brutally pounded the other team, and we won the game.

Coach Harry Neale was really pissed after the game. Apparently, at the pregame ceremonial drop of the puck, the mayor of Mankato presented Harry with the key to the city. Afterward, Harry was so upset that we had hammered his star players that he slammed open our locker room door and threw the key at us yelling, "Here ya go, you bums!"

The next day the Carlsons and I got sent down to the minors to play for the Johnstown, Pennsylvania, Jets of the North American Hockey League (NAHL). It was the Saints' top minor league farm team during 1974–75 and 1975–76 seasons. I would be making a $220 bucks a week wage at this point, which was good money in those days. I wouldn't be able to get the big dough, however, until I made it up to play in the WHA, with the Saints. I would have my work cut out for me, that was for sure.

Prior to the 1973–74 season, the NAHL had been known as the Eastern Hockey League, but the circuit folded and decided to change its name when it regrouped in order to try to present a new image. The EHL had a reputation for producing some outstanding hockey players, but it also was known as a "hatchet" league. Talk to anyone who played or watched it in its heyday and some outrageous stories about the EHL will flow freely. Needless to say, the arrival of the Carlson brothers and myself to the NAHL did nothing to help change the image of the league.

We flew from the Minneapolis airport to Buffalo, New York, where we got picked up for the trip to Niagara Falls, Ontario, for the Jets training camp. After staying in a very nice hotel in St. Paul during the Saints camp, the Olympia Hotel in Niagara Falls was a big dose of minor league reality. Let's just say it was a small step up from a fleabag doghouse. One of the interesting aspects of the hotel was its wake-up call procedure. When you left word that you wanted a wake-up call the next morning, the clerk would take your request and wish you a good night. At the designated time, a big German cleaning lady would slide open the unlockable hotel room window, reach inside to unlock the door, and enter the room with her vacuum cleaner blaring. She'd then start yelling at you that it was time to wake up.

When I went to the rink for my first practice, I met the team trainer/equipment manager. The trainer took me into a grungy room that was being used as the players' locker room, to unpack my hockey bag. He then took me down the hall to pick out my hockey sticks from a batch of about 50 used ones that were lined up around the walls of the room. He told me that they were used sticks left behind by players who played for the Jets over the last few years. I just looked at those old ratty things and thought, "Welcome to the minors, rookie."

Then, when I hit the ice, I realized that it was just myself, the three Carlsons, and about four other guys. That was it. Our coach was a guy by the name of Dick Roberge. Dick, a veteran of Johnstown hockey and a really nice guy, encouraged us to be patient as more guys would show up over the next few days from other training camps. Sure enough, every day someone new would arrive, which meant we had another guy for shinny hockey and another guy to buy the first round of Canadian beer at the bar down the street from the hotel. While we were in Niagara Falls, we spent more hours at the bar during training camp than we did skating.

During this time, I quickly got to know and gained respect for Coach Roberge. He would fly around the ice, skating effortlessly and scoring goals at will. As we sat around having beers after our practices, I learned that he had played in Johnstown from 1954–72 and was actually the league's all-time leading scorer with 1,699 career points. Several of the veterans, like Vern Campigotto, Galen Head, and Ron Docken, who had played with Dick, told me to listen and learn from him. It was great advice. Finally, just when we got what seemed like enough guys to run a full practice, we were told it was time to pack up and head to Johnstown.

Johnstown was a blue-collar steel mill city best known for the Great Flood of 1889 that wiped out the city and killed nearly 2,200 people. Prior to being sent there, I had never heard of the place. I distinctly remember my thoughts when I first set my eyes on the city. I rode in with Ron "Doc" Docken, a goalie from Bloomington, Minnesota, who played at the University of Minnesota and had been playing for the Jets since 1971. It was just getting dark as we came up over a ridge and started down into the valley toward the city. I saw stacks of gray billowing smoke piling up and over the city, and I could faintly see some city lights peeking through the dark clouds. Occasionally, I would see diabolical flames shooting up through the haze. My first reaction was, "Dear God, help me. I'm heading into the bowels of hell."

As we drove down the winding road, we drove past rows and rows of large dilapidated-looking steel buildings surrounded by a continuous wrought iron fence. Doc told me that this was the Bethlehem Steel mill where many of the citizens of Johnstown and the surrounding communities worked. As we traveled past these creepy-looking places, we came into the city where I saw a street sign that said, "All-American City." Doc told me all about the place as he drove me around.

He took me past the Incline Plane, a contraption that looked like two railcars being pulled up and down the side of a cliff on railroad tracks. He told me that it was built after the 1889 flood so it could carry horses, wagons, and people from the bottom to the top of the valley. I believe it is the steepest incline in the U.S. He also pointed out to me a statue of a four-foot-high dog standing on a corner of Main Street in the downtown plaza. Known as "Morely's Dog," legend has it that it saved a child during the great flood. We then drove past Point Stadium, an oddly shaped baseball stadium fitting into a rectangular city block and sitting on the banks of the confluence of the Little Conemaugh, Stoneycreek, and Conemaugh rivers. Baseball had been played there since 1926 with the likes of Babe Ruth, Reggie Jackson, Joe Torre, and John Franco running its bases.

We eventually drove by the Cambria County War Memorial Arena, built in 1950 and home to my new team—the Johnstown Jets. He then took me by a few of the local watering holes and restaurants that the guys frequented—Johnnie's Mission Inn, the Hendler Hotel, Brownies, the Professor's Inn, and of course, The Aces—the bar made famous in the movie *Slap Shot.*

Once the small tour and the brief history lesson were completed, he took me to the Town Manor Motel, where we were to check in and stay until we found a place to live. As we pulled into the parking lot, most of the parking places were taken. Right in front of the main entrance to the motel, however, was a parking space that had a wood sawhorse barrier in front of it. Doc said that spot was reserved for "Big Daddy," the team's general manager, who lived at the motel. Once we got settled, we headed over to the Hendler Hotel bar for a beer. Doc knew everyone in the place, including the bartender, so we drank more than our share until the joint closed.

From there, Doc took me to a real Johnstown landmark, the famous Coney Island Restaurant. Being from St. Paul, where White Castle slider hamburgers were the quintessential after-bar meal, I felt right at home. We walked in and there was this big lady behind the counter with a cigarette dangling from her lip, a greasy stained cooking bib draped from her neck, and a row of hot dogs lined up and down on her bare arm. She coughs a raspy "Hello, how yinz doin?" to Doc and me, whereupon Doc says he'll have six of his usual. She immediately slaps six hot dogs from her arm into six buns. She then poured this steamy chili sauce, complete with secret recipe, over each one, smothers them with onions, and sets them on a tray for Doc.

I watched this in wide-eyed disbelief and was about to say something, only to hear Doc tell me not to worry, and to just get ready for the treat of my life. I watched him take a big bite of the first dog and saw him roll his eyes with pleasure. So, I did the same and sure enough, my taste buds exploded. The hot dogs were heavenly. I wolfed down four of them until my belly finally said no more. We then headed back to the motel, where I immediately fell asleep. A few hours later, I suddenly woke up with my breath scorching the paint off the ceiling and my belly erupting like a Hawaiian volcano. So I rushed into the bathroom, where I violently deposited all of my delicious Coney Island hot dogs into the toilet at an alarming and disgusting rate. Meanwhile, Doc just kept snoring away, I'm sure with a bit of a smirk on his face knowing that I had completed phase one of my rookie initiation.

The next morning I didn't say a word to him as we walked over to the arena. From the outside, the place didn't look like anything special, but as soon as I got inside there was an immediate mystique and sense of history about it. I walked through the front lobby where the war veterans were honored with various displays and then entered into the actual arena, where the ice was. As I walked around I soaked in the old pictures and plaques, learning about all of the old teams that once played there. The town had a rich tradition of professional hockey going back to 1941, when the Johnstown Blue Birds first played in the old Eastern Amateur Hockey League. As I continued walking through the halls of the war memorial, looking at all of the great reflections of its hockey history, I knew then that I was about to become a part of something special. I just had no idea how special Johnstown would be for me.

• • •

After the team got together in the locker room for the first time, our coach, Dick Roberge, had us sit down and wait. (Dick was the referee in *Slap Shot* who threw the Hanson Brothers out of the game after their first brawl.) Then the door opened and this little old man in a gray business suit, with his pants pulled up like he was expecting another flood, walked in. He had a big wide tie, black-rimmed glasses, and a quick step to his stride. It was "Big Daddy."

John "Big Daddy" Mitchell was about 5′4." Whenever he talked to you, he would start out by saying, "Son..." He was a fiery Scotsman who knew, talked, lived, and breathed hockey. As a teenager he first worked as a stick boy for a hockey club. He then served as an NHL official en route to becoming a general manager for a couple of minor league teams. He also scouted for the Chicago Blackhawks and Detroit Red Wings. While he was with the Red Wings, he served as the director of their farm team and later became their assistant general manager. In 1959 he became the general manager of the Johnstown Jets and helped the fledging franchise reel off three consecutive EHL championships.

Mitchell knew hockey and was highly respected and known by everyone in the hockey world. He also knew how to be frugal with his money, as evidenced by the classic line from the movie where Strother Martin (who portrayed him) said, "See this quarter? It used to be a nickel..." Under Mitchell's tutelage from 1959–76, the Jets won championships, produced Hall of Fame players, and weathered many stormy seas. In the two years I played for him, I not only came to respect him as a great hockey man but also came to love him as a wonderful friend. "Mitch," as many of us came to call him, died in Johnstown in 1986 at the ripe old age of 85. Over the years, whenever I got back to Johnstown I would visit him as often as I could to reminisce and listen to him say, "Son, did I ever tell you..." He was a real throwback and one of my favorites.

One of my favorite stories involving Mitch happened one night after a game when Jeff Carlson, Ron Docken, and I consumed more than a few beers at the Professor's Inn. We decided that it was time to put Big Daddy's old wooden sawhorse out of its misery. So we went to the Town Manor Motel, and John's car was parked with the sawhorse set at its rear bumper. We quietly snuck up on the sawhorse, drenched it with gasoline, and threw a match to it. It immediately exploded into a towering inferno as we ran off like scared rabbits, giggling like idiots. The next day one of the guys on the team came into the locker room and told everyone about the big fire out in front of the Town Manor the night before. He said that someone had torched Big Daddy's sawhorse and that the Town Manor almost burned to the ground. He said that the entire Johnstown fire department came to put the fire out. Jeff, Doc, and I just looked at each other and didn't say a word. A few days later, I went by the motel and there in Mitch's parking spot was another sawhorse. Years later I told Mitch that it was us who torched his sawhorse. He just laughed and said he figured it had to be one of us goofballs.

Mitch was passionate about the game and about the guys who played for him. We were "his boys" and he was always trying to give us motivational pep talks. One time, when we were in a slump, he came into the locker room to talk to us about our excessive partying. He stormed into the room with his face as red as a ripe tomato and yelled, "Boys! There are two things in this world that will ruin your career: *booze* and *women*! Booze will rot your liver and turn your brain to mush! Women will steal your money and turn your legs into rubber!"

At that point, he ripped off his suit coat, threw it on the floor, and stood on top of it. He then says "If you want to be a hockey player, then this is how you need to treat booze and women!" He jumped up and down a couple times on his coat and then spit on it for good measure. He then snatched it up and stormed out of the room with it flung over his shoulder. We just sat there for a moment totally speechless and then all broke out into cheering applause.

Drinking and partying were just part of our everyday lives in Johnstown. The three Carlson brothers, Guido Tenesi, and myself all moved into a house together. The owners lived on the first floor, the Carlsons had the second floor, and Guido and

I were on the third floor. The house was a couple of blocks down the street from the War Memorial Arena. Guys would stop over after games, or after the bars closed, or anytime anyone wanted to come by for a beer. One of our favorite things to do together in the house was to race cars. Whenever we had a day off, especially after a long road trip, we would push all of the furniture to the side on the third floor living room and set up our slot race-car set. We'd then sit around and play with it all day, while listening to Jeff's Ozark Mountain Daredevil music. After a while, word leaked out about us playing with our toy cars and it became a bit of a standing joke among the guys on the team, until they started coming over to join in. Before long, guys were coming over for race-car parties, where we would drink beer, do a little bit of wagering, and just kick back. There was one rule for race-car parties though: no girls allowed. This was male bonding at its finest.

• • •

I will never forget finally getting to put on my Jets uniform and playing in my first professional game—it was amazing. By the time my two seasons in Johnstown were finished, I was a part of two of the more memorable teams ever to play in the North American Hockey League. (I would play briefly into a third season as well, before getting called up.) As a team we won the hearts of the Johnstown community. I really felt a connection with the fans, too. The fans loved a tough hockey team and especially players who were tough.

We certainly had some tough guys on those teams. For starters, there was big Jack Carlson, who, before he got called up to play with the Fighting Saints in St. Paul, managed to accumulate a whopping 246 penalty minutes in just 50 games. He also tallied 49 points as well, which showed that he could do a lot more than just fight out there. Meanwhile, Jeff Carlson racked up 250 penalty minutes in 64 games, while totaling 47 points. As for me, in 72 games I notched 34 points while spending 249 minutes in the penalty box. Jeff beat me by one penalty minute that first season, so I didn't get to collect my $1,000 contract bonus for leading the team in penalty minutes (PIM). Oh, I was pissed. So, the next season I made sure that it wouldn't happen again. I led the team with 311 penalty minutes in 66 regular-season games that year, plus another 54 PIMs in our nine playoff games.

The 1974–75 season home opener was against the Philadelphia Firebirds and we had more than 4,000 people in the War Memorial that night. The Firebirds were fashioned similar to their City of Brotherly Love's pro team, the Philadelphia Flyers, who were also known as the Broad Street Bullies. The Firebirds had some reputable tough guys, like Ray Schultz (brother to Flyers tough guy Dave "The Hammer" Schultz), Marc Bousquet, Lee Crozier, and Jack Chipchase. We wound up losing the game, 4–3 in overtime, but it was the start of a tumultuous and colorful relationship between our two teams.

Over the next two seasons we would have some tremendous games and outrageous brawls with those guys. One game worth mentioning took place in Johnstown during the 1975–76 season. Steve and I had gotten suspended for fighting and were forced to sit in the press box to watch the game. About halfway through the game, Jeff got into a fight with Marc Bousquet. Ray Schultz jumped into the mix and caused both teams to empty their benches. With our team short on players (because Steve and I were suspended), Jeff wound up battling both Schultz and Bousquet at the same time. No one from the Jets could help him because they were all tied up themselves. Steve and I rushed out of the press box, sprinted down the steps, hopped into our player's bench, and started spear chucking hockey sticks like javelins at Schultz and Bousquet. They backed off, realizing that their two-on-one attack was a big violation of the honor code that hockey fighters live by—and they were also fearful that they were going to get nailed by a flying Christian Brothers hockey stick. We emptied the entire stick rack on the bench as the rest of the players on the ice just stared at us in disbelief. Needless to say, Steve and I wound up having additional games tacked on to our suspensions—but it was worth it. We always had each other's backs out there no matter what.

• • •

Playing minor league hockey had its drawbacks to be sure, especially when it came to monetary matters. John Mitchell was notorious for being frugal with the team's money, of which he reminded us every day. For instance, hockey sticks were not so much a necessity in his eyes, but rather a luxury. In fact, he only ordered sticks twice a season, which sometimes left us without any lumber. You had to preserve your stick supply or you could run out and be forced to buy your own.

One time I broke my stick and was down to my last spare. I was sitting next to Steve Carlson on the bench at the time, so I leaned over to ask him if I could borrow a couple of his sticks. He told me that he was in the same boat and didn't have any to spare. I then asked Jack and he told me the same thing. So I sat there for a moment and then came up with an ingenious idea. I told Steve and Jack that on my next shift I was going to go after someone. As soon as I dropped my gloves I wanted them to race out there to start a bench-clearing brawl. They asked why and I said, "You'll see." I then turned to our stick boy, and told him what was up. I told him to run over and grab some of the other team's sticks when the melee ensued, and get them to our locker room before anyone noticed that they were missing. Sure enough, I started pounding on a guy and before I knew it, all hell broke loose.

When the dust settled, we had ourselves a whole pile of extra sticks to get us through to the next order. I later implemented a more practical way of getting a few extra sticks if I was running low. When the visiting teams would come in, I would arrange for one of the local kids to assist their equipment manager in bringing all of their stuff down to the locker room. I would slip the kid a few bucks and voilà, I had some extra lumber.

• • •

After battling and struggling through the first half of the 1974–75 season, we were in seventh place around Christmastime. Coach Roberge gave us a small break to allow some of the guys, especially the homesick rookies, to take time to spend Christmas at home. The Carlsons and I drove 80 miles through a snowstorm to get to the Pittsburgh airport so we could fly back to Minnesota. It was good to get home to see our families.

The Jets' marketing slogan for that season was "Aggressive Hockey is Back in Johnstown," and we lived up to the slogan with our physical play during the second half of the season. In fact, we wound up getting hot and went on a winning streak that didn't stop until we won the Lockhart Cup playoff championship.

By the end of the regular season, Jeff Carlson and I had earned an intimidating reputation throughout the league for our willingness to fight anyone who looked cross-eyed at us. (Jack, who was the toughest of the bunch, had gotten called up to the WHA Minnesota Fighting Saints by then.) Steve Carlson led the team in points that season, due in large part to the fact that nobody was going to lay a hand on him so long as Jeff or I were out there flanking him. We had a couple of other guys who could really put the puck in the net, plus some gritty players who would do anything it took to help us win. Not only did we have two of the toughest fighters in the league and a well-balanced skating team, we also had some solid defensemen in front of two of the best goaltenders in the league.

Our first playoff series was against the Cape Cod Codders and we beat them three games to one in the best-of-five series. They had a good skating team but just couldn't stand up to our relentless pounding. Then we took on the dreaded Syracuse Blazers, the defending Lockhart Cup champions, in the best-of-seven semifinals series. These guys owned us. We hadn't won in their building since 1971, a 41-game losing streak. The first game was in Syracuse and we lost a typical hard-fought game, 4–3. We then won the next two games in Johnstown, 3–2 and 5–3, in front of capacity crowds. With us leading the series after three games, our next two games were back in Syracuse. We lost both games by scores of 4–0 and 6–4 and left Syracuse down two games to three.

Then, on my birthday we beat Syracuse in Johnstown by a score of 6–3 to tie the series and send the seventh and final game back to their home ice. Two days later I stepped onto the familiar enemy ice of Syracuse's Onondaga County War Memorial Arena in front of about 4,000 maniac fans. My nerves were raw and my adrenalin was pumping. The game was a typical Blazers–Jets game with both teams playing hard with a take-no-prisoners attitude. I got into another fight, my fourth of the series, and Steve Carlson scored twice, and we hung in there and ended the five-year-long losing streak by beating the Blazers, 5–4, to advance to the Lockhart Cup Championship Finals. At the end of the game, the players met at center ice to shake hands. The Syracuse fans were so upset with the loss (a loss that they attributed to the referee who called a penalty late in the game against Syracuse) that they went after the three on-ice officials after the game. Fearing for their lives, the officials had to be escorted by the police through a mob to their cars while they were still in their officiating clothes. As we left Syracuse on the Old Iron Lung, we drank our Strohs and Schmidt's beer and couldn't wait to face our old foes from New York, the Binghamton Broome Dusters.

The game was scheduled to start in Binghamton two days after the final Syracuse game, but Binghamton's arena had booked a circus in it and the War Memorial Arena had an arts festival going on. It wasn't until 10 days later that we finally played the first game of the championship finals. Although Binghamton had finished ahead of us in the regular season standings, we started in Johnstown because the War Memorial became available first. The format was to play the first game in Johnstown, the next two in Binghamton, Games 4 and 5 in Johnstown, and Games 6 and 7 in Binghamton. We finally played our first game of the series on April 23 in front of a sellout crowd at the War Memorial, where we beat Binghamton, 5–1. Because the Johnstown versus Binghamton rivalry created such a frenzy in both cities, it was decided that every game of the championship series would be televised in both towns. We then traveled to Binghamton to play in front of a sellout crowd at the Broome County Veterans Memorial Arena the next night and came out on top once again, 7–4. Three nights later we beat them again in Binghamton, 2–1, and headed back to Johnstown with a commanding three-games-to-none lead.

In Oregon with my dad, who is wearing his softball uniform. He was a great athlete. Both my parents' athleticism inspired me to get involved in sports.

My mom and I overlook the Columbia River Gorge in Oregon.

Baby Durk and I dressed up as cowboys. Don't worry, the guns aren't loaded.

There is nothing more exciting than a horseback ride on Christmas Day. I am shown here enjoying a jaunt while my blow-up clown BoBo sits nearby. BoBo can attest to the fact that I threw punches at an early age.

A picture of me in my Humboldt Indians hockey uniform in 1971.

Here I am running (#11) the ball for the Humboldt High School Indians in 1971.

I got my first taste of acting in high school. I am shown here as Perchik, singing my love to Hodel, in the Humboldt production of The Fiddler on the Roof.

Playing football and baseball helped to make me a more competitive and driven player. Here I am scoring a run while my high school teammate Don Leseman signals.

The 1974–75 Johnstown Jets champion team photo, with John "Big Daddy" Mitchell in the center of the front row. I'm in the middle row, fourth from the left, next to Jeff Carlson, Steve Carlson, and Ned Dowd.

During the 1975–76 season, legendary Bill "Goldie" Goldthorpe (with the big blonde Afro and who was portrayed as Ogie Ogilthorpe in Slap Shot) and me battle during a game. I wonder which one of us the referee is calling a penalty on? (Courtesy Chuck Mamula)

In 1975 I was named an Honorary Citizen of Johnstown. This certificate, presented by the mayor, was given to me at our championship parade.

Here I am celebrating the NAHL Lockhart Cup Championship with the actual cup in 1975.

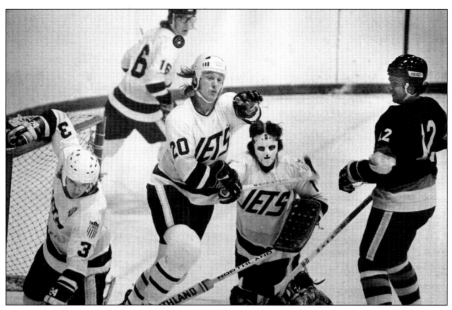

The 1974–75 Johnstown Jets in action against the Philadelphia Firebirds. Pictured here is Jets' goalie Ron Docken, me (#20), Jack Carlson (in the background, with glasses and the black helmet, #16), and Jets' defenseman Bob Boyd (#3).

As I squared off to fight Gilles "Bad News" Bilodeau in 1975, never in my wildest dreams did I ever think that we would later become teammates and good friends. (Courtesy Chuck Mamula)

On the set of Slap Shot, *director George Roy Hill stares off in disbelief after realizing that I really punched the guy in my first fight scene...*

...but the show must go on. (Both photos courtesy Chuck Mamula)

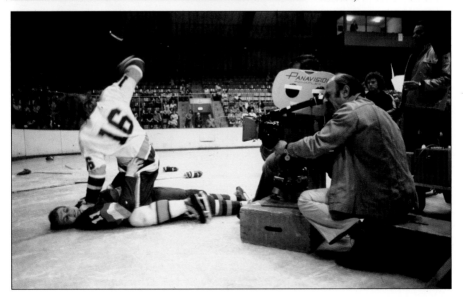

On Thursday, May 1, 1975, the War Memorial had a standing-room-only crowd. I had never really experienced anything as awesome as this and the majority of the fans hadn't either, since Johnstown hadn't won a championship since the early 1960s. When I came to the arena for our morning pregame skate, fans were lined up at the ticket office and when I came to get ready for the game, the ticket lines went out to the streets. When we hit the ice for warm-ups, the roar was deafening. We came out flying and never looked back. When the final buzzer sounded to end the game, we started to celebrate the 6–2 win over Binghamton. It was a mob scene on the ice when we tried to take our victory lap with the Lockhart Cup.

When we finally got to the locker room, the beer and champagne were waiting for us, and the suds started to fly. So much spraying, hooting, and hollering was going on that the TV and radio crews were hesitant to enter. Bill Wilson was a sportscasting icon for WJAC-TV, Johnstown's main television network, and he was a great supporter of our team. Bill also wore a toupee and I told him that if we won the championship, I was going to pull his rug off. Needless to say, Bill did not come into the locker room. He sent someone else to do the postgame interviews.

We won the NAHL championship around 10:30 PM and the celebration continued well into the wee hours of the morning. It really seemed like the entire town of Johnstown was going wild, all 40,833 of them. We all came back to the locker room later that morning, and Big Daddy said, "Boys, we have to go downtown."

Somehow, in a matter of hours, the City of Johnstown pulled together three high school bands, a fleet of showcase cars, and thousands of fans to line up and down Main Street. Many of us were still reeling from the effects of our all-nighter, but as we sat in the convertibles riding down Main Street to the incredible sounds of the bands and the excitement of the fans, we all felt like we were champions of the world. It was surreal, and as happy as we were for ourselves, we were even happier for Big Daddy. For a man who stood only 5'4", he was a giant that day and extremely proud of "his boys!"

Not only did we receive the overwhelming adulation from this proud steel town, but also, in the middle of Central Park, Johnstown Mayor Herb Pfuhl made us "Honorary Citizens" of his all-American city. Plus we each received a metallic mug with an inscription of our accomplishment on its side, along with a certificate for a complimentary polyester leisure suit at one of the downtown men's shops. Such were the rewards of a minor league champion in 1975, in Johnstown, Pennsylvania. Many years later, after Mitch passed away, Helen Hudac, his secretary before, during, and after I played for the Jets, paid for and presented to each one of the players on that championship team a Johnstown Jets Lockhart Cup championship ring. It is beautiful and one of my most cherished items I have to this day.

• • •

Among the many good things that happened to me in Johnstown, the greatest took place one afternoon when my buddy Doc introduced me to a gal at the Act III Restaurant. I thought she was the sexiest woman I had ever seen. Plus, she was a hockey fan. I was sold. She was just beautiful, standing about 5'9" with a sultry figure that would put Roger Rabbit's girlfriend, Jessica, to shame. She had long legs and straight brunette hair that hung to the middle of her back. Her name was Sue Kaschalk. She was a coal miner's daughter from Nanty Glo, a small mining borough about 15 miles outside of Johnstown, and she worked for a Johnstown radio and TV station, WJNL. We immediately connected, but I didn't see her again for a while, until our paths crossed again one night after a hockey game at the Hendler Hotel. She came up to me to say hi while I was eating a cheeseburger. My dorky response to her greeting was, "Ya want a bite of my burger?" Later, I took her to my apartment for some milk and cookies. Really!

Even though we started to date shortly after that, we seemed to constantly be sarcastic toward each other and behave like we didn't want to be with each other. But I would call her at work, bring her a yellow rose every Monday, give her tickets to the hockey games, and eventually we become a compatible couple. She then decided it was time for me to meet her parents.

Her plan was to leave me her car after one of my games so that I could drive out to Nanty Glo while she caught a ride home with a friend. Before she left, she saw me dressed in a very nice suit and tie with polished shoes. When she saw me again, however, I looked like a completely different person. I was extremely nervous about meeting her parents, so I figured I would stop at the Hendler for a couple of beers to settle my nerves. By the time I drank up some courage, I decided I didn't want to wear my stuffy suit and crampy shoes anymore. I went to the Napoleon Street house to change. When I got to Nanty Glo to meet Sue's parents, I was half in the bag, so I sat outside in the car honking the horn hoping she would come out and I wouldn't have to go in. She yelled to me to "park the damn car and get your ass in here!" So I parked the car, got out, walked up to the door, and got the look of shock and then scorn.

I showed up to meet her parents for the first time wearing grubby blue jeans, a T-shirt, and worn-out sneakers. I surely looked like a vagabond from the local mission. She was so pissed off she didn't want to bring me into the house, but her parents insisted. When I walked into the room, her mom and dad were sitting on the couch. As I stood there, I heard her dad say to her mom, "Gee, Mom, maybe we should buy the poor boy some shoes." I knew I had my work cut out for myself at that point. Sue and I continued to date and my feelings toward her grew stronger every day.

Our relationship came to a crossroads after the 1974–75 season. As I got on the small plane to fly out of the Johnstown airport, Sue was crying. She told me that my leaving would be the end of us, because we would never see each other again. When I got back to St. Paul, I told my mom that I wanted to marry her. I went out the next day and bought an engagement ring.

Two weeks later I flew back to Johnstown to surprise her by popping the question. My plan was to take her to a candlelight dinner at this fancy restaurant overlooking Johnstown on top of the Incline Plain. I had it all figured out. After ordering a bottle of champagne, I would slowly slip the ring case out of my pocket, get on one knee, and make a glamorous proposal. We got in the car and drove up to the restaurant, only to discover that it was closed. At that point I improvised. I nervously walked her out to the landing that overlooked the city and prepared to dazzle her with my proposal.

I checked my pocket for the jewelry box. I then remembered that I had wrapped the ring in a tissue and put it in my pocket because the jewelry box was too bulky to carry. I pulled the ring out of my pocket and handed it to her without saying a word. She had no idea why I was giving her tissue and just shook it like she was opening it to blow her nose with it. I screamed in horror as I envisioned the ring flying from the tissue and out over the cliff, never to be seen again.

Luckily I reacted with catlike quickness and was able to catch the ring in midair before it fell down the steep banks of Flood City. Sue just stood there wondering if I was having an asthma attack until I presented her with the ring. She hesitated just long enough for me to think that the answer was going to be no, but then she put it on and said, "Yes." We immediately drove to Nanty Glo to wake her folks up with the news that the poor boy with holes in his sneakers and grungy blue jeans was going to be their son-in-law. I can only imagine what was going through their minds.

• • •

That summer flew by as I spent much of my time going back and forth between Johnstown/Nanty Glo and St. Paul. As it got closer to training camp, I began to bear down on my physical and mental conditioning by intensifying my karate, boxing, weight training, and running workouts. Just before camp, I hit the ice at Augsburg College in Minneapolis with a bunch of local guys to play some pick-up games. Among the players were Brian Burke, Paul Holmgren, Bill Butters, Tom Younghans, and Jim Boo, who would all go on to have successful careers in professional hockey.

When camp started, I weighed in at a chiseled 195 pounds with 4 percent body fat and an attitude that I was going to whip anyone who got in my path. By the time the Fighting Saints camp ended, I got into a few fights, even one with my good friend and teammate, Jeff Carlson. But after having a good showing and doing what I did best, I still got the word that I was being sent back to Johnstown. The Saints had more than their share of tough guys again and apparently didn't need any more yet. As disappointed as I was about not staying, I was just as happy about returning to Johnstown.

After winning the Cup, getting to know the town, and having my own Dave "Killer" Hanson fan club where you could get a membership card for only 25¢, I did not mind at all about going back to be one of Mitch's "boys" again. The first day I got back to the War Memorial, Mitch was waiting there for me and greeted me with a $25.00 a week raise. I was now going to make $225 a week for something that I would've gladly done for free.

Many of the guys who were on the 1974–75 championship team came back that next season, plus we picked up some really good players to boot. Our two goalies were back, including my buddy Ron Docken, who was the reigning league MVP. Key veterans, including Galen Head, Vern Campigotto, John Gofton, and Reg Bechtold were back, as was our solid defensive core of Guido Tenesi and Francios Ouimet. Mitch added some good rookies too, including Bruce Boudreau and future Rookie of the Year Henry Taylor. Plus we had Steve and Jeff Carlson, who led the team in scoring and penalty minutes. What we didn't have, however, was our coach, Dick Roberge, who stepped down. I was named assistant captain that year and played 66 regular season games, tallying 29 points and 311 penalty minutes.

The NAHL expanded that year and was split into two five-team divisions. We played some great hockey throughout the year and wound up winning our divisional championship with 96 points. Only the Beauce Jaros had more points at 110, but we felt confident that we could defend the Lockhart Cup and keep it in Johnstown another year. We took on the Buffalo Norsemen in the first round and there was no love lost between our two teams. It was a best-of-five series that started in Buffalo, where we lost the first game by the score of 5–1. During Game 2, Greg Neeld of the Norsemen threw a hockey stick into the Johnstown stands and received a two-game suspension from the League, expelling him from Games 3 and 4. Neeld was a defenseman and a good hockey player, but he was a real agitator and cheap shot. He had a vision problem in one eye and wore a full-face shield for protection. He would stick guys and talk trash to everyone. I tried a couple of times to go after him, but he was difficult to fight because he refused to take the facemask off.

We won Games 2 and 3 at home, with the third game of the series being an 8–2 blowout. There was already some bad blood between us, and that blowout win only added fuel to the fire. Game 4 was held at the North Tonawanda Arena and was packed to the roof with Norsemen fans. We wound up losing the game, 3–2, but an ugly incident went down with Neeld, who had apparently been making disparaging remarks about an African American rookie on our team by the name of Hank Taylor. To make matters worse, some idiot Norsemen fans held up a derogatory sign stating that African Americans should be playing basketball, not hockey. That really pissed us off. Hank had scored 50 goals and 43 assists to lead our team in scoring that year and even won the NAHL Rookie of the Year award.

After the game I tried to go after Neeld, but the police grabbed me before I could nail him and escorted me to the squad car parked outside the back of the building. I still had my skates and uniform on, it was crazy. A couple of the other Jets players also tried to get at Neeld, most notably Vern Campigotto, but with no success. I was finally let go once order was restored inside.

We lost the game, which meant that Game 5 would be held in Johnstown. With over 291 penalty minutes called in the series up until that point, we knew it was going to be a wild one. On the bus ride back home, Campy and I discussed how Neeld didn't wear his face shield during warm-ups when referees were on the ice—the perfect time to get back at Neeld for his behavior toward Hank.

At the start of warm-ups, Campy skated up to Neeld and told him he was toast. Immediately they both threw down their gloves and went at it. Campy started to hammer Neeld, cutting him over the eye with a solid right punch. At the same time, everyone on both teams dropped their gloves and a huge brawl started. A Buffalo player tried to get off the ice, but the

Johnstown fans threw him back on. Neeld broke free from Campy and plowed his way through the crowd down a concrete corridor to the Buffalo locker room. He was later taken to the hospital on a stretcher where he was treated and released.

In the meantime, everyone was paired up except Jeff Carlson. Free to roam, Jeff came across his brother Steve, who had a guy down and was hitting him with the cast he had on his hand. Jeff told Steve to stop hitting him, so Steve let the guy up. Just then, Jeff walloped the guy with a left cross. It was insane. The rest of the Norsemen players finally left the ice to go to the locker room, never to return.

When it was time to start the game, the Jets came out, the referee and linesmen came out, but the Norsemen were nowhere to be seen. The head referee sent word to the Norsemen locker room that if they did not come out to play, they would forfeit the game. NAHL Commissioner Jack Timmons was in the building and witnessed the event. The commissioner even went to their locker room to try to get them to come out, but the general manager and the coach of the Norsemen refused to let the team go back on the ice. The Johnstown police and their dogs eventually had to escort the Buffalo team out of the arena to their bus.

The game was declared a forfeit and the Jets officially won the game, 1–0, and won the series three games to two. The standing-room-only crowd never saw a hockey game that night, but they were thoroughly entertained and even got a refund.

After beating the Norsemen we faced off against the Philadelphia Firebirds in the semifinals. We played tough but wound up losing the series four games to one. Following that final game, a wild 14–10 loss, I remember sitting in the second-floor locker room of the Philadelphia Civic Center and crying. I couldn't believe it was over. I really felt that we could win it that year and I tried my hardest to make it happen, but we fell short. We had a lot of injuries and the puck just didn't bounce our way that season. Hey, that's hockey.

And to make things worse, even though I led the team in penalty minutes, I never received the bonus that I had negotiated into my contract with the Fighting Saints because that February the franchise folded.

Chapter **5**

Bench-Clearing Brawls

Wild Times in Utica

We were playing in Utica, New York, against the Mohawk Valley Comets. They always seemed to have some of the strangest and rowdiest fans in the league. One time during a game some drunk fan managed to smuggle in a live chicken and threw it out onto the ice during our game. The arena maintenance guys came out in their street shoes and used brooms and trash cans to catch the thing. It looked like something out of a Charlie Chaplin movie. They chased that thing around the rink and when they eventually got it, they received standing ovations from the fans as well as from both team benches.

Once Jeff got nailed with a drink by a fan in the stands. Jeff, Steve, Jack, and I immediately climbed over the glass to go after the guy. Just like the scene from the movie, we were in the stands battling against a horde of fans, while our teammates and security guards were trying to get up there to help us out. Bodies were flying all over the place; people were screaming and wailing at us; and after it all got settled down, Jeff, Steve, and Guido got hauled off to jail by the Utica police.

I got off the hook somehow, so I took up a collection from the players to get the guys bailed out. The guy that threw the drink at Jeff later pressed charges against him. Jeff had to go to a hearing and wound up getting put on some sort of probation. Ironically, two years later, Jeff ended up playing for the Mohawk Valley Comets in Utica. And guess what? The fans loved him.

The Binghamton Brawl with Ted McCaskell

We went into Binghamton to play the Broome Dusters of Broome County, New York, about a month and a half before the playoffs were to start. During warm-ups all of the Binghamton players came out wearing the fake black-rimmed glasses with attached big noses. They were making fun of the Carlson brothers, but we didn't think it was very funny. After warm-ups, the Carlsons and I asked Coach Roberge to start us. The four of us planned to go after them as soon as the puck was dropped. They had some pretty tough boys on that team, but the scariest was a guy by the name of Ted McCaskell. Ted was a 38-year-old centerman who was a veteran of the EHL, the WHL, the WHA, and the NHL. He was a feared, vicious stick man who could quickly carve your eye "with the flick of his wrist" and with no remorse.

At the opening faceoff, he lined up at center across from Steve. Jack was on left wing, Jeff was on right, and I was on defense. Jack got to McCaskell first and the two of them started hammering away at each other while the rest of us paired off with one another. The benches poured onto the ice and the donnybrook went on for about a half an hour. Coach Roberge even threw a few punches from the bench when a Duster got too close. When it all finally got broken up, Ted McCaskell looked even scarier than before with blood running down his face. As he was leaving the ice, he yelled that he was going to cut the heads off of every Carlson brother before they left Binghamton. Later, after the game, we were in a Binghamton bar and Ted came in. He sent a couple of beers over to us, lifted his glass as we looked across the room at him, and nodded with a big smile and his sinister-looking eyes. Ted later had a role in the movie with us and we actually became pretty friendly, laughing about the Binghamton brawl. Binghamton would prove to be a regular place of mayhem for me. A year later I set an all-time NAHL record for most penalty minutes in a period—38—when I received four minors, two fighting majors, a misconduct, and a game misconduct. They sure didn't like me much in Binghamton.

Jeff Invents Rap Music

The Beauce Jaros played in the NAHL during the 1975–76. They were a very flamboyant and tough team with seven players who had over 150 minutes in penalties, the most notable one being Gilles "Bad News" Bilodeau. Bilodeau was a mean-looking French Canadian rookie from St. Pierre, Quebec. He was listed at 6'1" and 215 pounds, but looked like an NFL linebacker on skates. That season with the Jaros, Bilodeau racked up a whopping 451 minutes in penalties. He and I fought each other at least four out of the six games we played against each other that year, but the most entertaining fight that year between our two teams was the one when he and Jeff Carlson went at it in Johnstown.

Both started fighting each other by the public address announcer's table, which was located directly across from the players bench at ice level. Back then, there was not any glass protecting the PA and scorekeeper's table, which sat between the two penalty boxes. As Jeff and Gilles were exchanging punches, they started to grapple. Bilodeau had Jeff in a bear hug and bent him over backward onto the PA announcer's table. Jeff reached back, grabbed the PA announcer's microphone and started to whack Gilles in the head with it. Every time Jeff hit Gilles in the head with the mic, a loud thump boomed out of the overhead speakers. Jeff just kept whacking Gilles in the head until the linesmen finally broke it up. It was pretty hilarious. Jeff then calmly handed the broken microphone back to the PA announcer, who stood there in utter disbelief. The next day Jeff got a bill from Mitch for a new microphone. Steve, Jeff, and I contend to this day that Jeff may in fact be the originator of rap music.

The Syracuse Jail

Syracuse was a rough place to play and visit. The building was always full of loud and rambunctious fans who loved their Blazers and hated anyone they played. Both of our teams were very similar in style, but they were extremely tough at home. During the 1974–75 season, we played them 10 times during the regular season and never beat them at their building, the Onondaga County War Memorial Arena. That pattern carried on in the second round of the Lockhart Cup playoff championship, when we beat them, 5–4, in the seventh game of a best-of-seven series. It was the same story the next season too, where we managed just one win in six contests against them at home. They had a lot of tough players, including big Blake Ball—the guy who played "Gilmore Tuttle" of the Syracuse Bulldogs in *Slap Shot*. We finally wound up beating them pretty badly at home one time late that year.

Afterward, instead of riding on the bus for an all-nighter, we were allowed to stay the night in Syracuse. Most of the guys went to a bar across the street from the arena. While we there, some Syracuse fans who were at the game started in on me. By the time we left the bar, the crowd had gotten really rowdy. When we walked out of the bar, two policeman were standing outside for us. I recognized one cop from being at the game that night and he immediately grabbed me, put me in handcuffs, stuck me in the back of the squad car, and drove me to the police station, where he put me in a jail cell.

I wound up spending the night on a wooden bench. When morning came, I got escorted to a holding room. I sat in this small, stinky room with about six other disgusting and smelly people, while the guy next to me was puking all over his shoes.

As he was throwing up, I looked around at the other feet of my cell companions and noticed that three of them had the same shoes that I had. These were shoes that I had just bought on our trip to Lewiston, Maine, where they had a Dexter Shoe Factory outlet. I got them because they were really cool and unique. I figured that nowhere in my travels would I see anyone else who had a pair just like them. The shoes were powder blue with white platforms—yes, the old '70s disco platform shoes.

When I finally got to see the judge, he looked at me, said he was a big Blazers fan and that he had been at the game last night. He said if he ever saw me again in his courtroom, he would do more than keep me in jail for the night. He released me to our coach and we quietly walked to the bus that was waiting outside. As I stepped into the bus, I received a round of applause from the guys. As we pulled out of Syracuse, I threw my new powder blue shoes out the window.

Some Cape Cod Diarrhea

Playing in the "No Sunshine" bus league, there were times when it was tough to keep my energy high. Although I had youth on my side, the long bus rides, crummy food, lack of sleep, and other things would wear me down. On one extra-long trip that had us playing eight games in nine nights, we were in Cape Cod to play the Codders.

As we were driving to the arena, I mentioned to Jeff Carlson about how worn out I was feeling. He said he had a couple of pills that would help get my energy back and make me feel much better. Being a bit naïve and anxious to feel better, I took his pills with a can of Mountain Dew. I started to feel much more alert and energized as I changed into my uniform.

Right before we were ready to head out for warm-ups, I had the sudden urge to poop. As the guys left the room to go out for warm-ups, I rushed to the toilet. Once there, I undid my hockey pants, undid my garter belt that was holding up my hockey socks, pulled down my protective cup, unbuttoned my one-piece full-length union suit underwear, and sat on the toilet. Following a minor explosion, I quickly pulled up and redid everything, and headed out to warm-ups. Just as I got there, the guys were heading back to the dressing room.

I sat down without saying anything and waited to go out for the start of the game. I finally got out to the ice for a couple of laps, went to the bench, which was just across the hall from our locker room, stood through the singing of the national anthem, sat down and suddenly felt as though I was going to crap my pants again. I quickly left the bench, crossed the hallway, went back into the locker room, and proceeded to go through the same lengthy ordeal all over again in order to sit back on the toilet.

Once I finished, I put myself back together and headed out to the bench again, only to return to the stall minutes later. This time I didn't leave the toilet until the game was over. The team came back into the locker room, and I confronted Jeff and asked him what the hell it was he gave to me. He just laughed, as did the coach and the rest of the team. To this day, he will not tell me what it was that he gave me that night to throw my bowels into overdrive.

The Johnstown Incline Plane

Because we spent so much time on the road and had little free time at home, when it was time to have fun we made sure we took advantage of it. Whether it was a gathering to race slot cars in our living room, an open party at our house on Napoleon Street, or a night out at one of the local bars, we made sure that nothing stood in our way. One night a teammate was having a party at his place, which was located near the top of the Incline Plane. The Carlsons and I got primed at the Hendler Bar before deciding to head over to the party. Our plan was to ride the Johnstown Incline Plane up to the party and then ride it back down.

When we got to the Incline Plane's entrance, we discovered that it had stopped running for the night. We then made the courageous and ridiculous decision to climb up the gigantic apparatus in order to get to the party. We did not worry about the fact that it was over 900 feet up and had a very steep slope that included over 700 railroad ties. We just started climbing and didn't look down. Eventually we made it to the top and decided that there was no way in hell that we were going to climb back down at the end of the night. Needless to say, we caught a ride home when the festivities subsided.

The Golf Gloves

While I was playing junior hockey with the St. Paul Vulcans, I started to tape my fists because my knuckles would get so cut up from hitting helmets when I fought. It started out as a simple form of protection for me, but then became a way to cut my opponent easier and more often. I didn't put as much tape on them as a boxer does, but I put enough on to be effective. When I got to Johnstown, I showed the Carlsons my technique and they followed suit. About halfway through the season, word got to Commissioner Jack Timmons about our taped hands and he immediately instituted a rule that this practice was forbidden. Being the mischievous and innovative little buggers that we were, we came up with a new plan that would not violate the tape rule but would continue to give us an edge.

Our coach, Dick Roberge, was a golf pro at the Winder Country Club in the off-season. We had him get us some golf gloves, which in those days were made of leather, not the thin synthetic material of today. We would then scuff up the knuckles of the gloves with a wood rasp that we used to shave our sticks. From there, we soaked the gloves in water and set them on the locker room radiator to dry out overnight. The next day, just before game time, we would take the dried-out, crusty leather golf gloves off the radiator and put them on our hands under our hockey gloves. We would then be sure to get into a fight right away, before they got sweaty and softened back up. We thought this was an ingenious idea, but it lasted only a couple of games before Commissioner Timmons got wind of it and immediately put in a rule against it.

Cliff and the Old Iron Lung

We spent many hours, days, and nights on our team bus. We called it the "Old Iron Lung" and sometimes referred to the league as the "See No Sunshine" League, because we seemed to always be on the bus traveling to or from somewhere. Cliff was usually our bus driver and played "Walt" as the Chiefs' bus driver in the movie. No matter if the trip should normally take three hours or 12 hours, we could always count on Cliff finding a way to tack on at least two extra hours to our ETA. He was a great guy and everyone liked him, but he just never seemed to get us to where we were supposed to be at the right time.

We'd take nine-day road trips. It was crazy. We seemed to ride on the bus, get off at the arena, unpack, play, get back on the bus, travel, and repeat the process the next day. We spent very little time in hotels and a lot of time sleeping, eating, drinking, playing cards, and reading comic books on the bus.

We were on one of our long trips when suddenly we heard a loud screech, at which point we were all jerked from our bunks.

Everyone scrambled to see what had happened and after looking out the windows we realized that we were stopped in some kind of underground tunnel. Cliff had somehow managed to get the top of the bus stuck on the ceiling of an underground parking garage somewhere in Boston. How or why he was there still remains a mystery. We had to get out of the bus and let air out of the bus tires to try to lower the bus away from the ceiling in order to get it unwedged. While some of the team pushed the bus backward, others directed Cliff back out of the garage and back on the road again.

My favorite Iron Lung story came as the result of one of our road trips up to Cape Cod. We stopped at an outlet mall to do a little shopping. One of my teammates, Guido Tenesi (he played pretty boy Billy Charlesbois in *Slap Shot*), decided to buy an array of handcrafted exotic candles to use as Christmas gifts. During a meal stop, while everyone was in the restaurant, Jeff, Steve, and I snuck out to the bus, took every candle that Guido bought, taped them on all over the bus, and lit them.

We then hustled back into the restaurant and blended back into the group as though we never left. Then, as we all were getting up to leave the restaurant, someone looked out the window and yelled, "The bus is on fire!" We all rushed out to see flames galore flickering through every window on the bus. Cliff ran in and quickly determined that it was not an out-of-control flaming inferno. He turned around, spotted Guido, smiled, and said, "I think you better take a look at this." Guido then nervously peeked in and saw every one of his newly purchased candles brightly burning throughout the beautifully decorated bus. The Old Iron Lung looked like a tranquil Shaolin monastery. So we all started to hum and Guido just dropped his head in disbelief.

Goldy Goldthorpe

When Goldie and I wound up teammates at the Minnesota Saints training camp, we actually got along and spent some time together off the ice. As much as he was unpredictable and would do crazy things at times, he wasn't a bad hockey player when he stuck to playing the game. I think he respected honest, tough players and he viewed me as one of them.

He was friends with and really respected Gord "Machine Gun" Gallant, a fierce fighter who was a WHA penalty minutes leader for the Saints. Gord also wouldn't hesitate to fight anyone off the ice. In fact, he punched out Harry Neal, the head coach of the Minnesota Fighting Saints one night at his hotel room. Gord and I trained together before camp at the St. Paul Boxing Club and I'm sure that he told Goldie of our workouts and boxing matches together.

Many years later after we all were retired from playing, the Hanson Brothers were making an appearance at a Major Junior A game in Prince George, British Columbia. While we were there doing a promotional radio interview in a bar prior to the game, in walked Goldie. We recognized him right away, even though he didn't have an Afro anymore. We were shocked and even more surprised when he sat down with us and joined in telling stories of our past. We had a great time laughing our heads off.

Chapter 6

The Genesis of a Classic: *Slap Shot*

The 1975–76 off-season was the end of one chapter of my life and the beginning of another.

During the 1974–75 season, our teammate Ned Dowd carried around a tape recorder and recorded our conversations on the bus, in the locker room, in the bars, restaurants, parties—almost anywhere and anytime we were together. At times we thought he was going a bit loony because we would see him talking to himself. We later realized that he was voicing his own thoughts and observations into his recorder. After we bugged him enough about what he was doing, he told us that he had a sister living in Los Angeles who was a screenwriter and that she was interested in writing a movie about us.

As the season went along, his sister, Nancy Dowd, showed up and hung around with us for a while. She fit right in because, like Ned, she was fun, witty, and liked to party. She was a pretty and perky New England girl, whom we affectionately called Betty Boop, because we thought she resembled the cute little cartoon character. Nancy's idea to write *Slap Shot* came to her after her intoxicated brother called her from Johnstown one morning around 3:00 AM EST while she was living in Los Angeles. Ned told her that the team he was playing for, the Johnstown Jets, was going to fold or be sold because the steel mills in town were shutting down and all the mill workers were going to be unemployed. She asked Ned who *owned* the team, and Ned said he didn't know. She couldn't believe he didn't know who owned the team.

At that moment the idea to do a movie about our team was born. It would form in her head and develop through Ned's recordings of the Jets' exploits. Add in Nancy's personal observations, research, and imagination, and the script for *Slap Shot* was created. She pitched it to Universal Studios and they ran with it.

Her script was so good that they were able to cast legendary actor Paul Newman as well as renowned director George Roy Hill. She had plenty to work with, that was for sure, starting with the similarities between the fictitious city of Charlestown, a steel mill city that was going to lay off thousands of mill workers, and the real-life Johnstown, a steel mill city with similar circumstances. Then there were the Charlestown Chiefs, a floundering minor hockey league team that turned a losing season into a win in the Federal League championship thanks to the Hanson Brothers, three glasses-wearing, long-haired, goofy-looking tough hockey players who were the "terrors of the Federal League." In real life the Carlson brothers terrorized the North American Hockey League as members of the Johnstown Jets, which were losing halfway through the season but went on to win the Lockhart Cup championship.

All-out brawls in warm-ups, fights with fans, players thrown in jail, fashion shows, and telethons, the dog that saved a town from the flood, playing with toy race cars, and the list goes on and on of characters, happenings, and sites in *Slap Shot* that really took place during the Jets 1974–75 season.

In the movie my character was Jack Carlson, one of the Hanson Brothers. But my real-life persona in the film was played by Jerry Houser, who portrayed Dave "Killer" Carlson, a rookie fighting his way to prominence in the Federal League. *Slap Shot* had a lot more fact than fiction in it. In fact, in 1976, Nancy was quoted as saying, "The script calls for some rough language and bizarre action, but that's where hockey and the world are today. There's nothing in the film that hasn't already happened in minor league hockey. Besides, we're making a comedy. We think the picture will get laughs."

It created so much laughter that Dowd even got a Writer's Guild Oscar nomination for best comedy, only to be beaten by the eventual Academy Award winner, *Annie Hall.* Incidentally, she would win an Oscar the next year for co-writing the 1978 movie *Coming Home.*

Universal Studios wanted to cast professional actors to play key roles. They held auditions in Los Angeles and Montreal that included skating sessions. Even though Paul Newman's skating experience was limited to skating on the frozen ponds of rural Ohio as a kid with his older brother Art, he managed pretty well for himself. He said that when he knew he was going to be in *Slap Shot,* he started going to an ice rink to practice. Before he came to Johnstown, he'd sneak in to the rink close to his home in Westport, Connecticut, early in the mornings when no one was around to take skating lessons. He said the skating part came back to him pretty quickly, but he had trouble with shooting the puck, especially slap shots, mostly because he had never done it before. While we were together at the War Memorial Arena, he would often ask us how a player would do this or that. He really wanted to make sure he did things correctly. Whenever one of us showed him or told him how to do something, he would practice it. He was a perfectionist and really wanted to look right doing any action scenes on the ice. Although there was a double for him (Rod Bloomfield, who played for the Binghamton Broome Dusters), Paul did most of his own hockey stunts on the ice. Between his athleticism and the camera angles, Paul came across looking right in place with all the other hockey players.

One actor who had no trouble looking like he could play hockey was Michael Ontkean, star of two popular series, *The Rookies* and *Twin Peaks.* Universal cast Michael as Ned Braden, a former college player whose character in the movie was above fighting and wanted to play a clean and flashy game. Born in Vancouver, BC, he played on a scholarship for the NCAA Division I University of New Hampshire Wildcats from 1966–69, even scoring 111 points along the way. Michael could really skate and knew his way around the rink and the locker room. Rumor on the set was that he had been invited to try out for the NHL New York Rangers, but didn't go because he got turned off from pursuing a hockey career when a friend of his was apparently killed while playing hockey.

Universal executives really wanted to cast some big-name actors in the movie, including Nick Nolte, Scott Glenn, and Peter Strauss. They all tried, but no matter how hard they worked with these guys, they just couldn't get them to skate well enough to look like real hockey players out on the ice. During one of the practice sessions in L.A., Peter Strauss even broke his ankle. I was told that Donny Most, who played Ralph Malph on *Happy Days,* also tried out for a part but didn't make the cut. It was really difficult for George Roy Hill, the film's Academy Award–winning director, to find actors who could skate well enough to make sure that the on-ice scenes looked authentic, so he turned to his expert, Ned Dowd, who became his stunt coordinator and technical advisor, for suggestions. Ned's response was quick: "Go back to Johnstown and see if some of the guys, especially the Carlson brothers and Dave Hanson, can play the roles to George's satisfaction."

While we had known for some time about Ned's sister writing the screenplay, we didn't actually find out that we were going to be in the movie until the playoffs that season against the Philadelphia Firebirds. Steve, Jeff, and I were asked to meet with George, Nancy, and a few other studio execs involved in the casting of the film. The purpose was to see if they thought we could play the roles of the Hanson Brothers. I was originally going to be cast as Dave "Killer" Carlson, while the three Carlson brothers were going to play the "Hanson Brothers." They initially hoped to have Jack, the third real-life Carlson brother, play one of the Hansons, but he had signed with the Fighting Saints earlier that season. We thought he might return when we learned that the Saints franchise folded in February, but he wound up signing with the Edmonton Oilers instead. Universal removed Jack from the "Jack Hanson" role and plugged me in as the third brother.

When Steve, Jeff, and I arrived at the hotel, we got handed a couple of sheets of paper and were told to read the lines that were next to our names. I'm sure that the simple fact that we could read surprised and encouraged them, but once we got done with our verbal audition, they just sat there with concerned expressions on their faces. As bad as we may have sounded trying to read our scripted lines, I believe it was our looks and behavior in real life that convinced them that we were the guys to play the Hanson Brothers. Much of the cast and crew were in Johnstown to see some of our playoff games against Buffalo and Philadelphia, including Paul Newman, so they had been able to form a pretty good idea ahead of time about us. Plus, from all the time Nancy spent with us during the previous season and with Ned as our teammate during the 1974–75 season, they knew the kind of animated characters we really were. They eventually just told us to be ourselves, which is what we did. But we really didn't know or care what that meant at the time. We were just focused on playing hockey and defending the Lockhart Cup championship.

• • •

I remember taking my pregame nap when a knock on my door woke me up. I got out of bed wearing only my Fruit of the Loom briefs. My apartment was on the second floor, so the steps in the hallway outside my door led up to the landing. When I opened the door, I looked down and there staring up at me stood a guy with a pair of striking blue eyes and silvery gray hair. He looked just like Paul Newman, except he was about a foot shorter and forty pounds lighter than I imagined him to be. He put his hand out and said, "Hi, Dave, I'm Paul Newman. Sorry to bother you, but I got a couple of guys with me who want to see what a hockey player's apartment looks like. Would you mind if we came in to look around?" I said, "Sure, come on in and help yourself. But I've got a game tonight, so I'm going back to bed."

Paul apologized for the inconvenience and then asked if he could watch TV while he was waiting, because there was a race on. I showed him where the TV was, offered him a beer, which he accepted, and I went back to bed while strange men wandered about measuring things, taking pictures, and writing notes. They did a pretty good job, because Reggie Dunlop's apartment in the movie resembled my apartment pretty accurately.

Once our playoffs were over, Universal immediately jumped into action. Steve, Jeff, and I signed contracts that offered to pay us around $7,000 apiece, plus they paid for our rent and utilities and fed us every day we were in production. What I was going to make in three months to shoot *Slap Shot* was about the same amount that I got paid that year to play for the Jets—except with the Jets, I had to pay for rent, food, and beer. We all thought that this was a heck of a deal.

Our first day on the set at the War Memorial was spent mostly meeting everyone and preparing for the actual shooting of the film. We started out by meeting with hair stylists and makeup artists, who took Polaroids of us so they knew how to maintain our good looks throughout the filming. We then met with the wardrobe manager, who sized us for clothes and uniforms and had us try on stuff they wanted us to wear throughout the movie. This was when we got our first pair of Hanson Brothers glasses to try on, only these were round and really made us look foolish. The wardrobe manager, Tom Bronson, asked us to wear them around for a while to see how they felt while we played hockey. After about 10 minutes of trying to skate, pass, and shoot pucks with those glasses on, we got so dizzy with motion sickness that we felt like we were going to puke. Everything looked contorted. We brought them back and told Tom that there was no way we could wear them without barfing. The next day Tom came back with what would become one of the Hanson Brothers' trademarks: flat Coke-bottle-style lenses.

Jeff, Steve, and I then went around and met the camera and sound crews, gaffers, cooks, crew members, and other actors. It seemed like total chaos in the arena with people running around everywhere, scrambling to do this and that. Paul Newman poked his head through the arena side doors, waved us over, and whispered for us to follow him. We followed him into his big RV that was parked in the lot behind the War Memorial and he cracked open a couple of beers for us. This was really the start of a respectful and fun friendship that quickly developed and endured not only through the next three months, but for much longer. Jeff actually started calling Paul "Dad," because he dated his daughter Susan during much of the filming. Susan played the role of the pharmacist and was the goalie Denis Lemieux's sweetheart in the movie.

Newman's Own

Paul Newman was really fun to work with. What a great guy. I remember after we finished the filming, we had to do some voice-over work out in Hollywood. While we were there, Paul threw a party for us at his Beverly Hills home. He told us to invite anyone we wanted, so like doofuses, instead of inviting some sexy movie stars like Raquel Welch or Jacqueline Bisset, we invited the cast and crew from *Slap Shot*. We had a great time reuniting with the old gang, but in hindsight, I might've had a better time with Raquel. I'm sure she would've liked the glasses. Chicks love the glasses.

Another time, while he was racing in Brainerd, Minnesota, he invited me up to hang out with him. I brought my dad, who, ironically, strongly resembled Paul. While we hung out in his trailer at the racetrack, my dad, with a Budweiser in his hand, had people coming up to him, saying, "Mr. Newman, may I please have your autograph?" At first, my dad quietly told them he was not Paul, but after a while and a couple of Buds, he started granting people's requests and signing Paul's name for them. When Paul got back to the trailer, we told him what happened and Paul just laughed. He said he should have my dad go to all of his racing events and serve as his stand-in. My dad really got a kick out of that. Years later, sometime in the 1990s, when Paul had his Newman/Haas race team at the Detroit Grand Prix, he invited me to come enjoy the race with him. I brought my wife with me, and even though I hadn't seen him for about 10 years we had a great time hanging out together in his trailer and in the race pits. Mario Andretti was with Paul's team at the time and while Paul, Sue, and I were standing together, Mario walked up to me. As I put my hand out and started to say, "Hi, Mr. Andretti. I'm Dave...," he interrupted me by grabbing my hand and shaking it rigorously with the excitement of a little kid meeting Mickey Mouse for the first time, saying, "I know who you are...my kids love you! I love you! Can I have your autograph for them?"

I later mailed him some personalized pictures for his kids, Michael and Jeff, of the Hanson Brothers.

Mario kept saying to Paul that he needed to do a sequel to *Slap Shot* with the Hanson Brothers, but Paul said he didn't do sequels because they are never as good as the original. He said that because *Slap Shot* was such a great movie with hilarious and outrageous characters, that unless Nancy Dowd wrote the next script, he just couldn't see a sequel that could live up to the original. He really loved *Slap Shot* and often was quoted as saying that it was the most fun he ever had making a movie.

Paul came across as a very humble guy during the entire time we filmed together. He mingled with everyone and never copped a "high and mighty" movie star attitude with anyone. Although there was no disputing who the real star was, he behaved just like one of the gang.

His generosity and the great things he does with the entire profits from his Newman's Own food line for the Hole in the Wall camps for stricken children are amazing. But there are many nice things I know he does behind the scenes that he does not want publicized and only a few people know about.

I have two friends who got married shortly after high school. One of their children is mentally handicapped with special needs. I was talking on the phone one afternoon with my friend who was telling me how his wife had been trying to raise $5,000 for the self-funded school their son attended. The school needed to purchase computers that would serve the children. He said she had been contacting many major establishments requesting donations with no success. I suggested that he buy a jar of Newman's Own spaghetti sauce and look on the label to see if there is an address or phone number to contact, and to see if Paul's charitable organization would help with something like this.

He said he would, and after we got off the phone, I wrote a letter to Paul asking if it was possible for him to alert someone in his staff to keep an eye out for this letter from my friend in Minnesota who may be sending in an application for a financial donation. About a week later, I got a letter from Paul that simply said, "Done."

A few days later, I called my friend in St. Paul and his wife answered the phone in hysterics. I couldn't understand what she was saying, so I told her to put Don on the phone. When Don got on, he told me that they just got a check in the mail from Paul Newman for $5,000 and they hadn't even sent in the request letter yet. They immediately purchased the computers for the kids at the school and sent Paul a big picture of all the kids.

When my son was around 10 years old, he was eligible to play AAA hockey for a Tier I youth hockey organization, but the cost to participate was very high. I was concerned that I did not have enough money to allow him to play. He and I went on a little door-to-door campaign to solicit funds from small businesses in the area. Together, we went out with a letter explaining his goals to be a good student, a good citizen, and a good hockey player, and his hope that someday he could earn a hockey scholarship for college. We hit many places and placed many requests, but we were not very successful. After exhausting efforts, my son asked me what I thought of the idea of asking "Mr. Newman" to help. I said go for it. My son wrote to Paul, telling him of his dreams and needs in order to keep them going. Shortly after, we received a check in the mail from Paul that allowed my son to play. Christian is now attending the University of Notre Dame on a full athletic scholarship and had Paul not contributed, this likely would never have happened.

Hanson Brothers Take Action

When we finally got around to shooting the movie it started out fun, but got to be a big bore at times. There was too much time for us to have to sit and wait inside while other scenes were being shot or set up. We were not allowed to hang outside and bask in the sunshine for fear that we would have our winter white skin look pasty in one scene and then bronzed in another. Often we felt like we were going stir crazy. You know what they say about idle hands being the devil's workshop. To pass the time, Jeff, Steve, and I would think up pranks to pull on people, especially on these actor/hockey wannabes.

Jerry Houser was a really nice guy, but in the beginning he just didn't seem to fit our expectations of Dave "Killer" Carlson. Houser was the real-life voice of the Keebler Elf, and we felt like we needed to toughen him up. Back then, there was a ritual in hockey called the "Rookie Shave." Steve, Jeff, and I thought it only appropriate that he get initiated. In order to set it up and surprise him, we had to find a way to get him into the locker room with nobody else around.

Knowing that he was going to shoot a hockey scene on the ice, earlier that day we took his hockey stick, peeled back the cellophane strip wrapped around the bottom of the shaft, sawed the stick about three-fourths of the way through the shaft, and put the cellophane wrap back around the shaft to hide the cut. When Jerry got on the ice and went to shoot the puck, the stick immediately broke, which then forced him to come back into the locker room to get another stick. As he came through the door into the locker room, Jeff grabbed him in a bear hug, I shoved a hockey stick through his skate blades and all three of us picked him up and laid him down flat on the bench.

As he squirmed and yelled, we stuck a strip of duct tape over his mouth and taped his legs and arms down to the bench with more duct tape. Jeff then pulled up his jersey and I yanked down his hockey pants and popped open his long underwear, while Steve got the shaving cream and razor from the bathroom. By this time, Jerry was completely freaked out as to what was going on, especially when Steve sprayed shaving cream all over his hairy belly and private parts. I think Jerry then figured out what was coming next and just accepted it, until he saw me pull out a long string of skate laces tied together with a hangman noose on the end it. I threw the string up over the water pipe that ran along the ceiling and looped the hangman's noose around the head of his wiener. I then pulled the other end of the string and stretched his penis to look like a long thin night crawler being pulled out of the ground. At this moment, Steve and Jeff started to shave away. After a couple of strokes with the razor and tugs on the rope, the assistant director poked his head through the door and yelled Jerry's name.

He then came around the corner to see his poor actor strung up and taped down with three crazy-looking and hysterically laughing hockey thugs standing around him. After a moment's pause, the AD calmly said, "They're ready for you on the set, Jerry," and he walked out. We then untied and untaped Jerry so he could put himself back together and get on to the set. Had the AD not walked in, we probably would've shaved him clean and left him taped to the bench until someone else found him. Welcome to the show, rookie!

This was not the only prank we pulled on Jerry. Another form of friendly torment we imposed on our newfound friend came when he went into the toilet stall in the locker room to sit down and do his duty. That's when we snuck up on him with a bucket of cold water, dumped it over his head from the other stall, and then quickly followed that up by dumping an entire bottle of baby powder all over him. He looked like the Pillsbury Doughboy when he came out of the stall.

Jerry would later tell me that after the shooting of the movie was completed, he went back to L.A. to get psychiatric help in order to stop the uncontrollable nervous twitch he had mysteriously developed while in Johnstown. It was all in good fun, though, and Jerry continues to be my good friend to this day. He is one of the kindest people I know, truly a great guy.

When it came to pranks, we made sure we spread the wealth. Allan Nicholls, the outstanding actor who played Johnny Upton in the movie, found out that he, too, was not immune to our tricks. One time, after a long 12-hour day of shooting, Allan came into the locker room to change out of his Chiefs uniform. As he started to put on his clothes, he went to grab his boxer shorts, which he hung on a hook in his locker stall. To his surprise, however, he tugged and tugged them before realizing that we had nailed them to the wall. In fact, we nailed all of his clothes to the wall, including his pants, shirt, socks, and even his shoes. That one was a classic.

Then there was the time when we put a dab of Super Atomic Analgesic Balm in his jock strap. After he was on the ice shooting a scene and working up a nice sweat, the balm kicked in as his pores opened. His testicles lit on fire and he howled like a cow getting branded with a hot iron. We really thought we were going to lose Allan, or at least lose his balls, because we didn't know how to treat the balm's effects. We didn't want to try to wash it off with soap and hot water. That would just open the pores more and make matters worse. Putting ice bags on his sweltering nuts also didn't seem to do anything but shrink everything up. Eventually, it seemed the combination of soap, tepid water, and cool towels seemed to ease his pain, but it took a while before he felt close to normal.

As scary and as funny as that episode was, it didn't deter our desire to continue to strike fear and trepidation into the acting crew's hearts and minds. Even Paul Newman wasn't safe.

When Paul came to Johnstown, Universal got a place for him to stay that was out of the city. I think they rented one of our team doctor's homes for him to use. He also had a room at the Johnstown Sheraton Inn, where he would stay whenever he had to shoot late or had to be on the set early. When he moved into the Sheraton, he had his own private one-man sauna built so he could sweat out the beer that he drank the night before. He loved his Coors. In fact, he had 100 cases of Coors shipped in for his own private stash because Johnstown didn't serve it anywhere, and that was his beer of choice.

One morning Paul went to jump into his sauna and when he opened the door to step in, mounds and mounds of popped popcorn poured out all over his feet and legs. Paul thought it was hilarious and just rolled with it. He not only received jokes well, but he dished them out just as good. He had a really twisted sense of humor, and even became one of the biggest practical jokers on the set. After the popcorn episode, he had several live rabbits put into Tom Bronson's hotel room (Tom was the wardrobe director). I think he either thought Bronson was in on the sauna joke or he just wanted to get Bronson to loosen up a little. Either way, it was funnier than hell.

Paul and George Roy Hill had a special relationship that seemed to allow Paul to joke about with him without too much concern. Paul was quoted once in an interview about George as saying, "George and I have quite a marvelous relationship. He is, I think, an extraordinarily gifted man. He really has a concept of what a movie should be like. He has a great musical sense. He is loyal, affectionate, gifted, and the cheapest son of a bitch that I've ever met in my life."

Practical Jokes with Paul

During the filming of *Slap Shot,* Paul put that relationship to the test. He wanted to pull a joke on George that required the help of the Hansons and a few others from the gang. It was the scene where Paul rides up to Ned Braden's house in the woods, stops his car just before getting to the house, and gets out to call for Ned, who went tramping off into the woods. With the camera set up to shoot a side-angle shot of the car pulling up, George yells action and Newman races up the driveway in his brown GTO. Instead of stopping on his mark in front of the camera where George could see him, Paul streaked right on by, past the garage and out of sight of not only the camera, but also of George. Paul then slams on the brakes behind the side of the garage and hits the horn. Out of sight from everybody, Steve, Jeff, and I then start pounding on the side of the garage and tossed a bunch of garbage cans and tires out from behind the car to make it look like the car got into a bad accident. We heard George scream, "Oh my God!" and watched him rush over, expecting to see a crushed car and mangled Paul Newman.

Instead, he saw Paul laughing his head off, along with the rest of us. George did not think it was very funny though, and angrily yelled out that not only was everyone fired, but that he was shutting down production. Paul immediately ran to George to tell him it was all his idea and that he was sorry. George just carried on like he was extremely pissed off and that he was canceling the movie. We were all shocked by George's reaction as Paul relentlessly continued to apologize for his stunt. Finally, after a few minutes of this intense scene between the two,

George, with a Grinchlike crooked smile across his face, pointed his finger at us and declared, "I gotcha back!" We all laughed and then just let out a big sigh of relief. We didn't know he had that in him, but it was pretty good.

This was just one example of Newman's sense of humor. Another time we were shooting a scene late one night in a small town outside Johnstown. The scene was to have the Chiefs' bus pull over to the side of the road, followed by the Chiefs' booster club bus. The scene was such that both bus doors were to open with the players and boosters, mostly women, running off the buses to meet, hug, dance, and change places. For some reason, it was taking a long time to get everything set up to shoot the scene. And the longer it took the more beer we drank. By the time everything got set to shoot the scene, a bunch of us were half looped.

Just before we were ready to roll, we concocted a great stunt that we wanted to pull. When we heard we were minutes away from starting the scene, Jeff, Steve, and I talked to Paul about joining us in stripping down to our bare bottoms. Then, when the buses stopped in front of the camera and the doors opened, we would all run out completely naked. Paul said that was a great idea and encouraged us to do it, with the promise that he would be right behind us with nothing on but his socks. With the cry of "Action" the bus speeds down the road, pulls up to its mark, stops, the doors fly open and Jeff, Steve, and I run out buck naked, hooting and hollering, expecting Newman to be right there behind us. As we were hopping, flopping, and jumping around like dancing tribal Bushmen, we suddenly realized that there were many more spectators standing around than we expected.

Newman didn't join us, choosing instead to stay on the bus, hanging out of the window and laughing his head off at our foolish and embarrassing antics. Once everyone settled down, we looked around to see that many of the fine citizens of this little town came out to watch the filming, and the last thing I'm sure they expected or wanted to see was the Hanson Brothers flashing them the full monty. And it didn't turn out to be a laughing matter for Universal. The townspeople decided that they were not going to stand for such a flagrant display of indecent exposure in front of their families. They notified Universal that they were going to sue them and press charges against the Hanson Brothers for their unacceptable behavior. Universal had to get their legal department involved and everything, but thankfully it got all worked out. As for Newman, he just chuckled and said that was payback for us putting the popcorn in his sauna.

Paul was a carefree kind of a guy. He enjoyed having beers and some laughs with the guys after a day of shooting and often would show up at the bar unannounced. Unfortunately, it would not take very long for other patrons in the bar to recognize him and then mob him for autographs. Paul wasn't one for autographs and was particular about pictures being taken of him with cameras that had flashes. When he came onto the ice the first day in the arena with a full crowd in the stands, the place erupted into what looked like a lightning storm from all of the flash cameras going off. He hated flashing cameras. From that point on, it was announced that flash photography was not allowed. Paul had to be sure to take care of his baby blues. Violators were subject to going into the corners with the Hanson Brothers.

We had so much fun with Paul that we often told people that we took him under our wings so he didn't feel left out. One day in the locker room, Jeff, Steve, and I presented to him a bronze-plated plaque that we had specially made for him. It was inscribed with the proclamation of him being an "Honorary Loogan of Johnstown."

Loogan was a word coined by Ned Dowd to describe people we used to see hanging around the train station with their choice belongings in a gunny sack, or someone walking down the street with a silent boom box resting on their shoulder and singing off-key; just someone demonstrating unusual behavior. It became a word that was often used instead of calling someone a meathead, they were called a loogan.

We wanted Paul to feel like he fit in with the group and felt he was deserving of this ridiculous and outrageous award, so we granted him this very prestigious distinction. He said he felt extremely honored and would treasure the award above anything he has or ever will receive. I am sure it is sitting next to his Oscar at this very moment. What a loogan!

Leaving Our Mark

The Hanson Brothers never missed an opportunity to lighten things up if things got too serious or boring on set. Our pranks brought the Universal Studios executives to the decision that they needed a stronger presence of authority on the set in order to restore order and do things the way they are supposed to be done. They would see the dailies (raw unedited film footage) that showed unexpected things, like a guy suddenly walking through the background of a scene with a jock strap pulled over his face, wearing nothing but a pair of hockey gloves, or a "wet willie" (a finger stuck in someone's ear) during a closeup.

Universal Studios sent a "warden" to straighten things out on set named Tom Joyner. When he showed up to the set in Johnstown, he called everyone out into the arena and had us all sit in the stands as he stood in front of us to make his General George Patton address. He presented a very high-spirited message about why we were all there, what our objectives were, how we needed to work together, and how we all needed be on time, well prepared, and respectful of one another. He was actually quite moving and inspirational.

When he was finished, he asked the group if there were any questions. The crowd was silent, until Jeff stood up with his weiner hanging out of his pants zipper with his glasses resting on it. Then Jeff said as he was pointing down at his weiner, "I don't have any questions, but my friend does..." At that point, everyone in the arena burst out laughing, including Tom Joyner. It was pretty hilarious. From that moment on, we knew we had him on our side.

The Hanson Brothers continued to pull stunt after stunt on anyone and everyone we could. Not only were the actors not safe, but even members of the crew got a taste of our relentless attempts at humor. We had two makeup artists on set, Steve Abrums and Rick Sharp, and both were great guys. During the long shoots during the day and night, these guys always had to be on the set and would often fall asleep in their chairs. Whenever Rick dozed off and we saw it, the three of us would run up to him, bear hug him from behind, wrap rolls of tape around him and the chair, and then run away. We'd do something similar to another really great guy, our wardrobe director Tom Bronson. We'd see Tom lying outside in the sun, and we'd quickly run out, pin him to the ground, strip off all of his clothes, and run away with them leaving him to streak to his trailer to put something else on.

There finally came a time when the three of us got so bored that we just decided to take a week off. After about two months of being on the set at all hours of the morning, day and night, and sometimes not getting around to shooting a scene at all after waiting for hours, Jeff, Steve, and I decided it was time to take a break. Without telling anyone, Jeff took off for Gettysburg, I went to Washington DC, and Steve just went back to his place in Johnstown. After a day or two of not having the Hansons show up on the set, Tom Joyner got in touch with Steve at his place and told him that if we didn't get back to the set the next day, they were going to file a warrant for our arrest and have the state police track us down. They threatened to sue us for breach of contract and anything else that they could think of. So Steve tracked us down and we all skedaddled back to the set as fast as we could.

When we got back, we continued where we left off with the practical jokes, and we found other ways to deal with the boredom—such as drinking beer. We seemed to have an endless supply of Strohs and Schmidt's beer on the set. At first, we'd have a beer while we waited, and slowly sip at it just to pass the time. After a while that one beer became a six-pack; then the six-pack turned into a case; then the case turned into a big washtub full of ice-cold beer. There were a few times when, after a lengthy wait, George would yell that is was time for the Hanson Brothers to come on set to shoot a scene. But we were so looped from drinking that when we arrived on the set, George would take one look at us and say, "Okay, that's a wrap. We'll shoot the Hansons first thing tomorrow."

George allowed us to get away with stuff that no one else would have had the balls to do. He had a terrific sense for what was right with something and what was not. When we started out in front of the camera, George would set the scene up for us, give us our scripted lines and tell us what to do, then have the cameras roll—it did not go so well. We would try to do exactly what he said and we'd come across as being very unnatural. Finally, Steve, Jeff, and I said to each other, "Let's just behave how we normally would and not worry about what the script states or what George said we should be doing or saying."

A prime example of this was during the scene when Newman, as our coach Reg Dunlop, is sitting on the bench in the Chiefs locker room dressed in full game uniform, just before the team is ready to go out to start the game. He's giving a small, low-key, routine pep talk to the team, and the Hansons start in with intense yelling, "Nail 'em, pop 'em, stick 'em! Ya, we got a lot of losses!" George gave us our directions, but we decided to do it our way.

As soon as we completed filming the scene, George just looked at us with his crooked smile and that crazy gleam in his eyes and said, "Boys, that's it. From now on, don't worry about what the script says to do, just do what you think should be done." From then on, the Hanson Brothers didn't act any longer, we just played ourselves. It was a very sad day when I heard the news that George had passed away. He was a really good man and a fellow Minnesotan.

Injuries

While there were various injuries that occurred during the three-month ordeal of shooting the film, it is surprising that more people didn't get hurt. I mean, there was a lot of real hockey action and fighting scenes that went on with sticks, skates, pucks, and fists flying around. Newman and Chris Murney, the actor who played the goalie Tommy Handrahan, both pulled their groins and had to take some time off the ice. Chris also got hurt when he had to jump over the boards during a scene to get to Newman sitting in the penalty box. The crew had to build a ramp for him to jump up on in order to get over the boards because he had hurt his groin so badly and was too short to propel himself over the boards with all of his goalie equipment on.

Another injury happened when "Indian" Joe Nolan, who played Clarence "Screaming Buffalo" Swamptown, chased down Allen Nicholls on the ice and slid into the boards feet first. Joe popped both groins and afterward sat in the locker room with a big tub of iced beer between his legs. In addition, Steve Mendillo, who played Jim Ahern on the Chiefs team, got a pretty bad cut on his cheek that required stitches, but it didn't keep him out of the action for very long.

An injury that was really memorable occurred when Steve did the scene in which he skated down the ice past the opposition's players bench and slapped every player across the head with the blade of his stick. The stick that Steve used for this scene had a harmless rubber blade from the heel of the stick to the toe of the blade.

At the end of the bench was an extra who often came to our Johnstown Jets games. He'd sit in the stands and yell aggravating things at us, and this went on at every game he attended. We despised this guy. He somehow got cast in the movie as an opposing team player and was excited to be there. We wanted to get this clown and figured that this was going to be a perfect opportunity. So, on George's command, Steve skated toward the bench and went down the line, harmlessly slapping all the players with the rubber blade. Then, when he got to the heckler, he extended his stick in just a little bit and nailed the guy on the side of the head with the wooden shaft of the stick. He just nailed him.

The guy then pretended like it didn't hurt, especially since none of the others showed any signs of pain. They all were laughing except him. George then ordered everyone to do another take, and Steve proceeded to do the same thing again, only this time the guy went down with a big welt on the side of his noggin. Steve, Jeff, and I were just howling, especially after George yelled to do another take. This time, the guy reached down on the bench and pulled up a helmet to wear, which only prompted Steve to nail him even harder. Finally, after about fifth take, George said that we could put that one in the can and move on to another scene. Needless to say, the heckler was thrilled to be done with that. We later found him sitting in the stands with an ice pack on the side of his head. What a hoot.

The one injury that was probably the worst on the set, but the best for me, came during the scene that had me grabbing a guy at the shoulder to spin him around and nail him with a right cross on the jaw. When George described the scene to us, he said that when I swung him around, to just throw the punch like I would normally do (but miss him) and the camera angle would be set up to make the punch look real. The guy I was paired up with to do the scene was a professional player I had played against all year with a reputation for being a yapper.

During the game he would talk trash and stick you from behind. Then he'd skate away and refuse to stand up to the challenge of a fair fight. I didn't like this guy and was never able to get to him like I wanted to during the season. So when George yelled action, I skated into the camera's view, grabbed the guy from behind, spun him around, threw the wildest haymaker I could muster, and nailed him flush in the nose. He went down like a sack of potatoes and was knocked out cold. Everyone came rushing over as he lay there moaning. George asked me why I hit him. I told him that it was an accident and that I misjudged the angle. I later found out that his nose was broken and he never came back to the set. Oh, well. As they say, payback is a bitch.

Unexpected Occurrences

Sometimes it was very hard to keep from busting up even though the scene called for everyone to be serious. Strother Martin was not only a fun guy in person, but he was hilarious in character. We all had trouble keeping a straight face through his final locker room scene near the end of the movie. In the scene, we're all bloody, beat up, and losing the game, when suddenly General Manager Joe McGrath, played by Strother, rushes into the locker room. The scene really reminded me of the time Big Daddy Johnny Mitchell came in the room to admonish us about booze and women.

We could all hear Strother outside the door in the arena hallway walking back and forth practicing his lines. On "action," he flew into the locker room with his pantlegs pulled up, his face all red with emotion, and screams: "We're losin'! They're buryin' us alive! You're blowin' it!" At that moment, we all burst out laughing.

"Cut! Let's go again," yells George. Well, it took us at least five more takes to finally get through the scene. Every time Strother had to go out and start all over again, we could not get through the scene before someone, including Paul and George, would crack up. When we finally got through the scene and Strother had muttered his last line, "Not this bunch of pussies," George yelled "cut," and we all gave Strother a standing ovation.

Another funny scene that took forever to shoot was during the singing of the national anthem, right after the big warm-up brawl against Peterborough. The referee, actor Larry Block, kept looking over his shoulder at the bloodied Hanson Brothers, who were standing at attention on the blue line. He then turns, skates up to Steve in the middle of the anthem, and says, "I got my eye on you! You pull one thing, you're out! I run a clean game here and if there is any trouble I'll suspend you!" It is a great scene and Steve's response to the ref—"I'm listening to the fucking song!"— is one of the most quoted *Slap Shot* lines in the movie. But it was a real challenge to get it done.

The scene was originally set to show the entire act of the referee looking over his shoulder and then skating up to Steve, but Larry could not skate. Every time he went to turn around he would fall over. They even tried to shove him on his skates, so he could just glide across the ice to Steve, but he would either fall or run into Steve, unable to stop. We laughed and laughed, and Larry got more embarrassed with each take. Finally George worked his cinematic and directorial magic to get the scene completed without Larry having to skate more than two feet. They shot him just looking over his shoulder and then cut before he turned completely around. Then the next shot was spliced in just as he gets to Steve for his dialogue.

Some of the scenes we did cost Universal money that they weren't planning on spending. One came when we were shooting the scene in Indiana, Pennsylvania, at the Holiday Inn lobby. Newman is dialing on a pay phone while the team and the booster club are singing and dancing in a conga line and the Hanson Brothers are arguing with the desk clerk about getting three to a room. The scene called for the Hanson Brothers to pull the desk clerk over the counter and just shake him up and down. I decided to improvise. On the first take, we argue with the guy, grab him, pull him over the top of the counter, and—while Steve and Jeff are bouncing him upside down on the floor—I grab a skinny potted tree next to the front desk, pull it out of its pot, and start to hit the guy on the head with the sod and trunk. The tree belonged to the decor of the Holiday Inn's lobby and I guess they were pissed about it. George liked my impromptu creativeness so much that he just told the hotel to bill him for it.

Another incident occurred when we are all standing around the outside of the "Old Iron Lung," while our bus driver, Walt, was swinging a sledgehammer and banging in the side of the bus to "Make it look mean!" For some reason, Walt had trouble swinging the hammer the way George wanted him to swing it. After George showed Walt a couple of times how he wanted it done, George told him to practice the swing until he got back from setting up the shoot. Of course, the Hanson Brothers were right there encouraging Walt during his practice swings, but we figured it was time to pull something on Walt. The hammer was supposed to only hit the side cargo bay door, because Universal did not own the bus—they were just renting it for the movie. George just wanted to have the cargo door damaged because he figured Universal could easily replace the door panel at a reasonable cost after it got all banged up from Walt's hammer.

As Walt was banging on the door, practicing his swing to get it right for George, we suggested to Walt that he should go higher and not hit the door, because George wouldn't want it all banged up before he shoots the scene. Walt agreed and started banging away on the side panel and we're cheering, getting him all pumped up, until we see George coming. When George shows up Walt greets him with a big proud smile. He tells George he's got the swing down, but George's jaw drops when he sees that the side of the bus is all banged in and dented up. Turned out that Walt's sledgehammer job on the side of the bus was going to require repairs that were more than what the bus was worth. In the end Universal ended up buying the bus.

Then there was the incident that went down in the small town outside of Johnstown, where we were shooting the scene where the booster club and the Chiefs mooned the townspeople of Hyannisport. By the time it got around to gathering people to stick their bare bottoms out the bus windows, Steve, Jeff, and I had had more than our fair share of beer for the night. When the assistant director came to us to tell us what we had to do, Steve and I argued that there was nothing in our contract about being naked on camera. We were just bored, drunk, and ornery at that point and were trying to have some fun. We said we weren't being paid enough money to be doing a nude scene. So the AD went to George with our proclamation and George told him to offer us $50 each to do the scene.

We eagerly accepted, but couldn't find Jeff to tell him. We looked all over the place and finally found him passed out underneath the seats of the booster club's bus. Not wanting to lose out on $50 bucks, Steve and I pulled down his britches, propped his ass up through the bus window, and shot the scene. Talk about improvisation!

Actors on Ice

Throughout the shooting of the move, many of the actors would seek out our advice when it came to doing a technical scene out on the ice. One such scene occurred when it came time for the Dave "Killer" Carlson and Tim "Dr. Hook" McCracken to engage in a stick fight. The actors, Jerry Houser and Paul D'Amoto, didn't have a clue about what to do, so they came to me for advice. I had experience in this category because I had gotten into a couple of stick fights. A stick fight is simply when two hockey players decide not to drop the gloves to fight, but instead hang onto their hockey sticks to duel it out with wooden swords.

My first stick fight encounter was a typical rookie mistake. The Jets were playing against the Long Island Cougars in Commack, New York, and they had a cagey veteran on their team named George Swarbrick. At the age of 32, he was a fierce competitor who had seen and been in many on-ice battles. In this particular game, "Swarby" had taken a run at one of our players, so I stepped in and dropped my gloves on him. I was ready to start swinging when he stuck the end of his stick blade right against my nose and said, "Hey, rookie, you want to eat some beaver food?" Fortunately for me, George showed some mercy and didn't shove his lumber through my teeth. I learned a very valuable lesson that game about never dropping your stick around certain players, and it paid off for me later that season when I got into a tussle with Philadelphia Firebirds tough guy Ray Shultz. He hung onto his stick when I confronted him with a challenge and the two of us got into a stick fight that, fortunately, did not turn too ugly. After we flipped our blades over and jousted a bit, the linesman, whether due to bravery or stupidity, jumped in front of us both to prevent what could've turned into a bloody and scary mess. Nancy Dowd wrote a scene into the script that had Chiefs rookie Dave Carlson get into a stick fight with the grizzly veteran Tim McCracken.

The stick techniques employed in the movie were straight from the pages of Dave "Killer" Hanson's playbook. Turn the blades of your stick over so the tips are pointing down and jab in short controlled motions toward your opponent's face, staying away from wild swings. They both did a good job, with "Killer," in true fashion, winning the battle.

While we spent a lot of time with most of the actors on the set, Michael Ontkean seemed to be the most distant. His naturally intense personality seemed to be as close to the character of Ned Braden as we were to the Hanson Brothers. When we got on the ice with Michael, we could tell right away that he had played hockey at a high level. He was the best skater and puck handler of all the professional actors, but seemed to be in character the entire time we shot the film. Some speculated that he stayed pretty much a loner during the filming because that is what Ned Braden's character called for and that is how Michael prepared for and maintained his role.

We still had some fun with him, but he didn't hang around with us like the other actors did. Even though he was a very good skater, when it came time to do the striptease at the end of the film, he needed help. Universal opted to hire a professional figure skating coach to choreograph his routine. It was hilarious to watch Michael and this figure skater practice as they went through different sequences and gestures for his big finale. Through hours of intense practice, however, he managed to pull off an on-ice escapade with the expertise and grace of a professional figure skating stripper (probably the only one in the history of ice skating). When Michael finally got around to shooting the end of that scene, when he had nothing on but his jock strap and a smile, he was so concerned about exposing his cute little bare butt to everyone in the arena that he had the make-up guys cover his butt crack with flesh colored medical tape until his exit from the rink. Then it got ripped off just before he left the ice holding the Federal League Cup over his head. *Ouch!*

Slap Shot Premieres

Slap Shot's premiere showing was an exclusive, invitation-only affair held in the winter of 1976 at Yale University, George Roy Hill's alma mater. The initial audience to the outrageous comedy was a group of university professors, administrators, their colleagues, and their spouses. It was really an Ivy League black-tie and evening gown crowd, except for the *Slap Shot* crew, of course. Newman was there, along with some of us from the cast and crew, and it was the first time that we got to see the completed movie. By the end of the film, the only ones laughing out loud were the members from the movie. Everyone else in the audience seemed to be stunned silent by what they saw and heard.

Afterward, Universal and George sponsored a very elegant post-movie wine, champagne, and tea gathering in one of the prestigious halls of Yale University. As we walked around the room and tried to mingle with the guests, it seemed like most of the university invitees were afraid that we were going to yell something profane at them or maybe even punch them out. The few who did speak to us kept asking if that was the way hockey really was played in Charlestown, to which we responded, "Of course!"

After the movie was released, Universal Studios liked the wacky Hanson Brothers so much that they were planning on making more movies with us. In fact, Universal offered us a seven-year movie contract, with the idea of making a picture every summer.

At the time, I was playing in the AHL for the Providence Reds just before being called up to play with Steve and Jack Carlson, who were both with the New England Whalers of the WHA.

Jeff, meanwhile, was in Utica, playing with the Mohawk Valley Comets of the NAHL. When I received the contract offer, I sent it to my agent, Keith Hanzel, in St. Paul, Minnesota, for his review and to negotiate on our behalf. Universal said they'd keep us together and eventually work Jack in as the fourth brother. We told them that we didn't want movie making to interfere with our hockey careers. They promised us that it wouldn't interfere for the first two years, but after that they couldn't or wouldn't make any guarantees.

Universal already had a script written and wanted to shoot another movie with the three of us in the summer of 1977, but since we could not get them to guarantee no interference with our hockey careers by only shooting the movies between seasons, we had to say "no deal." I think we made the right choice. After all, Steve ended up playing a total of 14 seasons, Jeff played 11 seasons, and I played 10 seasons of pro hockey.

Chapter 7

Slap Shot Reflections

Allan Nichols, Actor

"*Slap Shot* was just a very vibrant, fun-loving approach to making a movie. I had only done two films prior to *Slap Shot*—*Nashville* and *Welcome to L.A.*—and both of them were with legendary director Robert Altman. Now, on an Altman film, he would screen the dailies with everybody there to watch. It was like a big party. Well, I just assumed all directors did it that way, but that was not the case with George Roy Hill. Instead, he was very private about it and didn't really want the actors around while he was reviewing them. Anyway, I thought it would be fun to check out the dailies, so I grabbed Dave, Ned Dowd, Jerry Howser, and Jeff and Steve Carlson to come with me to check them out. So we all grabbed some beers and went up to a room in the War Memorial Arena where they had the projectors set up. We just headed up there like it was no big deal and knocked on the door. We walked in and sitting there was George Roy Hill, Bobby Crawford, producer Dede Allan, the editor, and Paul Newman. That was it. He was in there very seriously doing business. Well, we all barged in and just sat down, basically unnerving his entire way of doing things. He was too tired to kick us out I think though, and just let us stay. We wound up having so much fun and giving him so much feedback that he let us come to all of the daily screenings and eventually he even wound up doing all of his movies that way. Eventually, however, Dave and the Carlsons would use that opportunity to get more screen time. So they would do all sorts of pranks on guys, getting them to screw up, so that we could all razz them at night during the dailies—sort of like our own blooper show. I remember one time Dave even walked right through a scene where Strother Martin

....

Andrew Duncan, who played the entertaining Chiefs broadcaster Jim Carr, said about his wig: "I remember watching the local broadcaster in Johnstown and studying him. That was the guy I was playing. When I went for the wig, George Roy Hill said, 'I don't care what you get, just get something outrageous.' I went to Glosser's Department Store and went to the wig department. The stylist started showing me wigs that made it look like I didn't have a wig. I said, 'No.' Then I saw one she pushed aside and I said, 'That's the one.' I stuck it on my head and looked in the mirror and started laughing. George looked at me and started laughing. He said, 'If you dare, I dare.'" The broadcaster that Andrew was portraying was based on Bill Wilson, the longtime sports broadcaster for Johnstown's WJAC-TV station who also wore an obvious hairpiece. I still kick myself for never getting the opportunity to rip that thing off of him. Oh well.

....

was all serious and he just strolled by bare-ass naked, wiggling his dink at the camera—it was absolutely hilarious."

Favorite Line from the Movie

"My most quoted line from the movie would have to be 'Fuckin' Chrysler plant, here I come!' That was just a classic."

Did You Have Any Idea the Movie Would be Such a Hit?

"No way, none of us had a clue. We were all wrapped up in the moment and really having a great time together. Dave and the Carlson boys were a huge part of that, too, because they made it fun for the rest of us. It was like a huge party, nonstop. It was by far the best time I have ever had on a movie set my entire career, without a doubt. We all became friends so quickly and just bonded. I have been on so many sets where there have been huge egos and where the actors didn't get along, but this was totally unique. Even the community embraced us. It was insane. I will never forget when we left and got on our bus for the last time, the Sheraton Inn put up a big sign for us that read, 'Goodbye *Slap Shot*, we'll never forget you…' People were waving at us like we were going off to war or something. It was surreal. What a sendoff."

Brian Burke, GM, Anaheim Ducks

"I remember where I was when I first saw it like it was yesterday. It was 1977 and I was in Phoenix on spring break. I had just finished up at Providence College and played briefly for Springfield in the AHL. So I had just had a brief taste of what minor league hockey was all about. Anyway, we had heard about this new hockey movie and were all excited to see it.

"The movie is a far cry from minor league hockey today, but it wasn't that far off the mark back then. Sure, they dramatized and glorified all of the fighting, but a lot of that kind of stuff was really going on back in those days. There was a lot of drinking involved with the players back then and because of that, a lot of crazy stuff went on, both on and off the ice. One thing I can say about the accuracy of the movie, however, was that nearly every character in the movie was based on someone who was playing at the time. The stereotypes were dead-on. I mean the French-Canadian goalie with fractured English, the over-the-top brawlers, and the guys who were always on the prowl for girls after the games—every team had those guys.

"The movie was just a classic. I have probably seen it more than 100 times in my lifetime. It is just hilarious. I remember doing TV for TSN up in Canada during the lockout and having Denny Lemiuex come in-studio one day for an interview with us.

• •

"When we shot the scene in Syracuse with the Hansons climbing over the boards to go into the stands, it got to be kind of scary for us. We had to do the scene so many times due to all the different angles and because there was a lot of difficulty in coordinating where all the fans needed to be. As a result, our hands got cut up and bloodied because of the number of times we had to grab the top of the glass to get over it. Then, when we finally got into the stands to battle with the fans, the extras, who were all Syracuse residents that hated us in real life, figured this was their time to get their payback on us. Sure enough, some of them got carried away when it was time to mob us and really let us have it. I wound up having to smack a couple and throw a few others off of my back during the fracases to not get beat up."—Dave Hanson

• •

· ·

"Even though the people on the set became a big family and everyone got along tremendously, which George Roy Hill, Paul Newman, Strother Martin, and the Hanson Brothers were largely responsible for, there were a few of the gals on the set we didn't get warm and fuzzy feelings from. Jennifer Warren, who played Red Dunlop's wife Francine, is one I don't recall meeting or seeing on the set. Lindsay Crouse, who did a fabulous job as Ned Braden's wife Lilly, and who later got nominated for an Oscar for Best Supporting Actress for her role in *Places in the Heart*, also gave us a lukewarm reception and kept her distance. A few of the ladies were a lot of fun though, including Swoozie Kurtz, who played Johnny Upton's wife. She was a sweetheart and a little cutie. The "Sparkle Twins," Janet and Louise Arters, were nice and a lot of fun too. The twins would skip down the street arm in arm, always seemed to giggle simultaneously at everything, and they were never apart. Originally, George Roy Hill was looking to have the Sparkle Twins be two teenaged hockey groupies with frizzy hair and retainers. But when he set eyes on Janet and Louise, he suddenly changed the part to two blonde bombshells with tight jeans and T-shirts."—Dave Hanson

· ·

Everybody recognized him immediately, it was amazing. I mean it was a real thrill for all of the players to talk to this guy. His popularity, at least in Canada, would rank right up there with a top NHL player. They were all coming up and reciting lines from the movie with him, it was great. 'Owwnnns… Owwnnns…' I just have to laugh when I think about that stuff, just classic.

"You know, I will never forget when we [the Anaheim Ducks] beat the Ottawa Senators to win the Stanley Cup in 2007. The clock was ticking down the final seconds and our video guy, Joe Trotta, yells out, 'And the Chiefs have won the championship of the Federal League!' I just burst out laughing, it was absolutely hilarious. I could just picture Jim Carr, the toupee-wearing play-by-play announcer of the Chiefs in my mind, screaming it out. It was just the perfect thing to say at this amazing time in our lives and we had all heard that line a million times over our careers. Even *Sports Illustrated* wrote about that moment in their big article about us winning the Cup. I still have to smile when I think about that."

••

The Carlson brothers first started out playing high school hockey together in Virginia, Minnesota. From there they all went to Michigan to play with the Marquette Iron Rangers, and then on to Johnstown, Pennsylvania, where they played for the Jets. They all really did wear glasses, too.

••

On Fighting In Hockey

"The only part of *Slap Shot* that was far-fetched in my eyes was the notion that skill players would get attacked out of the blue. Not everyone had to fight, it just wasn't that way. There is an honor code in hockey and even though the movie took some great liberties in how it portrayed fighting, that kind of stuff didn't happen. Fighting is and always has been confined to players who want to partake in it. Sure, guys have been attacked over the years, but that is rare. Even the old Philadelphia Broad Street Bullies didn't do that. Sure, they intimidated guys and threatened them, but they didn't attack smaller skill guys out of the blue. I mean to think that guys like the Hanson Brothers would just arbitrarily beat the crap out of an opposing player, a smaller skill guy, for no reason would be a stretch. It might have happened, but those guys would in turn get killed very soon after.

"Even now, with the Ducks, we want our guys to be tough. We led the league in fighting majors and that was a part of our style of play. We weren't going to be intimidated and we stood up for ourselves. If we lead the league again this year in fighting majors, that would be fine with me. You have to play this game

••

Before the last game, Reggie Dunlop says he wants to go out "clean" and play "old-time hockey," mentioning Toe Blake, Dit Clapper, and Eddie Shore. Hector "Toe" Blake played for the Canadiens from 1935—48 and was a three-time All-Star and one-time MVP, later becoming a legendary coach. Aubrey "Dit" Clapper led the Boston Bruins to three Stanley Cups from 1927—47 and was later inducted into the Hall of Fame. Eddie Shore was a four-time MVP who played defense for the Bruins from 1926—40.

••

· ·

Yvon Barrette, the actor who played the asthmatic French-Canadian goalie for the Chiefs, Denis Lemiuex, had his audition in Montreal. He played some pond hockey growing up, but he was hurt when it came time to shoot the fast-action hockey scenes. So Ron Docken, the real-life All-Star goalie for the Jets, had his hair streaked with gray by the makeup guys to look like Yvon's. He then put on Denis's mask to stand in for him as his double for the on-ice action scenes.

· ·

with respect, and if you don't, then you will have to be accountable for your actions. That is just the bottom line. Fighting regulates the amount of violence that goes on out on the ice, no question. You have to stand up for your actions out there no matter what, that is how this game polices itself. It keeps the clown show to a minimum, that is for sure."

Jack Carlson

"Back in those days the minor league teams were patterning themselves around the proven model for success at the time, which was the Philadelphia Flyers. The Broad Street Bullies were tough and could intimidate their opponents to gain a psychological advantage. They had won a couple of Stanley Cups using that philosophy and everybody wanted to copy their formula for success. Organizations figured that if they could build their teams around a combination of tough guys and skill players, then they, too, could have success. So top-end tough guys in the minor leagues were suddenly in big demand.

"The old Eastern League was a tough league in those days and all of the players were trying to move up to either the NHL or WHA. There were a lot of job opportunities in those days and if you could play well and were tough, then you could get a shot. It was a tough league, though, with tough players and tough teams. The Johnstown team was full of characters, and the movie wasn't that far-fetched. Sure, it was a little bit over the top, but most of that stuff really happened out there."

On Being Left Out of the Movie

"I had gotten called up with the WHA's St. Paul Fighting Saints when the movie started, so I was a little bit bummed out about that. I later wound up signing with Edmonton when the Saints folded and the movie started. I was a little disappointed that I couldn't be in the movie with my brothers, sure, but on the other hand I was thrilled that I was going to be able to realize my dream of playing professional hockey at that level. The WHA was on par with the NHL in those days and it was the big time. Professionally, it was a good, smart move for me at that point in my career. But personally, it would have been fun to have been in the movie. Steve and Jeff and I had all played together for the past five seasons, and it was ironic that I finally got called up right at that exact time. At the time, who in their right mind would have ever guessed that the movie would be so popular? Nobody saw that coming, no way.

"I just wish I had a dollar for every time somebody mistakenly thought that I was in the movie. I'd be a rich man. The one thing that still amazes me about the movie even to this day, though, is the fact that so many kids have seen the movie. They know all the lines and just love it. Everybody loves it, it is just pure fun. What can you say, it is a classic. Hey, as far as I am concerned the Hanson Brothers should have won Oscars!"

On the Hanson Brothers Legacy

"As for their success today as the Hanson Brothers, it is great to see. I performed with them one time when one of the guys was sick and I had a lot of fun with it. What a feeling it is to be out there with those guys, so much fun. They are really into it, even now when they are all well into their fifties. They travel around and perform in arenas all over North America. It is pretty amazing when you think about it. It is a business for them, a franchise. They all keep the long hair and truly get into character whenever they are on stage, so to speak. They have done very well for

••

Paul Newman's older brother, Arthur, worked on the movie as the unit production manager.

••

··

There were many other little interesting tidbits about the various actors and the film. For instance, because Allan Nicholls and Jerry Houser had similar curly brown hair when they got selected to be in the film, they made Allan wear a helmet to cover up his head so that they wouldn't be confused with one another. Allan was also a big fan of Larry Robinson, an NHL All-Star defenseman for the Montreal Canadians who donned a mustache, so he grew a Fu Manchu mustache in honor of him.

··

themselves and I couldn't be happier for them. The thing that I am most impressed about, though, is just how much money the Hanson Brothers have raised for charity over the years. That is the neatest part as far as I am concerned. They have helped to raise literally tens of millions of dollars over the years and that, more than anything else, should be their legacy as far as I am concerned.

"You know, those guys weren't acting in the movie. They were just being themselves and having fun. That is why they were such popular characters, they didn't force anything, they just skated and had a great time out there with the fellas. People just love them. Wherever they go they are always instantly recognized and welcomed with a smile. Even at the celebrity events that they are a part of, they are usually among the most popular people there—especially with the pro hockey players. It's wild. Who could have ever imagined that they would be touring the world 30 years later? My hat goes off to them, it is just a great, great story."

John Brophy

"*Slap Shot* was a real classic, it really was. They got it down to a tee. That is how minor league hockey was back in those days. From the bus trips to the brawls, those were some wild times. When they brought in the Hanson Brothers in the movie, to turn the club on and get the momentum going, that kind of stuff really happened. They were a spark plug, new blood, and they were a kind of tactic that teams would use to rally their players. The movie was wonderful and they nailed it to perfection as far as I am concerned."

Paul D'Amato (aka "Tim 'Dr. Hook' McCracken")

"My performance in *Slap Shot* was my first role as an actor. I had just finished performing in an off-Broadway show and heard about the movie. They were looking for actors who were hockey players and, luckily, I had been a hockey player back at Emerson College in Boston. Anyway, my agent called me and told me that my audition time was at 1:00 AM at Sky Rink in New York City. So I put my skates on and took a couple of shots on goal. Apparently they liked it because the next morning I was in George Roy Hill's office reading for the role of Tim 'Dr. Hook' McCracken. I was lucky. I was in the right place at the right time and, thankfully, it all worked out for me. I mean they looked all over the place to find actors who could skate. I can't tell you how excited I was the first time I went out onto the ice to audition and saw how many actors were out there that could barely stand up on skates. I knew I had the part at that point, which was really exciting. My heart was beating out of my chest.

"The notoriety from the movie has always been great, even now, some 30 years later. I still get people that will come up to me looking inquisitive and ask me if I played hockey. They will recognize me, but aren't quite sure from where. Whether its in gyms or in bars, people always want to come over and ask about the movie and they want you to tell them stories. It is an amazing thing, it really is.

"Nobody knew either. None of us had any idea that the movie would still be this popular all these years later. No way. We were all basically young actors and young hockey players who were trying to make as good a film as we could, while still being able to have a lot of fun—and that is exactly what we did. Even though we were on the ice some days for 13–14 hours, we were

••

After claiming that he swore very little in real life before making *Slap Shot*, Paul Newman said to *Time* magazine in 1984: "There's a hangover from characters sometimes. There are things that stick. Since *Slap Shot*, my language is right out of the locker room."

••

"When we heard that Paul Newman was going to shoot a bed scene with a naked girl we, of course, wanted to be around for it. George had already announced that was it was going to be a closed set and only the immediate cast and necessary crew people were going to be allowed to attend. But, figuring that we were going to crash the shoot, he moved it to the Johnstown Armory just to be safe. Undeterred, Steve, Jeff, myself, and Allan Nicholls all decided to sneak onto the set. When we got there, however, there were literally U.S. Military guards standing outside the door with strict orders to watch for the Hansons. We tried to schmooze them over, but they wouldn't budge. We were able to persuade a couple of soldiers into allowing us to drive one of the tanks at the armory though, which was really cool. I'm sure that if George knew we were just outside the door driving an armor tank around, that they wouldn't have felt so comfortable in there."—Dave Hanson

all still having a great time. It was a really unique situation, it really was. We laughed a lot and rarely took anything seriously. It was a wonderful experience.

"I do a lot of charity work around the movie, too. I still get together with some of the guys to raise money for good causes. I have done some golf tournaments with Yvon Barrette up in Canada, and I still see Chris Murney, who played Handrahan in the movie too. We do stuff with the New York Islanders and also for the New York City cops and firefighters in their fundraisers for 9/11 events. So it is fun to still be involved with the movie to help good causes and to still be able to hang out with those guys.

"The thing that is so neat about the movie is that it didn't use any special effects or have any big stunt doubles. It was just great hockey played by guys who did all their own acting. You don't see that in movies today, where the next explosion has to be bigger and better than the last one. This was just a great story told by really funny actors and hockey players. The realness and the rawness of that is what makes the movie so special, I think. We were just a bunch of young guys who loved hockey and were having a great time. And the fact that we were getting to be in a Universal Pictures movie alongside the legendary Paul Newman and directed by George Roy Hill, that just made it even sweeter."

Who Did You Channel to Become Dr. Hook?

"Dr. Hook is actually an amalgam of several characters, specifically former '70s tough guys Dave Schultz (Philadelphia Flyers), Bobby Schmautz (Boston Bruins), and then the shark from the movie *Jaws*. I was a hockey player growing up and used to love to watch the old brawlers go at it. Those guys were great. Add to that the fact that I had just finished performing in an off-Broadway show in which I played a guy who became a murderer while in prison. So, combine all of that together and that was the history behind Dr. Hook."

Your Most Quoted Line

"Without question, it's 'Dunlop, you suck cock.' Now, you have to remember, that was my first spoken line I ever had in a motion picture, too. So it was a real doozy and I still get asked to say it all these years later. I love it. In fact, my fingers have ached because I have signed that line so much. Whenever I sign autographs on *Slap Shot* stuff I always quote that line. It's great, a true classic."

Roy Mlakar, President of the NHL's Ottawa Senators

"I have probably seen *Slap Shot* at least 50 times. We watch the movie constantly, it is an absolute classic. Even now, with Ottawa, we all still love it. Guys are constantly quoting lines from the movie, especially in the locker room. My favorite is 'Handrahan, your wife's a dike!' People have no idea just how accurate of a depiction it really was of minor league hockey in the 1970s. It was

••

"In the scene during the final where Clarence "Screaming Buffalo" Swampton chases down Johnny Upton from behind before slamming into the boards, the war cry that Clarence yells out was actually my voice pre-recorded and looped in. Originally there was no call in the script for the war cry, but when they practiced the scene before shooting it, I did the yell as a joke. George Roy Hill liked my imitation so well that he had me do it a couple more times on audiotape and then inserted it into the sound track as Screaming Buffalo's."—Dave Hanson

••

••

"Brad Sullivan, who played Morris "Moe" Wanchuk, had a habit of chewing each bite of food he put into his mouth at least 15 times before he swallowed and took his next bite. We got intrigued whenever he was around for mealtime. We could drink beer and watch him eat all day, just fascinating stuff."—Dave Hanson

••

dead on, just dead on. I remember when I was with New Haven, and we were about to embark on a seven-hour bus trip to God knows where. We would all try to guess the number of cases of beer and packs of cigarettes that we were going to go through along the way. It was crazy. The guys would play cards in the back of the bus the whole way and tell lies. It was wonderful."

Guido Tenissi (aka "Billy Charlesbois")

"Being in the movie was a great experience for me. It was an ideal situation because I was a hockey player and didn't have to do too much acting. It is just amazing to think that the movie is still so popular all of these years later. None of us had any idea that it would take off the way that it did. It is sort of like a cult movie today. I mean all of the young kids know the lines, it is pretty funny to see. They can turn off the volume and practically recite it verbatim. As for the legacy of the movie, it is just fun to still be remembered all of these years later. I am really happy that the Hanson Brothers are still out there, doing their thing, so that we can keep it all going. Those guys have raised a lot of money for charity and had a lot of fun along the way, so I salute them and thank them."

Paul Holmgren, GM of the Philadelphia Flyers

Slap Shot is a cult classic, what else can you say? I, like most hockey fans, have seen it a million times. I love it, it's great. Heck, even my kids love the movie. It is just timeless. The movie was not very far off from reality either. People ask me all the time if it was really like that in real life and I always tell them, 'Heck yeah, it's pretty darn close!' I was actually playing with

Johnstown right before the movie started filming, but got called up to the WHA's St. Paul Fighting Saints. So, had I not gotten called up, I too would have been an extra or something in the movie like so many of the other players on the team.

"The movie was art imitating life in many regards. I mean the Philadelphia Flyers of the early 1970s, or Broad Street Bullies as they were known, revolutionized hockey at the time. They were so tough and intimidating that teams were literally terrified to play against them. They used fighting as a tactic and it worked, I mean they won two Stanley Cups during that time. I think the movie fed on that and then took it to the next level. And while the fighting scenes weren't like that in the NHL, there were times that it came pretty close to reality in the minor leagues. You know, people oftentimes tend to think of the old Flyers of that era as just brawlers, but they had some great players on those teams—guys like Bob Clarke, Billy Barber, Reggie Leech, Jimmy Watson, and Bernie Parent. And then they had tough guys like Dave Schultz, Bob Kelly, and Moose Dupont who gave the other guys a whole bunch of courage. Certainly, though, that toughness will always be a part of the legacy of those teams.

"You know, I have been with the Flyers organization for many years now and I will always remember a story that Mr. Snyder, the

• •

"Jeff, Steve, Allan Nicholls, Jerry Houser, Susan Newman, and myself created a little musical group that we affectionately called "The Loogans." We'd sit around with each other during our downtime coming up with little ditties, one of which became the song used in the hotel scene when the Hansons grabbed the desk clerk. Together we created a unique song we called, "It Had to Be Johnstown," and we even ended up going into a studio to record it. I had a friend who was a salesman for the local radio station and I got him to get the station's DJ to play it on the air. We then got invited to play and sing it live on a morning TV talk show in Pittsburgh. At the end of our performance, the show's hosts and the 30-plus old women who were sitting in the studio audience were tongue-tied. I don't think they appreciated some of the risqué verses we belted out during our performance. It was a real hoot."—Dave Hanson

• •

longtime owner of the Flyers, once told me. He told me about the time that the St. Louis Blues came into the Spectrum and literally beat up the Flyers. He never forgot that game and vowed right then and there that something like that was never going to happen again. So they brought in some tougher, more physical players and it wasn't long afterward that the Flyers started to turn the corner. Once they achieved a level of success winning that way, other teams tried to follow suit during that era. So the movie, I think, reflected a lot of what was going on at all levels of professional hockey at the time. Teams were looking to get tougher and the guys in the minor leagues knew that if they were willing to fight, then they too might get a shot at playing in the NHL."

Barry Melrose, Hockey Analyst and NHL Coach

"All I can say is that the movie was awesome. Even if you are not a hockey fan, it is a classic. I would argue that it is the best sports movie ever made. I have seen it hundreds of times, literally, and I still chuckle when I see it. How great is that? Any self-respecting hockey player knows every line from the movie, too. I remember when the movie was being shot, I was finishing up my last year of junior, up in Camloops, BC. I played with and against a lot of the guys who were in it while I was in the minors and have just gotten to know practically everybody who has been associated with the movie through the years of being in professional hockey and now in the media.

"As for the movie being a case of art imitating life, unfortunately, I would have to agree. I like to refer to those days as the 'dark ages' of hockey. Those were some tough times, literally. I tell you what, I wouldn't have wanted my son to play in that era, no way. That was the wild, wild west, where vigilante justice was a big part of the game. There were bench-clearing brawls and five-on-five line fights going on all the time—it was brutal. The movie was really not that far off, to be perfectly honest. Personally, I think the best part of the movie was how it just captured the essence of what minor league sports were really like at the time. I mean the fashion show, the bus trips, the owners pinching pennies—that stuff was dead-on. Beyond that, the music was great and the story is just fun.

"The Charlestown Chiefs jersey has got to be the most popular jersey in all of hockey, without a doubt. Whether it is hockey, broomball, ringette, or slow-pitch softball, a Chiefs jersey can always be seen worn proudly by some die-hard fan. It is great. You just have to smile and chuckle when you see that, too, because it represents fun. Or like they say in the movie, 'old-time hockey.' I love it.

"What is so great about these guys—Dave, Steve, and Jeff—is that they don't age. They are timeless. They look exactly the same today as they did 30 years ago. Hey, with the steroid scandal in baseball right now, maybe we should check these guys out because they are looking way too young and in shape! Really though, they are wonderful people and do so much for hockey—both on and off the ice. They bring joy to fans on the ice and they do so much for charity off of it, so they are to be commended, in my eyes."

Ron Docken (aka "Yvon Lebrun")

"*Slap Shot* was based on our 1974–75 team where we beat the hell out of anybody and everybody. We were a farm team of the St. Paul Fighting Saints, of the World Hockey Association, and that league was struggling financially at the time. As a result, a lot of top players who were with St. Paul wound up with us that season. So we were pretty tough, no question. We lost a lot of games

••

Slap Shot was the first Hollywood production to use hockey as its subject matter and story line.

••

....

According to the 2006 book *The Joy of Swearing* by M. Hunt, *Slap Shot* was peppered with the F-word, but when it was shown on TV, it became the first film to be dubbed with the word "freakin'." In the U.S., the replacement word soon took on a life of its own and is now frequently used in everyday speech.

....

early on in the season because we were usually a couple of men down late in our games, having lost them to fighting ejections. Because of the Carlson brothers and Dave, nobody wanted to play us. If you hit one of those guys, the other two were going to come after you and make you pay. We had a lot of donnybrooks out there and those guys were usually always right in the middle of it. Those guys beat the hell out of a lot of teams. Well, we were a couple of points out of last place at Christmas and then rallied to make the playoffs. We eventually rode that momentum and wound up winning the league title. It was a great story. We had a good team that was full of great characters.

"Shooting the movie was a lot of fun. Paul Newman couldn't have been nicer, either. We used to go out and drink beers and shoot pool at night together. He was just a normal guy, really a nice person. He was just very down to earth. Everything in the movie was pretty much true, too. Ned Dowd, whose sister wrote the script, would bring a recorder with him everywhere he went that year in order to capture the things that were being said in the locker room and on the team bus. So what you saw on screen was really what was going on. Sure, it was highly exaggerated, but for the most part it was all based on real events. Every character in the movie was based on a real player, or maybe a combination of players. Everybody in the movie, actor or skater, sort of channeled somebody to base their characters on. It is fun for us now to go back and watch the movie and try to figure out who each guy was trying to be.

"They asked me to be the back-up goalie, so it was a no-brainer for me. I thought it would be fun and figured I would make a few bucks hanging around a movie set that summer. Little did I know that it would turn into what it did. It was the

'70s, I had just gotten out of college, and I was ready to have a good time. It was a lot of fun.

"As for the movie itself, the Hanson Brothers stole the show, they really did. I don't think it was intended either, I just think that those guys were so funny and so good at playing those characters that they wound up stealing every scene. They were cast perfectly for their roles because they truly just got to be themselves. It was great and we all had a fun time doing it.

"There was a lot of downtime while we were shooting the movie. Sometimes we would get dressed and ready to go by seven in the morning and then sit around all day without ever doing a scene. We would play cards and just do whatever we could to stay busy. There was a lot of drinking going on, which naturally led to a lot of pranks being pulled. My personal favorite was the time we lit the assistant director's shoelaces on fire. We were always doing stuff like that because we knew that our jobs were pretty secure. I mean, what were they going to do, fire us? We were hockey players and we knew that we couldn't just be replaced. It wasn't like we were all auditioning for our next movie or anything, like the other actors were. So we used that to our advantage at times, maybe even too much. But it was all in good fun.

"Another time we were all at the local armory, where we had to show up to do a night scene. Well, we were bored silly from sitting around all night, waiting for our calls. So, a bunch of us hockey players decided to go over to the local tavern for some beers. Eventually, they came looking for us and we all headed back to the set. On the way back Dave Hanson ran over to this big tractor with a front-end scoop on it that was parked

• •

During filming, all of the actors and many of the hockey players were put up at the Sheraton Inn in Johnstown. Because the cast and crew were so friendly to each other and everyone they met on the streets, after three months of shooting everyone just kind of blended in with the locals. When the movie wrapped and the actors got on the bus to leave Johnstown, droves of people stood outside the hotel waving good-bye and even held up signs that read: "Good-bye, *Slap Shot*."

• •

••

The movie was filmed almost entirely in Johnstown, with a few scenes shot at the Syracuse Onondaga County War Memorial Arena, the Utica Memorial Auditorium, and at Colgate University in Hamilton, New York.

••

out front. He hopped right in and started the thing up. We all jumped on and he drove us up to the set like we were all rock stars, it was crazy.

"The legacy of the movie is far reaching. I remember serving as an assistant coach at the University of Minnesota back in the '90s and hearing references to the movie all of the time. It would be subtle too, like a guy casually saying 'and none of the stinking root beer...' Little lines, here or there, they just sort of permeate the locker room and add a whole new level of vocabulary to it. For me, personally, I literally can't go more than two days without somebody bringing up the movie to me. It may be a line or a question or something, but it always comes up somehow. It amazes me because I was just a back-up goalie who walked from point A to point B, and never really did a lot to stand out in the movie. They needed bodies, though, and I made the cut. I ended up with one speaking line in the movie. It came after the scene in the movie where Newman beat up Handrahan. I walked into the dressing room and said 'Way to go, guys!' That was it, my 15 minutes of fame, I suppose."

Jerry Houser (aka "Dave 'Killer' Carlson")

"The movie to me is like a huge scrapbook of wonderful memories. Nobody had any idea that this movie would turn out the way that it did. The fact that we are talking about it all of these years later is amazing to me. For me, it was such a great time in my life both personally and professionally. As much fun as the movie looked on screen, it was even more fun shooting it. It was just a great experience. It captured the spirit of a lot of things that were going on in sports at the time and put them in a context that everyone could enjoy. It might sound corny to say, but we were all a team. We bonded together and I think we all felt that connection. I have been on a lot of movie sets over the years, and this one was special. It was very unique and I have never been around anything like it since. Most actors are individuals and pretty private. They keep to themselves for the most part on set and when they are not working, they are in their trailers by themselves. Well, in this movie, we all hung out and totally got along with each other. There were no big egos or anything and that is what made it so cool. I fed off of that energy and gained strength from it. It was truly a wonderful feeling.

"It was a big deal for Johnstown, the community, to have a movie shot there, too. The locals were so excited about it. I mean, they had the legendary Paul Newman living there and all of these actors right there amongst them. It was pretty cool. I will never forget the time we went on a road trip together to Pittsburgh. We were at this bar and I asked this hot girl some great pick-up line like 'What time is it?' Well, we started talking and before I knew it, some guy got all up in my face. He was apparently her boyfriend or at least wanted to be her boyfriend. He is getting really physical with me and trying to intimidate me. He is like, 'Do you have a problem, you pussy?' I just wanted to back off and get out of there, I mean I did not want to get into a fight with this guy. For starters, he probably would have killed me, and beyond that I didn't know if this guy was crazy or something. So I am trying to back out of there as this guy gets right in my face and then all of a sudden I see his eyes get real big as Dave and the Carlson brothers come up behind me and say, 'Hey, Jer, what's the problem? Is this asshole giving you a hard time?' They were all calm about it and just looked at the guy like they were going to kill him. It was like the cavalry came riding in to rescue me, it was one of the greatest moments of my life. At that point I was like, 'Hell yes! This asshole has a

....

"During our Johnstown Jets days, after practices some of us would go over to Brownies Bar to sip on 25¢ drafts and watch soap operas, just like the scene in the movie when Dave Carlson first reads Dickie Dunn's article about the team being sold to Florida."—Dave Hanson

....

••

Almost all of the ice scenes were photographed on the ice using innovative sleds with cameras mounted on them. A skating Ned Dowd often
pushed around Vic Kemper, the cinematographer, on a sled and also on
a wheelchair.

••

problem and I got all up in his face!' Dave was like my personal
bodyguard at that moment and I was so happy to see him. The
guy took one look at those guys and just totally backed down.
He knew that he was about to get his ass kicked and got the hell
out of there. It was awesome. I really felt like I was a part of the
team after that. I mean, these guys really did have my back, and
that was a great feeling.

"I will say this, though. Some of the fight scenes were a bit
too realistic for my own good. I will never forget this one scene
where I had to square off with a guy and I seriously got pounded
on. Our bodies were angled to the camera as such that when he
pretended to punch me, my head would snap back. Well, he
started punching me in my shoulder, in order to make it look
and feel authentic, so I just went with it even though it hurt
a little bit. Then he just starts wailing away at me and George
Roy Hill is really getting into it. He is like, 'Great, perfect, keep
going!' Anyway, this guy grabs me by the hair and starts pounding on my face like crazy. I mean, he was really punching me,
it was like he lost it or something. I am bleeding everywhere
and am like, 'Hello? Please stop beating the hell out of me!'
Meanwhile, George is still screaming out that he loves it and
that it looks so real. Little did he know that it actually was real,
I was getting killed. Afterward, the guy goes, 'Ah, I am really
sorry I got carried away there, I sort of forgot this wasn't real.' I
just had to laugh, what was I going to do at that point? The only
good thing that came out of that scene was that I finally earned
some respect from the Hanson boys for being tough. It was as
if I had popped my fighting, tough-guy cherry at that point and
was now one of the guys. They were all so excited for me that I
was really beat up and bloody, it was great.

"George Roy Hill loved the Hanson Brothers because they were just out there to have fun and to keep everybody loose. He knew that they were hockey players and had no aspirations of becoming actors, so there was no pressure or anything like there was with other actors who were always looking for their next job. Most actors kissed his ass, but the Hansons didn't care about any of that stuff. They just wanted to have fun, drink beer, and play hockey. I think deep down he envied that carefree attitude. It was very different from anything he had been used to in the movie business, that was for sure. The Hansons didn't give a shit about any of the protocols involved with the movie. It was hilarious. They didn't read the call sheets to figure out what times they were going to be needed on set or anything like that. They would go out drinking all night and just kind of show up when it was convenient. Or, if they needed to know what time they were supposed to show up, instead of calling an assistant or something, they would just wake up George after bar time and ask him what time he wanted them there in the morning. 'Hey, George buddy, what time do you want us there tomorrow?' As actors, we couldn't believe it. But we knew that they couldn't replace these guys. I mean, who in the hell could you find to bring in on short notice that could skate like that? They had them by the balls, it was great. George just loved them and really let them get away with murder. He didn't like it when actors tried to kiss his butt, so these guys were a breath of fresh air to him, I think. He loved the fact that they were just real, not phony actors.

"There were a lot of people who got pretty bent out of shape with all of the violence and fighting in the movie. It was a pretty vulgar movie, with a lot of bad language that some people were offended by. But hey, the movie was an artist's depiction of what was really going on in hockey in those days. I mean, the Broad Street Bullies were having great success in terrorizing the

••

Paul Newman was quoted as saying: "This is the raunchiest film I've ever done. The language is quite a bit beyond blue and heavy into purple almost, and I think it will be tastefully vulgar."

••

While the crew was setting up the scene in the locker room where the Hanson Brothers were foiling up their knuckles, Jeff and Steve wrapped my entire body from head to toe with tinfoil. Then, when George called us to the set, I wobbled in to show him that I was already "foiled up." He got a big kick out of that one.

hockey world and the minor league players knew that if they wanted to make it at that level, then they were going to have to be tough. So the movie was trying to show what was really going on in those days, with all of the struggling minor league teams and how they needed to make money and use violence as a tool to not only make money but also to showcase young fighters who were looking to get a shot in the NHL. We caught some heat about it though, no question. It was controversial at the time. The NHL was not happy with it at all. They did not want the rest of the world to think that *Slap Shot* was all that hockey was about in those days. Even if it was the truth, they didn't want that image out there. So there was a lot of controversy surrounding the movie that first year, for sure. I personally took some heat, too, from parents saying that we were bad role models and stuff like that. We would just tell them that most everything that they saw in the movie was based on true events. They couldn't believe it, but it was true. That was always the basis for my argument. Sure, there was some pretty horrible stuff going on in those days, with racism, with violence, and the movie tried to make light of that and bring it to the forefront.

"You know, I have been fortunate enough to be an actor my entire life. Each role is different and you never know what it is going to be until afterward. I have done a bunch of different things, from *The Summer of '42* to *The Brady Bunch* to being the voice of one of the Keebler Elves. But this role as Killer Hanson was one of my all-time favorites for sure. It was memorable and meaningful. I mean, nobody ever comes up to me and says, 'Hey, I loved you in *Barnaby Jones*…that really changed my life.' *Slap Shot* was special, though, and I think we all feel that way about it, even three decades later. People are always coming up to me and asking me about this movie, it is amazing. As an actor, you always hope that you can land a role that you will be remembered for. This was certainly one of those roles for me and it will always be special to me in that regard. The movie was great, but it is even more than that for me. The entire experience of living in Johnstown and getting to act and play hockey with all of those guys was just a wonderful time in my life. It was truly a remarkable experience. As an actor I got to work with Paul Newman under the direction of the great George Roy Hill. It doesn't get much better than that. Then, as a hockey player wannabe I got to perform with the Hanson Brothers and all of these professional athletes who were just outstanding athletes. It was a marvelous experience, it really was. I was a 25-year-old kid at the time and it still ranks right up there with one of the greatest highlights of my career. People just love the movie, it has a cult following. It really struck a chord with hockey fans and I am just thrilled to have been a part of it."

Funny Hazing Story on Set

"The Hansons totally treated me like any other rookie that was coming into training camp. They hazed me and totally put me in my place. It was pretty hilarious. They were hockey players and the locker room was their domain, we were truly guests in their domain. I just went along with it because I wanted to experience it for what it was and try to learn as much as I could. I wanted to get down the lingo and totally soak it all in. It was great. They were always pulling pranks and practical jokes on set, too, which was always an adventure.

"In fact, when I got home from shooting the movie, I think I had post-dramatic stress disorder from sleeping with one eye open all of the time. They were constantly ribbing everyone and waiting for that opportune moment to get you. You had to

••

Paul Newman loves auto racing and is a crackerjack bridge player, an all-around athlete, an excellent caricaturist, and a popcorn connoisseur.

••

∙∙∙

Ogie Oglethorpe is often considered the *Slap Shot* character that was loosely based on the real-life Bill "Goldie" Goldthorpe. Ogie played for the fictitious Syracuse Bulldogs, while Goldie played for the Syracuse Blazers. Both had big blond Afros. Ogie was referred to by Reg Dunlop (Paul Newman) as "the worst goon in hockey," while Goldie was infamous for his rookie season with Syracuse when he amassed 25 major fighting penalties before Christmas. Ogie was deported to Canada, while Goldie was arrested for brawling with teammates at a U.S. airport and put in jail, while the rest of the team flew on to Canada. Goldie was released the next day and was escorted across the border by Canadian immigration officials.

∙∙∙

totally be on guard, or you were going to be their next victim. The Hansons terrorized the set, they really did. I remember one time when they ransacked one of the makeup guys. He was this little guy, a really nice guy who kept to himself. Well, they came running in there one day and taped him up from head to toe with hockey tape, tossed him in the shower and then took off. It was nuts! Another time the poor guy was eating outside just minding his own business and the Hansons ran up and stripped him naked, right in front of all the extras, and took off with his clothes. One time they lit his shoelaces on fire when he was sleeping.

"Nobody was safe from them. One of their favorite pranks was to put this Ben Gay–type wax stuff, which relaxed sore muscles through intense heat when it was rubbed on, all over guys' underwear while they were out skating. They would come back from a hard day of work, shower, and then get dressed—only to keel over in pain once that stuff kicked in on their you-know-what. Those bastards got me with that trick a few times and it totally sucked. That stuff got all over your balls and would just burn. You would jump in the shower and the hot water would just open your pores, so that the medicine could penetrate even further. It was horrible. They would just laugh and laugh, and then take off like sharks on the prowl for their next victim.

"I will never forget the time I had to go to the bathroom in the locker room. There was this one stall in there where there were four walls, but it was open on top. Well, I snuck in there hoping to God the Hansons wouldn't see me. So I am in there for about a minute, doing my thing, when all of a sudden I got completely drenched by a garbage can full of freezing water. Then they just doused me with baby powder, totally covering me from head to toe. I was just a mess and couldn't do a thing about it. They all took off running, laughing like hell at my expense. I would see them later and they would all totally deny it, even getting offended that I would accuse them of such a thing. I couldn't even be mad at them because it was so damn funny.

"Then, after I got cleaned up, I went to put my shoes on and they were filled with shaving cream. It never ended with those guys. Another time I came up to my room after a long day of shooting and they had totally trashed my room. I mean my mattress was in the shower and my clothes were all tied in knots and hung out the window, hanging several stories below. I nearly went insane with those guys around. They abused everybody, not just me, but I would like to think I got the brunt of it.

"We weren't safe on the ice either. I will never forget the first time those guys got me with the old 'sawed stick' trick. Sticks in those days had a little silver sticker decal near the bottom heel, for decoration or something. Well, they would take your stick when you were doing a scene or something, peel back that sticker, and saw the wooden shaft halfway through with a skinny hacksaw blade. They would then put the sticker back and wait for you to grab your stick. I grabbed my stick one time after they had booby-trapped it, and wound up taking a big slap shot with it. Well, sure enough, the thing snapped right in half and I fell right on my face. Those guys just started laughing their asses off and all I could do was shake my head.

"This prank actually led to the worst offense of them all, though, my 'rookie initiation.' After breaking my stick, I had to

• •

Paul Newman was 51 years old when he shot *Slap Shot*. In 1976, he had been acting for 21 years and had already made 36 films. By the time the movie was shot, Paul had already received five Best Actor Oscar nominations and won an Academy Award for the 1973 movie *The Sting*.

• •

· ·

The Hanson Brothers have been a source of inspiration for many people in the last 30 years. They inspired a popular WWE professional wrestling tag-team duo called the Dudley Boys, who wore the black-rimmed taped glasses as part of their appearance. The Hanson Brothers of *Slap Shot* have also provided inspiration to a Canadian rock band called the Hanson Brothers.

· ·

go into the locker room to get a new stick. So I walk in there and who do I see waiting for me? Dave, Steve, and Jeff. They are the only ones in there and right away I am nervous. They go, 'Hey Jer... How ya doin?' I am like, 'Fine guys, what's up?' I just knew something was going on, they made me so damn paranoid. Sure enough, they grabbed me and pinned me down on one of the training tables. They are holding me down and I am struggling to get loose, and that is when I realized what was going on. They then proceeded to pull my jersey up over my head and then yank my pants down. At this point I knew I was in trouble.

"So, I just relaxed and stopped fighting, figuring that would bore them and I would escape on a bit of reverse psychology. Nope. They just kept at it and the next thing I knew they had put shaving cream all over my crotch. Then, to make matters worse, they tied a string around my dick and strung it up on the water pipes in the ceiling. It was like a makeshift torture chamber. If I moved, they would just yank on the string. They literally had me by the balls, I was trapped. Before I knew it, Dave Hanson pulled out a razor and started shaving my crotch. There was nothing I could do. They were laughing so hard I was terrified that they were going to cut my dick off. I started screaming 'Help! Help!' and thank God one of the assistant directors walked in. He comes in and says, 'Hey, what the hell are you guys doing? We need Jerry on the set!' So they let me go and I untied the string, accepting my initiation like a man. I got dressed and headed out to the set with my head held high. Yes, I was now officially a hockey player.

"The pranks were never ending and we all got into the act. One of my favorites was the time when we got Newman. Paul had this sauna installed in the hotel where we were staying, so he could go in there at night and relax over a couple of beers. So one time we went in there and filled the entire thing with popped popcorn. I mean every inch of that thing was packed with the stuff. It was absolutely hilarious. He came in there and just about died; he thought it was pretty funny. Another time we got Tom Bronson pretty good. Tom was the movie's wardrobe guy, a real nice guy. Anyway, I can't remember who did it, but they filled this poor guy's room with rabbits. He came back to quite a surprise, let me tell you. They made a hell of a mess in there."

Yvon Barrette (aka "Denis Lemieux")

"None of us ever could have imagined that the movie would be as successful as it was. It was really a surprise for me to see just how many people loved the movie from around the world. It was unbelievable. Of course, it was huge in the U.S. and in Canada, but there are thousands and thousands of fans of the movie all over the globe. It has a cult following over in Europe, which was just wonderful to see.

"The neatest thing about the legacy of the movie now is the fact that we have raised so much money for charity. I think we have really made a big difference in a lot of peoples' lives because of this and that means a lot to me. It has brought a lot of joy to my life over the years, that is for sure. I don't think

• •

Ned Dowd was born in Boston and graduated from Bowdoin College in Maine in 1972. There, he was involved in track and hockey—even setting a school scoring record in hockey that stood for almost 25 years. He later went to McGill University in Canada where he gained his master's degree before playing pro hockey. He played two years of pro before taking on the role of Ogie Oglethorpe, his first job in the film industry. After pursuing an acting career, he went on to become an extremely successful movie producer.

• •

....

During the 1973—74 hockey season, the coach of the USHL Marquette Iron Rangers placed a $50 bounty on the head of the Green Bay Bobcats player Ernie Dupot. Jack Carlson, of the three bespectacled Carlson brothers, was the first to catch old Ernie and promptly collected the loot. No word on if he shared with his two brothers or not.

....

there is a day that goes by where somebody doesn't mention a line from the movie to me, it is really a lot of fun. I recently did a signing in Montreal where there was a little boy, his father, and his grandfather, all there to meet me—three generations of *Slap Shot* fans. That kind of thing is just amazing to me, that it would still be so popular all of these years later.

"Being on the set of the movie was so much fun. It was a fantastic experience, for sure. The camaraderie on the set amongst all the guys was really unique and unlike anything I had ever been around before. To be able to work with Paul Newman and Strother Martin was unbelievable for me as a young actor. The script was so well written, too, it was a great story. Nancy Dowd did a fantastic job in capturing the essence of what minor league hockey was really like at that time.

"Then George Roy Hill did a great job in directing it, too—he was a real legend in the industry. You know, I have been sober for 20 years now, but back then when we shot the movie I was drinking a lot. I was a young actor and was really insecure about how I was doing. So, one night after drinking quite a bit, I called up George Roy Hill at midnight to ask him how I was doing. Needless to say, while he was pleased with my acting, he was not pleased with my late-night antics. I was just thrilled to be a part of it, to tell you the truth.

"One of the worst moments of the movie for me came during the latter part of filming when I got a serious knee injury. A guy took a slap shot at me from inside the blue line and it got me right inside the knee. I was in so much pain I couldn't even open my eyes. So I went to the hospital in George Roy Hill's limousine to get checked out. But when I got there I had to wait in line behind this guy who had just gotten shot by a policeman. I didn't know what the heck was going to happen after that because it started to get pretty crazy in there. There were some pretty rough characters in Johnstown, that was for sure. Luckily I got checked out okay and I wound up having to stay off of it for about 10 days. Everybody came to see me afterward and brought me gifts, everything from nudey magazines to fruit baskets to booze. Allan Nichols even wrote a song for me and they all came and sang to me. It was great! We had a great camaraderie on the set, all of us, it was neat. We all genuinely cared about each other, which was very special.

"The movie was a comedy, plain and simple. Sure, it was a parody of what was really going on in the world of minor league hockey, but we weren't out to make some big political statement. I mean, there was so much fighting going on at that time in history. It was ridiculous. So our goal was show what was going on in an over-the-top way and try to have fun with it. The violence in the movie was there to make people laugh, but to also show

• •

Slap Shot's budget was $6 million and it barely broke even in theaters. Although it opened in theaters to less than raving reviews, it remains one of the most rented videos of all time. NBC film critic Gene Shalit's review of *Slap Shot* claimed, "Any parent who'd take their kid to see this movie should be 'slapped,' or, in some cases, 'shot!'" Gene Siskel, of the famous Siskel and Ebert movie critic duo, once noted that his greatest regret as a critic was giving *Slap Shot* a mediocre review when he first saw it. After watching it several more times, he later listed it as one of the greatest American comedies of all time. When Jay Gould Bounum, a respected film critic for the *Wall Street Journal*, watched *Slap Shot*, he seemed entertained and repulsed by a movie so "foul-mouthed and unabashedly vulgar" on one hand, yet so "vigorous and funny" on the other. Since then, *Slap Shot* has reached legendary status by some. "One of the Top Ten Sports Movies Ever!" proclaimed *Sports Illustrated*, ESPN.com, and *The Sporting News*. In 1998 *Maxim Magazine* named *Slap Shot* as the "Best Guy Movie of All Time." The 50th Anniversary Issue of *GQ* magazine named *Slap Shot* as one of the "30 films that changed men's lives," and in their November 2007 issue, author Dan Jenkins proclaimed *Slap Shot* "the best sports film of the past 50 years."

• •

··

In the 2007 July issue of *Sports Illustrated* magazine, the Hanson Brothers were featured on the cover. It was the only hockey-related cover on *SI* for 2007. When Paul Newman was asked by *Sports Illustrated* writer Austin Murphy about the Hanson Brothers, he said, "They were very professional, and they were crazy. We drank a lot of beer."

··

that if pro hockey kept up its ways that perhaps someday it might look like that. Personally, I don't understand why there is so much fighting in hockey even to this day. I don't like it at all, I don't think it adds anything to the game, to be honest.

"You know, for the Hansons, the movie was a really special part of their lives. So much was based on their real-life story and about all of the antics that they had gotten into as minor league players. But for me, it was much different. Even though I was from Canada and grew up playing hockey, I was not a professional player or anything like that. I played when I was a kid and that was it. I was an actor and that was my profession. So it was very challenging to learn how to play hockey again at a high level and still be able to act and perform at a high level. I was very different in real life from my character, Dennis Lemieux. Beyond that, I would just say that for me, personally, it was tough to put on all of that goalie gear every day. It got hot and stinky and after a while I wanted to just burn it. I got through it, though, and the end product was something I am still very proud of."

Jim Boo, Former Teammate

"I was in *Slap Shot* as a goon with the Hyannisport Presidents. I had just finished up playing with the Gophers, where we won the NCAA national championship in 1976 under Herb Brooks. That summer I got a call one day from a guy from Universal Pictures and he told me that I was holding up the movie. I was like, 'What in the world are you talking about?' He then told me that Dave had informed them that unless they got me in the movie, that he was going to quit. That was Dave, always looking out for his buddies. So, I hopped on a flight

● ●

Nancy Dowd, *Slap Shot*'s screenwriter, won an Oscar for co-writing the 1978 movie *Coming Home.*

● ●

for Johnstown and wound up sneaking into a few scenes. It was a real thrill to be out there and to be a part of such a great movie. It was a fun few weeks, that was for sure. The thing about the movie that nobody realizes is that it was a true story. Sure, they made the scenes a little funnier and took some liberties, but for the most part all of that stuff really happened in one way or another.

"As far as the movie went, it was a lot of standing around and waiting all day. It was the old hurry-up-and-wait deal, where you would sit around for three hours in your gear in order to film a scene that took two minutes. It got boring at times, but we made the best of it. We actually wound up getting to play some good pick-up hockey while we were out there, which was fun, too. We had some pretty intense scrimmages, let me tell you. There were some bitter enemies on those rival teams, and sometimes guys would go at it. Then we would get cleaned up and go out and party together at night. It was great.

"Getting to know Paul Newman was neat, too—what a guy. He would drink beer with us and just loved to hang out with the guys. For as big of a star as he was, he was really just a normal guy. What a nice guy, not egotistical at all. I think he was more fascinated with us than we were with him, to tell you the truth. He couldn't believe that we got to play hockey for a living. I actually stayed in touch with him for a few years and would see him when he came to Minnesota to race his car up at the

● ●

Duluth, Minneapolis, Syracuse, and Utica were all considered the primary location for the movie, but Henry Bumstead, Universal's art director, insisted on Johnstown because he wanted a park in the middle of town with a statue of a dog in it. Needless to say, Johnstown won out.

● ●

....

The movie employed some 5,100 non-speaking extras and paid them a whopping $2.30 an hour to be a part of the movie.

....

Brainerd Speedway. It is amazing to think about what an acting icon he has become around the world. What a great guy."

Glen Sonmor, Former Coach

"*Slap Shot* was such a wonderful movie. I just laugh like hell every time I see it. My father-in-law, a guy by the name of Johnny Mitchell, was the team's general manager. The actor Strother Martin played his character, Joe McGrath, and they actually used his real office in the movie as well. We were always in touch, talking about which kids were playing well and which ones weren't. I used to fly into Pennsylvania from time to time to check out certain players we were considering bringing up. It was our farm team and I had to stay on top of those things. We were both real high on the Carlson brothers and knew that they were going to be something special, too. Jack got called up to play with us here in St. Paul just before the movie started to shoot, otherwise he would have been in the movie as the third brother. Dave, of course, wound up taking his spot instead. The thing about the movie that not many people realize is that it was pretty accurate. Sure, they took some liberties here and there, but for the most part everything that happened in the movie was stuff that really happened down there. Those were some wild times. It still amazes me that the movie remains so popular even 30 years later. That is really something."

Chapter 8

Married at the Aces...
And Then Off to the Races

WHEN WE FINALLY FINISHED FILMING IN JUNE, MY BRIDE-TO-BE, Sue, said it was time for me to focus on our upcoming wedding. I did score a few points by getting her and her co-worker at WJNL radio into a scene in the movie, however, which was pretty cool. They played a couple of groupies riding with the Hanson Brothers and Killer Carlson on the backseat of our convertible during the parade. It was fun, but she made it clear that playtime was over for her big boy after that.

Up to this point, she and her family had been working on all of the arrangements, while I did virtually nothing to contribute to the end of my bachelorhood. I did go to Sue's home in Nanty Glo one afternoon to sit with her mom and sister to help out with the wedding plans. When I started to give them my input on how I thought some things should be, they jumped all over me like a pack of starving wolves on a wounded rabbit. That's when I said, "Okay. I'm going back to Minnesota. Just send me the invitation to let me know when and where to show up for the wedding." My friend Jim Boo was still with me after spending some time in the movie, so we packed up some clothes and my white shepherd pup, Caesar, hopped into Sue's green 1970 Monte Carlo, and drove to Minnesota.

About a week before the wedding, I flew back to Johnstown with my friend Steve Sandback. The night before the wedding we all went out on the town to celebrate my last night as a free man. We really didn't do anything too crazy, but we did manage to find a bit of trouble after a few too many beers. My brother, who was 20 at the time, got into a bit of a fuss with another guy at a bar. Luckily, before a big scuffle could break out one of the guys in the bar yelled out, "Hey, it's Dave 'Killer' Hanson!" Fortunately at that point tensions eased and we got drinks bought for us the rest of the night.

The next day, July 24, 1976, was my wedding day, and it was really hot outside. We all got up late in the morning with hangovers and panicked when we couldn't figure out whose tuxedo was whose. We got them all mixed up when we brought them into the house together. It took over an hour of scrambling and trying on different pants, shirts, coats, cummerbunds, and shoes from the five sets of tuxedos before we finally figured out what went with what. We showed up in front of St. Mary's Church in Nanty Glo at about 1:15 PM, fifteen minutes late. As soon as I got out of the car, it was a mad rush to get into the church to start the ceremony. My mom and dad were there, along with my sisters, Joni and Joyce, my uncle David, and Don's future wife, Pat. On Sue's side, the entire Kaschalk family was there to fill up most of the church, as were many of our friends from Johnstown. After the church ceremony, it was off to the Aces.

The Aces Lounge, where Paul Newman offered to take Lilly Braden out for a night on the town in *Slap Shot*, was a real place in Johnstown. The Aces had a huge stage where a live band was playing when we walked into a massive crowd of over 500 wedding guests. As soon as we got there, I was handed two Western Union telegrams. One was from George Roy Hill and the other from Paul Newman. Both sent their regrets for not being able to attend, along with their best wishes. Paul added that when we were in Los Angeles on our way to Hawaii for our honeymoon, we should call him so he could throw a post-wedding party for us.

Even though George, Paul, and the others from the movie did not make it, everything about the reception was perfect. The eating, drinking, socializing, and dancing was a blast for everyone. After six hours of craziness, we finally got to our hotel suite at the beautiful Cottage Inn on trucker's Route 22 in Ebensburg. The first thing we did was count our dollar-dance money, which turned out to be a tidy amount that helped us pay for the reception. Then we hit the sack and passed out almost immediately.

The next day we went to Sue's parents' house to open wedding gifts, and I wound up playing tennis all day with Sue's brother-in-law, Joe Horgas. We then went out for some post-tennis refreshments and did not get back to the house until late in the evening. As such, I wound up spending my second day of married life sleeping on the floor at the foot of Sue's bed with my dog and a six-pack of Iron City beer. Sue made it very clear that if I thought I was getting into bed with her to enjoy what I missed out on the night before, I was sorely mistaken.

After a long night on the floor with my trusted four-legged companion, Sue and I patched things up and headed to St. Paul for another wedding reception with all of my family and friends who were not able to make it to Johnstown. There, another 150 guests gathered at the Trend Bar on University Avenue for more drinking, eating, and dancing.

Finally it came time for our official honeymoon to Hawaii. Believe it or not, I had actually won the trip the year before when I randomly entered a contest put on by Hotel Intercontinental. The timing couldn't have been better; what a wonderful vacation. On the way home from Maui we stopped in L.A. and decided to stay for a few days and go to Disneyland. When we finally arrived back in Minnesota, we moved into an apartment with my Uncle Dave, who was also sharing it with another guy. Our plan was to stay there temporarily until I went to training camp and figured out where I was going to be playing.

I would go off every morning to skate at Augsburg College with a bunch of other guys who were also getting ready for training camp. After that, I would go lift weights or go the boxing gym to work out and spar with Jim Boo, and then I often headed to the bar for a few beers with the guys. During this time, Sue was stuck in the apartment, and oftentimes alone with my Uncle Dave's roommate, who was a creepy character, to say the least. Sue had no way to get around, because I had the car. I later found out that she made several calls to her parents in Nanty Glo crying about her loneliness, telling them that she didn't think she wanted to be married to me anymore. Fortunately for me, her dad, God bless his soul, insisted that she stick it out. In hindsight, while I wanted to be married to Sue, I wasn't prepared to make the commitment that a good husband makes. I give Sue all the credit for hanging in there with me during this initial stretch.

When training camp invitations finally rolled in I was in terrific shape. I weighed about 195 pounds with about 4 percent body fat. I had worked very hard on honing my fighting skills in the boxing ring. My first invite was with the NHL's Atlanta Flames in Marietta, Georgia. When I arrived, head coach Fred Creighton had a team meeting with everyone who was in camp, most of whom seemed like giants to me. There was 6'3" Pat Quinn, 6'3" Willie Plett, 6'3" Curt Bennett, 6'3" Ed Kea, and a lot of 6'2" guys, plus many others—big ol' farm boys who stood right along with them. There I was, a 6'1" long-haired kid with an earring that I just had put in.

Camp went very well for me, as I didn't let the size or experience of the other guys affect my play. I played my typical physical game and got into a couple of scraps with some of their tough guys. When it came time for the roster to be trimmed, Coach Creighton told me I did not make the cut, but that he wanted to sign me with their farm team instead, the Tulsa Oilers of the CHL. I had planned to accept his offer, but that night at the hotel I received a call from Glen Sonmor. How he tracked me down, I don't know, but he told me that the Fighting Saints were back in business. The franchise had folded in February, but had been purchased by a new ownership group and brought back to life as the "New Fighting Saints." He told me that he wanted me to come back to St. Paul to join the team. I was thrilled and left immediately.

The Saints had already started their training camp when I arrived to the St. Paul Civic Center. It was a typical Glen Sonmor camp loaded with mix of talented skill players and enforcers. Glen loved tough guys and really viewed fighting as a tactic. He was old school and felt strongly that in order for a team to be successful it had to have a handful of players who could intimidate the opposition. He had the Carlson brothers, Pat Westrum, Bill Butters, John Arbor, and Gord Gallant, among others who were all looking to become one of Sonmor's soldiers.

At the end of camp, Glen signed me. He decided to send me to the minors again, though, but this time with the promise that I would be back sooner rather than later. The Saints had changed their farm team from Johnstown to Hampton, Virginia, so I headed out to play for the Hampton Gulls in the Southern Hockey League. Once there, Sue and I found a neat place on the Chesapeake Bay to rent. It was a small two-story house built on stilts. A young military couple lived on the first floor and we were on the top floor. When the bay's tide would roll in under the front of the house, the place would sway on the stilts. It had a big deck out the front that faced the bay and it was really relaxing to sit out on the deck watching the ships and the sea gulls. When the tide went out, however, it took a while to get accustomed to the stinky fishy smell that was left behind on the beach. It became the popular place for some of the guys to gather for some relaxing beers and barbecue.

The Gulls were led by a coaching legend, John Brophy. Brophy was about 43 years old, had a full head of white hair, spoke with kind of a quick step to his speech, and had a no-nonsense manner. He garnered immediate respect by just his presence, because you knew he was a man who had faced many battles during his time on the ice. "Broph" had a well-deserved reputation of being a fierce competitor and for doing almost anything to win. He played 18 seasons as a defenseman in the old rough-and-tumble Eastern Hockey League from 1955–73, and he retired with nearly 4,000 career penalty minutes, the most in EHL history. (He would go on to coach for about 50 years before retiring at the age of 74. He won 1,034 games, second only to Scotty Bowman's 1,244 professional regular-season victories.) He was a man after my heart and became one of my favorite coaches.

One of the first indications I had that John and I were going to really get along was during our first week of practice. John was demanding at practice and really pushed everyone to always skate hard and hit hard in practice. At the end of a practice one morning, I was standing next to him when a rookie on the team skated up to him and said, "Broph, what do I do if I get into a stick fight?" John asked him if he was sure he really wanted to know and the kid said, "Hell yes!" John then squared off in front of the kid and told him to drop his stick and gloves. When the kid did, with lightning speed John whacked him on top of his head with his hockey stick. The rookie dropped to the ice like a sack of potatoes and had blood oozing from the fresh split in his scalp. As the kid looked up from the ice at John in a bit of a daze and a state of shock, John simply said, "Kid, lesson No. 1: Don't ever drop your stick first." Then he just skated off chuckling to himself.

The Southern Hockey League didn't seem to have the same intensity and hockey mayhem that I was accustomed to after two years in Johnstown. As much as I enjoyed playing for Brophy and in the SHL, where the weather was always nice, my goal was to get back to St. Paul to play with the Saints.

Just before Christmas, I finally got the call to fly to St. Paul to dress for my first game at the St. Paul Civic Center against the San Diego Mariners. I was so pumped and excited to finally have my new red and gold Saints uniform on—I wanted to make a statement. So, early in the first period and before I even got out onto the ice for my first shift, one of our players got into a small scrap with Paul Shmyr, a hard-nosed defenseman for the Mariners. On the way to the penalty box, Shmyr skated by our bench and made a nasty gesture toward us. Not even thinking, I dropped my gloves and catapulted straight over the boards and rushed straight at him. No way was I going to let him get away with disrespecting my team. But before I could even get close to him, the linesman grabbed me and shoved me into the penalty box. Shmyr just skated away laughing. I wound up getting ejected from the game for leaving the bench during an altercation, and even though I got my name on the score sheet, I never got to play a shift in my first big-league game in front of my hometown fans.

When I arrived in St. Paul, there was talk about guys not getting paid or even getting their meal money. I didn't care because I just wanted to play. But as time went on, it got more intense with guys threatening to boycott games or even leave the team to go play in the rival NHL. We went on one trip where our coach, Harry Neale, and our GM, Glen Sonmor, got a bag full of cash from the owner in the airport hallway just before we got on the plane to use as meal money. It was crazy. Sadly, the fateful day came in January when the plug was officially pulled and the Saints folded for the second and final time. When it was all said and done I wound up playing there for a little over a month. I got into seven games, accumulated two assists, and racked up 35 penalty minutes. Before I left, Don Nedercorn, the equipment manager, gave me a pair of Saints hockey gloves and hockey pants because he knew I hadn't been paid since I got there and was really dejected to leave. I was living the dream by playing in "the show" with incredible players like Dave Keon, Johnny "Pie" McKenzie, and John Garrette, not to mention my Minnesotan friends Jack and Steve Carlson, Bill Butters, Pat Westrum, and Mike Antonovich. This was the big time, we were playing against legends like Gordie Howe and Bobby Hull, but now it was over. I called my wife and said, "I'm coming back." When I got back, however, I was in for yet another shocker.

As soon as I got back to Hampton and went to the coliseum where we played, Broph pulled me aside to tell me that the league was on the verge of folding. I couldn't believe what I was hearing. First the Saints and now the Gulls? Already a couple of teams in the league had gone out of business, which is why Jeff Carlson was in Hampton when I arrived. His team, the Greensboro Generals, had closed their doors, so Broph brought him in to be a Gull. We played one game together in a Gulls uniform and then the SHL folded.

Sue and I moved out of our scenic beach house, grabbed the dog, and stuffed everything we owned into the van we had bought while in Hampton, including Jeff, and headed back to Johnstown. When we got back, I dropped Jeff off in town while Sue and I went to Nanty Glo to unload everything at her parents' house.

I immediately phoned the Jets to see about playing there again and they jumped at the possibility. When I went to Johnny Mitchell's office, instead of meeting with Mitch, I was met by one of the owners, Ed Hoke. I asked him where Mitch was and he told me that Mitch had resigned, which I couldn't believe because the Jets were Mitch's life.

I did not have a good feeling about playing for the new ownership, but I had no other choice at the time. The team had many of the guys back on it from the year before, which I thought was a good thing. But by this time, they also had a flood of players come and go through their roster, which was not a good sign. Around the time I arrived, the team was dwelling near the bottom of the NAHL standings and their home attendance was very poor. Ed Hoke signed me to a contract for $275 a week and then offered to pay me an extra $50 for every fight I got into. I felt insulted by his offer and told him that I don't fight for money, I fought for my team. After playing six games and accumulating three assists with 27 penalty minutes, I wound up signing with the WHA's New England Whalers.

I signed a two-way contract with the Whalers and was told to report to their farm club in Providence, Rhode Island. The team played in the American Hockey League, which was the league where most of the NHL teams put their players, and it definitely was a huge step up for me. The team was called the Rhode Island Reds and the logo on the front of the jersey was a big chicken head. By the time I got there, it was like a revolving door. By the time I left, they had close to 50 players go through the organization, which was one of the reasons why the team ended up in last place in the AHL and missed the playoffs.

When I told Sue that I had signed with the Whalers and was going to Providence, she said she had enough of packing and unpacking or driving around the country. Sue knew I wanted to chase my dream and she was completely supportive, even at her own sacrifice. I packed up my hockey bag and another suitcase, then hopped onto the little commuter plane out of the Johnstown airport and flew off to Providence, where I would live in a hotel until the end of the season.

After playing in the SHL, the AHL was really a change. The skill level of the players was much higher and the tempo of the game much faster. Players were bigger, stronger, quicker, and more disciplined. It was not the level of play that the WHA offered, but it was just a short step below.

I was still playing defense when I went to Providence and one of my defensive partners was Bill Mikkelson. Bill had spent time going back and forth between the AHL and the NHL. One night we were playing in Rochester against the Americans. During the game, their goalie, Jim "Seaweed" Pettie, chopped me in the leg and I started a bench-clearing brawl with him.

After my brawl with Pettie, the Rochester fans were all over me, throwing insults as well as objects at me as I was escorted off the ice. Later that night, after the game, Bill and I went to a nightclub across town. While we were there enjoying ourselves, I got a tap on the shoulder from one of the bar's bouncers. He asked if he could speak to me outside because it was too noisy in the place. He said he was a big hockey fan of the Amerks and really enjoyed watching me play in the game that night.

As I walked with him, I passed Bill and nodded at him to follow, because I thought something was up. As soon as I stepped outside, the guy, along with a couple of the other bouncers, grabbed me and started slugging me. Just then, Bill came flying out the door and jumped on them, trying to get them off me. As fists were flying and people were screaming, I got spun around by someone who I immediately cold cocked. The guy went down and yelled, "Hey, I'm just trying to help you!"

It was Jim Pettie, the goalie from Rochester who I got into a fight with during the game earlier that evening. Jim helped get everything settled down just as the cops pulled up. He spoke to the cops and they agreed to drive Bill and me back to the hotel. When we got back, Bill discovered he had lost his plate for his false teeth and I lost my watch. We both had some major lumps on our heads and bloodied knuckles, but we laughed about the whole thing as we rode the elevator to our room.

The team ended up in last place in the AHL and didn't make the playoffs. But just as the season ended I got called up to be with New England Whalers in Hartford, Connecticut. When I arrived, it looked like the Saints team all over again. Many of the former Saints had gone to play with the Whalers when Minnesota folded, so it was nice to be back with some familiar faces and friends.

While I was there, the team had a set of twins from Sweden, Thommy and Christer Abrahamsson. Thommy was a defenseman and Christer was a goalie. They were not fully accustomed to the American culture and the English language, so a couple of the guys told them that in the States, when you want to make a friendly gesture to someone, you stick up your middle finger at them. The brothers were eager to be friendly, so as they drove through a tough section of town the next day on their way to the rink, they flipped the bird to a group hanging out on a corner, only to be chased all the way to the arena by the angry mob. We came clean with them on that one after sharing a good laugh.

The Whalers, which finished the regular season in fourth place, played the first round of the playoffs against the league champion, Quebec Nordiques. Harry Neale had me dress for the first game in Quebec. Midway through the game, Neale sent me out onto the ice to put their tough guy, Paul Baxter, a rugged defenseman, in his place. I did everything I could to get Baxter to drop his gloves with me, but he wouldn't. I was never one to just sucker-punch a guy and always prided myself in taking a straight approach in order to get someone to fight me.

When I got back to the bench, Harry yelled at me because I didn't clock the guy, and from that point on, he never played me again. The Whalers wound up losing the series in five games and the Nordiques went on to beat Winnipeg for the Avco Cup playoff championship. Meanwhile, after being with six different teams in four different leagues during the 1976–77 season, I was worn out and ready to get home to my new wife. So I went back to Nanty Glo to reunite with Sue and my dog.

After spending half the summer at Sue's folks' home, we traveled to St. Paul to stay with my parents. My new agent, Keith Hanzel, had contacted Ted Lindsay, the new general manager of the Detroit Red Wings. Ted wanted to sign me and Keith was able to negotiate a five-year contract with the team, including a one-way escalating yearly salary, whether I played in Detroit or the minors. It was a great deal. I have to believe that Ted was influenced by not only my penalty minutes statistics, but also by the movie, *Slap Shot*, because right after he signed me, the

Red Wings adopted a familiar promotional slogan: "Aggressive Hockey Is Back In Town." The Detroit *Free Press* newspaper even sent a photographer and sportswriter to St. Paul to interview me for a story and to take pictures of me hitting my speed bag in the backyard. I didn't care; I was thrilled to be playing for a top-flight NHL organization.

When I arrived at the Red Wings camp in Kalamazoo, Michigan, Ted Lindsay called everyone into the hotel's ballroom for a very important meeting. After greeting us and telling us, "Every spot on the team is open and we won't cut you, you will cut yourselves," he announced to us that Kalamazoo had the largest per capita record of people contracting gonorrhea of anywhere in the U.S. So, he said, be sure to keep your focus on training camp and your pecker in your pants.

There was a flood of players at this camp. After just a couple of days into it, Larry Wilson, the Red Wings' top minor league coach, stepped onto the middle of the ice to tell everyone where they stood. Some guys were going home, some were going to Detroit, some guys were staying in Kalamazoo, their second-tier farm team, while others were going to their top farm team, the Kansas City Red Wings. As for me, I was heading to Kansas City. They would not allow me to return to Nanty Glo to get Sue and drive to Kansas City, so Sue packed up the van and, along with her brother, mom, and dad, drove close to 15 hours to meet me in Shawnee Mission, Kansas. Once they got there, we moved into a nice apartment, flew her parents and brother back to Johnstown, and got settled just long enough to feel like it was home.

I really liked playing with the guys on this team and playing in the Central Hockey League. The cities we played in were fun places, like Dallas, Fort Worth, Oklahoma City, Tulsa, and Salt Lake City. The movie was big news in the hockey world and the notoriety was all right.

After playing 15 games for the KC Red Wings, I got a call late one night from our equipment manager. He told me to come to the rink and get my hockey gear. Larry, our coach, told him that Ted Lindsay called and that he wanted me in Detroit. This was it, the call I had been waiting a lifetime for.

I took the first flight to Detroit. I was really excited about being called up to the parent club and felt that I was finally going to make it to the NHL. After arriving in Detroit, I had no idea what I was supposed to do or where I was supposed to go. I picked everything up and started for the door when Ted Lindsay came walking in. I said, "Hi, Mr. Lindsay," and he said, "Here's your ticket to fly back to Kansas City. I just traded you to Birmingham. Good luck." He handed me the ticket, turned around, and left, while I stood there not believing what had just happened.

It turned out that Lindsay and Gilles Leger, the general manager of the WHA Birmingham Bulls, had just made the first-ever player trade between the NHL and WHA and I was a part of it—Steve Durbano, who signed with Detroit as a free agent, and I got traded from Detroit to Birmingham for Tim Sheehy and Vaclav Nedomansky.

Still in shock, I flew back to Kansas City to prepare to head to Alabama. Just before we were ready to leave, I got a call from Mr. Leger, who informed me that he wanted me to first report to the Hampton Gulls. So, we reworked our map to drive 1,200 miles back to Hampton, Virginia, and my favorite coach, John Brophy. When we got to Hampton, we quickly found an apartment in an Amish part of town. My stay in Hampton lasted a whopping five games before I got summoned to Birmingham. After my travels of the year before, and the way this one was starting out, both Sue and I figured it was going to be another *Gulliver's Travels* season. What was unique about this one, though, was that Mr. Leger had brought in Glen Sonmor to serve as the team's head coach, and I knew that Glen wanted me on his team.

It felt good to be wanted, let me tell you. So Sue and I packed up the van to drive another 800 miles to go play hockey in the Deep South.

Chapter 9

Sing Dixie to Me

WHEN I WALKED INTO THE BIRMINGHAM-JEFFERSON CIVIC Center for the first time and found my way to the dressing room, I couldn't believe my eyes—my new teammates were menacing. I wondered if we were going to play hockey or if we were going to a gang fight. I soon found out that we were going to have gang fights while we played hockey.

On Thanksgiving Day, the Cincinnati Stingers came to Birmingham. Glen started Steve Durbano, Frank Beaton, Serge Beaudoin, Gilles Bilodeau, and Bobby Stephenson, a group that by season's end accumulated over 900 penalty minutes. The Stingers started Robbie Ftorek, Del Hall, Jamie Hislop, Ron Plumb, and Barry Legge, who accounted for about 220 penalty minutes all season. The puck dropped and just 24 seconds into the game the Bulls started pounding on the Stingers like they were sacrificial turkeys. Needless to say, we ended up beating the Stingers 12–2. The next day the newspapers called the event the "Thanksgiving Day Massacre." Another Cincinnati publication wrote, "It was like watching the German army invading Poland...absolute carnage everywhere you looked."

The next time Cincy came to town, they brought with them an old nemesis of mine from my NAHL days, Paul Stewart. Stewie was a real gamer and a pretty tough character. He had a Boston accent and would always talk to me before or after a fight. We'd go at it for a couple of minutes and after the linesman broke it up, he'd say things like, "Hey, Killer, I bet the fans really loved that one."

He could throw punches with the best of them, and through the years we had our share of bouts. Paul was a bleeder, though, and whenever we fought he would inevitably dirty up my game jersey with his bright red blood. My equipment managers hated it when we would play against Stewie, because they knew they would have to spend time after the game trying to get his blood stains out of my jersey. Paul went on to become, in my opinion, one of the best referees in the NHL. We've since gotten together a few times at various charity functions, and have enjoyed rehashing some of the old-time stories.

Glen Sonmor, the architect of the Minnesota Fighting Saints and now the mastermind (with Gilles Leger) behind building the team that became known as the "Birmingham Bullies," was once asked which team did he feel was scarier, the Saints or the Bulls. He said, "I think for sheer terror, you couldn't beat that Birmingham team." Glen's mandate from the team's owner was to put together a team that would sell tickets in the South.

Glen knew that Birmingham was Coach "Bear" Bryant country, the legendary coach of the University of Alabama Crimson Tide football team. Bear Bryant always used the saying, "We're going to put a hurt'n on them," whenever asked about what he was going to do to his opponents. Glen knew the rough and tumble kind of game was what would sell in Birmingham, so the 1977–78 Bulls were built to win through toughness and intimidation. We set a professional hockey record for the most penalty minutes in a season, a distinction that was previously held by the NHL's Philadelphia Flyers' "Broad Street Bullies." Collectively, our statistics were mind-boggling. Dave Hanson: 42 games, 241 penalty minutes; Gilles Bilodeau: 59 games, 258 penalty minutes; Steve Durbano: 45 games, 284 penalty minutes; Frank Beaton: 56 games, 279 penalty minutes; Serge Beaudoin: 64 games, 115 penalty minutes.

The team paid almost $24,000 in fines to the league. Glen would always put on his black suit whenever he had to go to our suspension hearings, which became known as his "goin' to a meet'n suit." We'd see him skipping by with a big grin on his face and he would say, "Off to another trial, boys…wish me luck."

Glen Sonmor ranks right next to John Brophy in my book as my favorite coach. The two of them were cut from the same cloth and they were what is referred to as a player's coach. Glen was one tough hombre and was never afraid to get in the middle of anything. He had a promising professional hockey career cut short at the age of 25 when in 1955, while playing in a game with the AHL's Cleveland Barons against the Pittsburgh Hornets, he lost his left eye when he got hit by a deflected puck. He felt that there was honor in toughness and respected players who would be willing to make those sacrifices for the good of the team.

The Birmingham squad was a once-in-a-lifetime team. I think we would've been more successful in the win-loss column, however, had we played more disciplined, and better picked our spots as to when and when not to fight. But because Glen loved the physical game so much, and knew that the Birmingham fans were buying tickets with certain expectations, he didn't rein his hounds in as much as he maybe should have.

I remember one night in Winnipeg when Pat Westrum got benched. Pat was a really solid stay-at-home defenseman who played an honest game and would fight whenever he had to. About halfway through the game it became obvious that Glen had purposely removed him from the regular rotation. Pat asked Glen why he was benched and Glen told him it was because he wasn't fighting enough. Pat threw up his arms in frustration and said, "Glen, whenever I try to fight, I got three other guys jumping in ahead of me."

Glen had an infectious personality and was loved by all. He also liked to drink in those days and sometimes the booze would get the better of his good judgment. After a game in Winnipeg one night, I went to the hotel lounge to relax and have a beer. Glen was sitting at the bar, singing to himself and tapping his toe. I sat down next to him and he immediately turned to me with his big smile. It was obvious that he was feeling his oats. He told me that he was trying to pick up the gal sitting next to him, but she was giving him the cold shoulder. His face then broke out into a devilish smile and he said he was ready to unleash his secret weapon on her. He reached up and took his glass eye out and plopped it into the gal's drink. He then tapped her on the shoulder, and as she turned around, he pointed to her drink and said, "I've got my eye on you, baby..." Needless to say, she was not impressed.

Frank "Never" Beaton was one tough cookie. He wasn't a very big guy, but he was ornery and fearless and would scrap with anyone. He was like the Energizer Bunny, he just keep on going and going. We were playing a game in Cincinnati against the Stingers one evening and there was an outstanding warrant for Frank's arrest. He had apparently beaten up a Cincinnati service-station attendant the year before when the guy spilled gas on his Corvette. During the game, a couple of cops showed up on our bench. Frank spotted them while he was on the ice, so he skated directly to the Stingers' players bench, jumped off the ice, and ran to hide in the Stingers' stick room. In between periods, the cops came into our dressing room looking for Frank and made everyone get out their IDs. They then went over to the Stingers' room to do the same and eventually discovered Frank's hiding place. They allowed him to shower, then cuffed him and whisked him off to jail.

Gilles "Bad News" Bilodeau was one scary and mean-looking dude. We had played against each other and fought each other a couple of times when we were in the NAHL. It was much better to have him as a teammate instead of an opponent. Johnny "Pie" McKenzie played for the New England Whalers and whenever we faced them he would always yap at Gilles, trying to get under his skin. One time during warm-ups, McKenzie asked Gilles at center ice how he ever found a helmet to fit his big head. Gilles looked down at him and said, in a heavy French accent, "I had it special made." Pie just stared up at Gilles for a second and then burst out laughing hysterically. Gilles never cracked a smile; he didn't get the joke. He also never caught McKenzie.

Steve "Durbo" Durbano was a big, mobile defenseman with offensive skill and a considerable mean streak. He could really shoot the puck and make steady plays, but you knew he was always a click away from snapping and going out of control. He and I got along really well and I liked him a lot, but he would really freak me out sometimes. One afternoon before a big game against Gordie Howe and the Whalers, he was in the hallway sharpening the edge of the blade of his stick with a wood rasp. When I asked him what he was doing, he told me he was getting ready to cut the old man's heart out. I just shook my head and wished him luck.

Durbo was married to a really hot-looking gal, Lisa. Word around the locker room was that she was a former stripper or go-go dancer, and that she was just as wild as Durbo. We were at Pat Westrum's birthday party one night, and everyone brought something to eat and a gift for Pat. Lisa brought a tray of brownies, but no one would eat them for fear that they were laced with dope. When it came time to give Pat his birthday presents, Lisa stood up in front of Pat, pulled her blouse up to expose her breasts, and invited Pat to grope them for his birthday gift. Pat's wife, meanwhile, was not too thrilled with the offer. Durbo, oddly enough, just laughed.

One time we were on the road in Cincinnati when Lisa called the hotel room looking for Durbo. Frank Mahovlich was his roommate and had to tell Lisa that Durbo was not in. Lisa went ballistic. She told him to tell Durbo to call as soon as he got in and hung up. When Durbo arrived, he called and she told him that he had better get his ass home because so far she'd thrown his stereo and all his clothes out into the street, and was about to strangle his dog. Durbo then ran up to Glen Sonmor's room at about 4:00 AM with tears in his eyes, telling Glen what was happening and that he had to get back to Birmingham to save his dog. He said, "Glen, I really love that dog." Glen just shook his head and wished him luck, giving him a few days off to get his affairs in order.

In Winnipeg, Durbo got thrown out of the game for going after Bobby Hull. Afterward, while we were all in the locker room showering, Durbo was standing by our bus, which was parked inside of the arena near our locker room. He was just standing there when along came a group of drunken Winnipeg fans who jumped him. As luck would have it, Glen Sonmor stepped out of the locker room at that exact moment and saw what was going on. He immediately ran back into our locker room and yelled to all of us, "Durbo's in trouble!" We all ran out, including guys straight from the shower, and all hell broke loose. Naked guys were fighting with clothed guys and girls were standing by watching. It was crazy. Finally, the cops showed up and got things under control. One of the naked Bulls got a bit defensive when one of the female bystanders commented on how small a package he had. He angrily yelled back at her, "What do you expect? It's cold out here!"

• • •

Frank Mahovlich was an incredibly nice and mild-mannered man who also had a few odd quirks about him. He never wore blue jeans and oftentimes came to practice dressed in clothes that looked like he was going out for tea on his yacht. He had a pet mud turtle named Sammy and would bring him to practice in a cardboard carrying box. He'd take Sammy out of the box and put him across the room and try to coax the turtle to walk to him by saying, "Here Sammy, Sammy. Come to Papa." The "Big M" was a great hockey player, a 20-year veteran of the NHL before jumping to the WHA. Frank used to drive Glen crazy because Glen wanted guys who would hustle all the time and go into the corners without fear. Frank would often just skate like he had it on cruise control, making big swoops and, occasionally, taking a big slap shot. But every once in a while, someone or something would get him fired up and he would skate the length of the ice and rifle a laser shot over the shoulder of the

....

Frank Beaton on the Infamous Brawl in Winnipeg

"That was one hell of a brawl, let me tell ya. I remember sitting in the locker room after the game up in Winnipeg and seeing all of my team-mates jump up to help out Durbo. I wasn't going to be the last guy out there, so I just instinctively jumped up too and ran like hell to help him out. I had just gotten all of my wet equipment off and had nothing to put on, so I just ran out there in my birthday suit in front of the women and children and everything. It was one wild scene, that was for sure."

....

• •

Frank Beaton on Hockey in Alabama

"Back in those days you didn't get a game misconduct penalty until your third fight. So you had to earn your penalty minutes, it was some tough hockey. The fans loved it and sure, we needed to sell tickets down in Alabama. Hey, we didn't care. We wanted to keep our jobs and do what we were expected to do. There were some pretty wild brawls in those days, that was for sure. Think of the lawsuits you would have now if that kind of stuff took place. That was just a different time back then."

• •

startled goalie. My guess is that Glen would've liked to get rid of Frank, but because Frank was a good tennis player and so was the owner, John Bassett, the owner wouldn't allow it. (Bassett's daughter was Carling Basset, a teen tennis phenom back in the '70s.) One time, Glen put Frank on a line with Beaton and I, just to get him fired up. Later, after the game, when a reporter asked Frank what was wrong, he replied, "I don't know, but I seem to play a lot better with Howe and Delvecchio." I'm glad Frank stayed, because I really enjoyed watching him play hockey, getting to know him, and even watching him play with his turtle.

One night we were playing the Edmonton Oilers in Birmingham, and during the game this big 6'2" Frenchman named Pierre Guite elbowed me in the jaw. I immediately dropped my gloves and went after him for taking a cheap shot at me. We fought and got banished to the penalty box, with both of us receiving five minutes for fighting. Plus, he got an additional two minutes for elbowing. When my five minutes were up, I left the box and skated past Guite, where he was still serving his two-minute minor.

As I skated by, he yelled something at me in French. I didn't understand a word he said, but figured he was yelling some kind of insult at me. I took exception, sprinted to his box, dove over the dasher boards onto him, and started pounding away. The two of us were going at each other in the penalty box while the linesmen were trying to get through the door to break up the fight. When I got into the locker room between periods, my teammate Serge Beaudoin said to me, "Do you know what he said to you?" I said, "No, but I'm sure it wasn't good." Serge said, "He said he was sorry for elbowing you." I said, "Well…maybe next time he'll learn to apologize in English."

• • •

When I came to the Bulls, Glen made the decision to move me from playing defense to left wing. He put me on a line with Ken "the Rat" Linseman and Phil Roberto. Glen wanted to be sure there was always someone on the ice with Ken who could protect him. Ken was a good player, but one of the chippiest and dirtiest guys I ever saw. After playing with him, I completely understood why opposing players wanted to rip his head off. I couldn't understand why he thought he had to play that way, because he was a very skilled and crafty player. He would go out and jab guys with his stick, slew-foot them, talk trash to them, and get them to go after him. Then he would run and hide while I had to jump in to protect him.

I finally got fed up with it one game and told him if one more guy comes after him that night that I was not going to defend him. Of course, that didn't change the way he played and, of course, I still had to stick up for him. He was our top goal scorer, what was I to do? I played 47 games that year and tallied seven goals, 17 assists, and 289 PIMs. At the end of the season, Glen presented me with the Most Improved Player award. It could've just as easily been the Most Tolerant of Rats award.

• • •

In Game 1 of our first-round playoff series against the Winnipeg Jets, I really wanted to set the tone of the game by taking a shot at knocking Bobby "the Golden Jet" Hull down. Early in the game he came rushing down the side of the rink and I stepped into him with all I could muster. He hit me like a freight train hitting a Volkswagen, and I was the VW. Down I went and he never broke stride.

After going to the bench with my tail between my legs, the opportunity presented itself again and this time I made sure I was more prepared. I hit Bobby hard and got my elbows a little higher than he appreciated. Off went our gloves and we proceeded to exchange a flurry of lefts and rights. Suddenly we both stopped and Bobby looked much different to me. I then realized that he was bald and I was holding his hairpiece in my hand! The roar of the crowd turned from ear splitting to a deafening silence. I frantically threw his rug out toward the center of the ice and went directly into the penalty box without assistance or saying a word. Bobby then sheepishly skated over to pick up his toupee before going off to the locker room.

The league's rule against pulling hair called for an automatic match penalty and ejection from the game. However, the referee, Bill Friday, only assessed me a minor and major penalty because, technically, I hadn't pulled Bobby's real hair. Bobby, who received no penalty for his part in our scuffle, then came out of the locker room with a Jofa helmet on and proceeded to score a goal a few minutes later like nothing had happened.

Toward the end of the game, I found myself in a face-off with Bobby next to me. I said, "Mr. Hull, I'm really sorry." He just looked at me with a grin and said in his raspy voice, "Don't worry, kid, it was time for a new one anyway." The next day, in newspapers across Canada, there was a picture of Bobby and me with his hairpiece in the background. The headlines read, "Is Nothing Sacred?" For the next couple of weeks, I got threatening letters and phone calls from people across Canada. It was really intense. Over the years, however, Bobby and I have crossed paths many times and have even done charity work together. He's never once mentioned the incident to me and I've never once brought it up with him. I will never forget meeting Bobby's brother, Dennis, though, whose first words to me were, "Aren't you the guy who pulled my brother's rug off?"

We ended up losing to the Winnipeg Jets, four games to one, but it was still a good season for us. As was our normal routine by now, Sue, Caesar, and I all packed up the van and headed back to Nanty Glo to spend the summer at her folks' place. By now Sue was pregnant with an expectant due date of December. So with a little one on the way, I decided to become a bit more aware of my responsibilities as a husband and settle down from my wild ways—especially out on the ice.

Moving On

When I got back to Minnesota to prepare for training camp that August, my agent told me that the Detroit Red Wings made a conditional trade for me with Birmingham with provisions that somehow gave them the option of returning me to the Bulls if things didn't work out. I was thrilled to finally get my shot in the NHL. With that, I headed to the Motor City for another unforeseen adventure. My wife would soon follow me out there and we moved into an elderly couple's home in Dearborn.

Bob Kromm was the head coach in Detroit and his coaching style was the exact opposite of Glen Sonmor's. After spending a season with the charisma and positive energy of Glen, this guy seemed like a mannequin. He had won a couple of championships with teams he coached in the minors and even won the WHA Stanley Cup–Avco Cup championship with the Winnipeg Jets. But my impression of his personality and coaching techniques was that he couldn't inspire a starving dog to eat a filet mignon. The team's record and nickname, the "Dead Wings," bore that out. He led them during the 1978–79 season to only 23 wins and out of the playoffs. We had a competitive team, but had more plumbers than high-flyers. It was a tough environment to thrive in but I hung in there.

Before leaving I witnessed one of the most brutal incidents I have ever seen. We were playing the Colorado Rockies at home in Olympia Stadium on October 25, 1978, and I was sitting in the press box as a healthy scratch. I had found out earlier in the evening that I was not playing that night when I showed up to the locker room before the game and did not see my jersey hanging in my stall. This was Coach Kromm's way of communicating to his team who was and who wasn't in the lineup.

During the game, the puck was passed up to Detroit's Dennis Polonich, who was stationed along the sideboards of the Wings' defensive zone. Just as Dennis relayed the puck to his center, Colorado's Wilf Paiement came to finish his check by hitting Dennis with his shoulder. Dennis, who stood 5'5", instinctively raised his stick as Wilf, who stood 6'1", went to hit him. Wilf ran into Dennis's stick, which hit Wilf in the face. In the blink of an eye, Wilf, who was an excellent hard-nosed hockey player, swung his stick in the manner of a baseball player swinging the bat, and nailed Dennis flush in the face, breaking his nose and inflicting other serious facial injuries. The blow knocked Dennis to the ice and left him unconscious in a pool of blood. Polo was notorious for the illegal use of his stick and for being an agitator, but even he didn't deserve this kind of retribution—and a jury agreed. Polonich sued Paiement and won the first civil suit resulting from an on-ice incident in NHL history. Wilf ended up getting a 15-game suspension and Dennis was awarded $850,000 from a U.S. federal court. I went to see Polo in the hospital after the incident and his face was totally wrapped up like a mummy, swollen to twice its normal size.

There were a few other choice moments with the Wings as well, including the time I took out Barry Beck with one punch. We were playing the Colorado Rockies, but this time it was in Denver and I was in the lineup. I got tangled up with their goalie and the scrum turned into a brawl with the goalie and me going at it. Out of the corner of my eye I see Barry Beck, a gigantic defenseman for the Rockies, skating over toward me and getting ready to drill me. Beck stood 6'3", weighed about 225, and was just a behemoth on skates. He was an outstanding hockey player and well known for destroying people when he hit them. There was no doubt in my mind that taking my head off was what he had in mind for me. Just as he started to throw his big meat hook, I ducked and heard a *swoosh* as it went by my head, followed by a scream of pain. I looked up and poor Barry was bent over holding his arm in agony. Turned out he dislocated his shoulder while trying to knock my block off and had to leave the game.

One of my other memorable moments with Detroit came during a game against the Chicago Blackhawks and the incredible Bobby Orr. After 10 illustrious seasons with the Boston Bruins and some devastating knee surgeries, Bobby was trying to make a comeback with the Hawks. I was so thrilled and captivated with watching him that when I got on the ice against him, I freaked. I found myself coming down the ice with the puck going one-on-one against him. When I realized that it was Bobby Orr that I was going against, I was so intimidated and caught up in the moment that instead of trying to beat him to get to the goalie, I blindly dropped the puck back hoping it was going to one of my teammates. Instead, it went right onto the stick of another Blackhawk, who quickly turned up ice and scored. Coach Kromm was so pissed that I didn't get another shift after that. Bobby retired for good following that game.

I wound up playing in just 11 games with the Wings that season, although I was there for many more as a healthy scratch. On December 4, 1978, I became the proud papa of a little baby girl. It was one of the greatest days of my life. Then, on December 5, I was told that I was being sent to Birmingham again. I definitely welcomed the news, but the timing couldn't have been worse. Erin was born on a Monday, I was required to be in Birmingham by Friday, and Sue was not going to be released from the hospital until Wednesday. What a whirlwind. When I picked her up on Wednesday, I brought her and the baby home to Dearborn, kissed them good-bye, and hit the road for the 700-mile trek to Alabama. Sue and Erin, meanwhile, went back to Pennsylvania to stay with her folks.

When I arrived in Birmingham, checked into the hotel, and got to the locker room the next day, things were nowhere near the same as I left them the previous spring. Glen Sonmor had gone off to coach the NHL's Minnesota North Stars and my other favorite coach, John Brophy, was now at the helm. The "Big M" and Phil Roberto had retired, while Frankie Beaton, "Bad News" Bilodeau, Ken Linseman, Mark Napier, Rod Langway, and John Garrett were all sold to other teams.

The guy I was most surprised to see gone was Steve Durbano, my old partner in crime. In fact, I would never see Durbo again after that tumultuous "Birmingham Bullies" season. He played briefly with the St. Louis Blues before retiring to Yellowknife, the "Gateway to the Arctic," in the obscure Northwest Territories of Canada. He later got sentenced to seven years in prison for his part in a cocaine import scheme and then another trip to the clink when he mistakenly offered an undercover cop a job in his sex escort business. Sadly, he died of liver failure one month shy of his 51st birthday in 2002. I really liked Durbo a lot as a teammate and as a friend. I never saw him do dope and he was always a gentleman toward Sue. He truly ranks up there on my list of most memorable people that I am glad to have known. One thing was for sure, I was definitely glad that I played with—and not against—old Durbo.

So in the place of all these tough guys and veterans, team owner John Bassett went out and signed a bunch of kids for the 1978–79 season. They would be called the "stars of the future," but soon were known simply as the "Baby Bulls." In all, there would be six underage junior stars (underage then meant players under 20 years old), including: goalie Pat Riggins, defensemen Gaston Gingras, Rob Ramage, and Craig Hartsburg, plus forwards Michel Goulet and Rick Vaive. Ramage, Hartsburg, and Vaive eventually became NHL All-Stars and Goulet became an NHL Hall of Famer.

Ricky Vaive was one of my favorites. He was like a young, spirited colt. He could really skate and shoot, but also didn't know when to stop running his mouth. He ended the season with 26 goals and led the WHA with 248 penalty minutes. I tried my best to protect the young buck and help steer him along, but he was one who just couldn't be tamed, and that often got him into more trouble than he could handle.

Later in the year, while we were in Edmonton playing against the Oilers, Rick got into a verbal sparring match with Glen Sather, the Oilers' coach. Glen was never one to be shown up or spoken to in a derogatory manner, especially in his home rink, so he immediately sent his resident tough guy, Dave Semenko, out to speak to Rick. Rick didn't get many words in before Semenko hammered him into an unconscious submission. After that, Rick grew up quite a bit and would go on to NHL stardom with the Toronto Maple Leafs, where he became the first 50-goal scorer in Leafs history.

Michel Goulet was a pure goal scorer. He had exhilarating speed, craftiness with the puck, and a sixth sense of how to find the back of the net with his quick release of the puck. When I arrived, Brophy pulled me aside to express his concern to me about Michel. He said the kid was one hell of a player, but that he was an introvert and seemed a bit fragile. He said he was not concerned about the other kids, because they could take care of themselves, but he was worried that Michel was going to get eaten up by the other teams when they start to go after him.

John had me take Michel in the back room and teach him how to box. It became quite comical because here I was, Killer Hanson, trying to show this skinny French-Canadian kid who could barely speak a lick of English how to throw punches at an imaginary foe. I'd show him how to hit the bag and Broph would be in the background cheering us on. We tried and tried, but to no avail. Thank God that Michel went on to become one of the NHL's most prolific goal scorers, because that warranted someone else watching over him instead of him having to defend himself regularly against thugs.

When I first met Rob "Rammer" Ramage, I immediately knew he was really a unique kid. Physically, he was solid at 6'2" and over 200 pounds of pure muscle. As a 19-year-old, he had the poise and maturity of a veteran with a confident yet quiet way about him. I could tell he was a natural leader and I saw many similarities between the two of us. He was as tough as nails and had a very competitive spirit. He was skilled, headsy, a very good playmaker, and he played with a lot of character.

Right off the bat I kind of took Rammer under my wing and tried to keep him from many of the unnecessary distractions that many young athletes fall victim to. I started taking him to the gym with me and taught him the value of taking care of himself off the ice with weight training and proper nutrition. He and I used to hit the weights pretty hard together and as frequently as we could, which really helped both of us. He got 48 points that season, along with 165 PIMs, before going on to be selected by the Colorado Rockies first overall in the 1979 NHL Entry Draft. The ingredients I saw in Rammer as a player for the Baby Bulls would lead him to two Stanley Cup championships over his 15-year career in the NHL.

Playing with the kids, being with Broph as the head coach again, and spending the season in Birmingham again was great, especially after my dismal experience in Detroit. It was fun to play with the kids and to be their guardian angel out on the ice. We had our growing pains and lost a number of close games early in the season, but Brophy had a reputation for getting the best out of young players and as the season wore on, his influence began to show.

By the last half of the season, the Baby Bulls were earning respect and playing excellent hockey. The toughest thing for us was dealing with all of the payback from the other rival teams that the "Birmingham Bullies" had intimidated the year before. We ended up finishing 10 games under .500 and out of the playoffs. We really created some exciting times for the fans in Birmingham, though, especially for the young southern belles who had their hearts set on snaring one of those young studs. My reputation grew as an enforcer as well. In fact, I was even offered to fight as a headliner in a Toughman Contest exhibition. I turned it down, though. I just didn't think it was right to exploit what I was doing as a profession for my team and for the sport that I loved.

Meanwhile, Sue and I had really grown to like the area, the people, and the lifestyle of the Deep South. At the end of the season we decided it was time to finally plant some roots so we bought a house. I figured that I had pretty good job security with the Bulls under Brophy, and that we could settle down for a while there.

Little did I know, however, that behind the scenes the WHA was about to go belly-up. Sure enough, just before the 1979–80 season started, the league folded. Four WHA franchises did manage to merge with the NHL, but Birmingham was not one of them. With that, I received word that I would be sent packing to Detroit for the next season. My gypsy saga would continue.

I spent the summer hitting the weights and training very hard at my gym. While I was in Birmingham, I became good friends with a guy by the name of Gene Brasher, who owned a local gym in town. Gene was a former football player for Bear Bryant at the University of Alabama and we hit it off really well. I eventually went into business with him and we opened a training facility called Dave Hanson's Nautilus Health Club that later split off into a Gold's Gym. It was my first business venture. We had many amateur and professional bodybuilders working out at our gym. The summer went by fast with Erin and Sue in our new home, where we made new friends and went to the Gulf of Mexico many times to enjoy the ocean.

When September rolled around, it was off to the "Soo"—Sault Ste. Marie, Michigan, for training camp with the Red Wings. Never one to give up hope or give up trying, I went to training camp with every expectation of making the team, even though Bob Kromm was back again as head coach. I got the message pretty quickly that I had no shot at making the team. I wound up getting sent to the Wings' farm team in Glens Falls, New York.

The Adirondack Red Wings were Detroit's new AHL minor league club after departing from Kansas City of the CHL. Larry Wilson, their coach in KC, moved with the team to Glens Falls and was scheduled to be their coach, but just after he moved there to get ready for the new season, he died from a heart attack. It caught everyone by surprise—Larry was a relatively young man and thought to be in excellent health. His sudden heart attack happened while he was out for his regular jog.

When I got there, the general manager of the new franchise and of the new Glens Falls Civic Center, Ned Harkness, met me. He told me that I was not allowed to practice with the team because Detroit was trying to work out an arrangement to send me back to Birmingham. Birmingham was no longer a WHA franchise, but now a minor league team in the lower CHL. John Brophy was still the Bulls' coach and he had requested that I get sent to them if I was not kept in Detroit.

For a couple of weeks, I was put up in the Queensbury Hotel and had to skate all by myself at the Civic Center while I waited. During my short stay, Ned Harkness went out of his way to do whatever he could for me. He offered me the use of his car whenever I wanted it, he invited me to breakfast or lunch, and he often invited me into his office just to kill some time. When the time came for me to depart Glens Falls for Birmingham, Ned made arrangements for me to get to the airport and we shook hands good-bye, never dreaming that our paths would soon cross again.

The Birmingham Bulls were now the farm team of the NHL's Atlanta Flames and still played out of the Birmingham-Jefferson Civic Center. I was disappointed that I didn't stick with the Red

Wings, but it was nice to be back, especially since it meant that Sue, Erin, Caesar, and I didn't have to pack up the van to leave our new home to go somewhere else to play. But even though we were wearing the same uniform and still had the same coach, the atmosphere surrounding the team was not the same. We still had some of the old Bulls on the team, Paul Henderson, Serge Beaudoin, Peter Marrin, and a few others, but the fans didn't turn out like they had in the past and the league certainly wasn't as exciting.

About 20 games into the season, Broph pulled me into his office and asked me if something was wrong. I really didn't know why he asked that until he said that the Minnesota North Stars had been calling him about me and wondering if I was still playing with the same intensity and fire that I had shown in the past. I told him that it seemed to me that the Central Hockey League was more of the issue, because this league was nowhere near as physical or intense as the WHA or AHL or NHL.

I had guys on other teams telling me to take it easy, no reason to be banging or fighting so much in this league. Broph said Glen Sonmor was looking for someone to take the injured Jack Carlson's place with the North Stars and he was interested in me. He was concerned, however, that I may have lost the fire. I said to Broph that the fire would be reignited and I immediately went on a tear where I hit everything that moved and fought everyone I could get my hands on. A few weeks later I got a call from Broph telling me it was official; I was heading back to Minnesota to play for my hometown North Stars.

Chapter 10

The Odyssey Continues

WITH THAT, THE HANSON CLAN ONCE AGAIN PACKED UP AND headed north. I was really excited to be there and welcomed my return to the Twin Cities as a good chance to get back into the NHL with a coach who knew me and wanted me.

One of my first games was against the terrorizing Flyers of Philadelphia, which had my friend Paul Holmgren leading the way as their resident enforcer. I was playing left wing with Mike Eaves as my center. We were at a face-off in the Philadelphia zone and Mike was going against Bobby Clarke. At the drop of the puck between Eaves and Clarke, bodies started moving, I started to jockey for position, and Mike Eaves dropped down to the ice in a pool of blood. I never saw what happened, but the whistle blew and play stopped so the trainer could come out to tend to Mike. When I got back to the bench, Glen says to me, "Why the hell didn't you go after Clarke?"

I asked why, and Glen screamed, "Because he just put a zipper in your centerman's lip!" I never saw it happen, but apparently Clarke came up with his stick and really cut Eaves. The one thing I quickly learned about the great Bobby Clarke was that anything he did with his stick was never an accident. I knew that I had messed up and as a result didn't get back onto the ice until late in the game. When I finally did get out there for my next shift I immediately went right after the first Flyer I could. I knew that I had to make up for not responding to Eaves's slice job. So I just grabbed the first Flyer I could and pounded him. When I came back, Glen patted me on the shoulder.

There was an old saying about the Flyers when they were known as the "Broad Street Bullies" back in the early '70s. Because players feared them so much, they used to mysteriously come down with what was known simply as the "Philly Flu." It was an ailment that struck some of the weak-spirited players just before the opening face-off, because they simply figured it would be easier to play possum rather than lose any teeth against those thugs.

Well, the next time we played the Flyers, Glen challenged the entire team at practice the day before to stand up to their intimidation. On the day of the game, wouldn't you know it, I got the flu, the real full-blown flu. It was so bad that when I tried to get out of bed and walk down the stairs to get ready to go to the game, I passed out and fell down the stairs. Sue had to help me back into bed and dial the phone so I could call Glen to tell him that I couldn't make it. Glen literally begged me to get to the game. He would not accept the fact that I was so sick that I couldn't even put my own pants on. Sadly, all I could do was watch it on TV, in between barfs. When I finally got well enough to go to the rink, Glen told me they were sending me to their farm team to get some more ice time and to "get my game back." I was devastated.

It was difficult for me to get into the groove with the North Stars. I knew I was brought in to serve as their "policeman," but every team I had ever played for, I played regularly. By playing regularly, your conditioning is good, your coordination is good, your timing is on par with everyone, and you feel like you're a part of the team.

In Minnesota, I was dressing and sitting on the bench for most of the game, getting very limited ice time. This routine really throws everything off track and makes it very hard not only to fit in when you do get in a shift, but also makes it difficult to even fight with confidence and effectiveness.

So, it was down to Oklahoma City to play for their farm team, the Oklahoma City Stars of the CHL. There, I met up with my good friends Jim Boo and Bill Butters, which was a lot of fun.

When I checked into the hotel, I really wondered where this road was going to take me. However, true to Glen's word, after just six games he called me back up to the North Stars.

My first game back was against the Bruins at the old Boston Garden. The Bruins had a pretty tough and intimidating team with players like Terry O'Reilly, Al Secord, Stan Jonathan, and John Wensink. Since it was my first game back, I wanted to show Glen that I was committed to playing his style of hockey. I went out and nailed Peter McNab, one of Boston's top centermen.

Sure enough, out came Terry O'Reilly, a 6'1" enforcer who had established himself as one of the league's toughest guys. We dropped the gloves, squared off, and ended up bear hugging each other to the ice after we both threw haymakers that missed each other. Back in Minnesota for a rematch a couple of weeks later, we went at it again, and this time we both got some good shots in. As the linesmen were separating us I remember saying to him, "We have to stop meeting like this or people are going to talk." We both got a good chuckle out of that one.

My one and only NHL goal was scored against the Detroit Red Wings at the Joe Louis Arena in Detroit. I was on a line with Tommy Younghans and Mike Polich. We were cycling the puck in the Red Wings zone when Tommy passed the puck to me in the slot. I quickly let a wrist shot go at the net. To my surprise, the puck zipped through the five-hole of Rogie Vachon, a Vezina Trophy winner and NHL All-Star. After the game, Glen presented the puck to me in the locker room and said, "Congratulations, I hope you get many more."

He was actually probably hoping I *didn't* get many more. Oftentimes when enforcers start thinking they are goal scorers it can lead to their downfall. Well, Glen didn't have to worry because that would be my one and only career NHL goal. I had no illusions of becoming the next Gretzky, that was for sure.

I ended up playing with the North Stars for most of the second half of the season. We made the playoffs, something the team hadn't done the prior two seasons, and did pretty well. We swept the Maple Leafs in the opening round, then beat the Canadians four games to three in the quarterfinals. We met up with the Flyers in the semifinals, where we lost four games to one. I made all the trips, but didn't play in any of the games.

Typically, in the postseason teams will sit their tough guys so that they don't become a liability and cause the team to be short-handed. Teams can't afford penalties in the playoffs, so we are usually dressed but benched. I really thought I would see some ice time in the Flyers' series, but I was told I didn't play for fear that I might start something that the team couldn't finish. With the first two series wins, the leadership decided that it was good team strategy to stay away from getting into fights. Instead, they wanted the players to not retaliate and to just take penalties so they could capitalize on power-play situations.

I knew this was totally against Glen's personality, but I suspected the general manager, Lou Nanne, persuaded him to take this approach. As much as I was really proud to be in a North Stars uniform, I was really disappointed that I did not contribute to the team's success in the manner to which I was accustomed. I also felt that I let Glen down and that bothered me. I made sure to thank him for the opportunity and for the chances he gave me. After the 1978–79 season I would never have the opportunity to play for Glen again, nor would I ever get another shot in the NHL.

When it came time for the start of the 1980–81 season, Detroit, which still held my contract rights, told me to report directly to the AHL's Adirondack Red Wings and plan on staying there. So we packed up yet again and moved up to Glens Falls, New York, where we found a nice house to rent on beautiful Lake George, a 32-mile-long spring-fed lake dubbed the "Queen of American Lakes." We lived on one of the bays of the lake in a remote community called Cleverdale, complete with a beautiful view of the Adirondack Mountains. Sue's mom and dad, Gram and Pap, came to visit us in Cleverdale early in the year and stayed with us practically the entire season because they just fell in love with the area.

I was excited about being back in Adirondack. The team, despite missing the playoffs the year before, was selling out its arena and giving the fans a good show night in and night out. When I arrived to the Civic Center, Ned Harkness was one of the first to greet me. He immediately told me that he would do everything in his power to see that I stayed with Adirondack because he wanted me to be a part of this exciting franchise. I was really surprised, because other than a couple of weeks that I spent with him a year ago while I was waiting in Glens Falls to be sent to Birmingham, I really hadn't gotten to know Ned very well. I must have made quite an impression on him, though, because he was adamant that I was not going anywhere. The small town was abuzz over their Red Wings and it was a great feeling to be wanted again.

We had some solid players on our roster that season, including Pete Mahovlich, Tom Bladon, Greg Joly, George Lyle, and Bill Hogaboam, among others—all of whom had prior NHL experience. Detroit had cleaned house and sent a bunch of guys down to the minors, which was going to make for an interesting mix of veterans and young rookies. It would take a while before everybody's egos got put in check, but eventually the team came together and played some pretty terrific hockey toward the end of the season and through the playoffs.

Because Ned Harkness had shown such confidence in me, and because we had such outstanding support from the Adirondack fans, I got a renewed sense of spirit and played my heart out every game. Tom Webster, who had retired the season before due to a chronic back injury, and J.P. LeBlanc, a rock-solid veteran player, teamed up to coach this team and played me in almost every position. I played wing, center and defense, and probably would've played goalie if they had ever needed me to. I really felt like I was contributing and the fans in Adirondack got a taste of something they hadn't witnessed yet, Dave "Killer" Hanson. I went through the league once and fought almost everyone there was to fight. After that, I went through it again and did it again, and again. I was having fun and we were winning.

One night early in the season we were playing rival Hershey, which had a very disciplined team with their fair share of legitimate tough guys. One of their defensemen and I got into a fight and both of us got put into the box. I really wanted a piece of this guy, so I went directly to his penalty box before he could get out to challenge me again. He obliged, and with the boards between us (him standing in the penalty box and me on the ice), we exchanged punches nonstop for a good two minutes until I finally caught him with a straight right that put him to his knees. The Civic Center fans had never seen anything like this before and from that point on, they couldn't wait to see what my next shift would bring.

One night I caught Bill Riley, an honest player and solid-built winger for the New Brunswick Hawks, with an open-ice body check. I hit him so hard that his helmet popped straight up into the air and hit the bottom of the center ice scoreboard at the Civic Center. Later, in the bar after the game, I bought Bill a friendly beer and he shook my hand while telling me that was the hardest he'd ever been hit. During a game against the Rochester Americans in Glens Falls, a player came out of nowhere and butt-ended me in the mouth with his stick, splitting my upper lip into a "Y" shape. Blood was pouring all over my face and onto the ice, but I kept skating until I chased the guy down and pounded the crap out of him. The scar from that vicious attack is the primary reason I wore a mustache for the rest of my life. The doctor had to put in about 30 stitches inside and outside my lip to close it all up and for about a week my face was a real mess.

After my disappointing season the year before with the North Stars, playing regularly again with a bunch of good guys in front of awesome fans and living in that beautiful part of the country had made hockey fun again for me. By the time the regular season started to wind down, we began to get the feeling that the best way to stick it up Detroit's behind and give Ned Harkness and our fans what they deserved was to win the Calder Cup. So the group of outcasts went on a mission.

We beat the Binghamton Whalers in the first round, followed by the defending champion Hershey Bears in the semifinals. The Bears had finished the regular season 28 points ahead of us and were a scoring juggernaut, but we hung tough and took them four games to two. From there, we faced off against the Maine Mariners, the Philadelphia Flyers' top farm team, which were led by their young, brilliant Swedish goalie, Pelle Linbergh, who

There isn't anything like an impromptu get-together or sing-a-long. Here Jerry Houser (left), me (middle), and Allan Nicholls celebrate the joys of hockey, friendship, and beer.

Our many after-hour parties were the stuff of legend, and screenwriter Nancy Dowd (shown at left, with her brother Ned, aka Ogie Oglethorpe, at right) captured these events, as well as the ups and downs of hockey, in Slap Shot.

Pictured here are most of the people responsible for a classic—it's the cast and crew of Slap Shot. I think you'll be able to pick out the jokers for yourself, but isn't it obvious that we're a pretty happy family?

Dave "Jack" Hanson is shown here biting the ear of an opponent in a pregame brawl during a scene in Slap Shot.

Here Paul Newman as the coach addresses the Hanson Brothers about "puttin' on the foil" in Slap Shot.

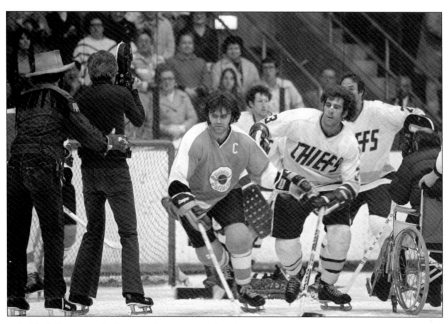

A behind-the-scenes look at Paul D'Amato (aka Tim "Dr. Hook" McCracken) and Jerry Houser (aka Dave "Killer" Carlson) in action. Notice the cameramen in the wheelchair and on skates—innovative camera work at the time. (Courtesy Chuck Mamula)

Steve Carlson, Paul Newman, and me after we presented Paul with a plaque for being an honorary loogan.

Jeff Carlson (left), an unknown woman, Steve Carlson (middle), my future wife Sue Kaschalk, and me (far right) in the backseat—with Yvon Ponton aka Jean-Guy Dourin in the front seat—wave to Paul Newman off set. This was Sue's big (and only) scene in Slap Shot. *(Courtesy Chuck Mamula)*

Paul taking a break with that sly fox look on his face of "Who can I pull a prank on next?" To think that Al Pacino was initially going to play the role of Reg Dunlop…I just don't think Pacino would've looked as good in a blue Chiefs uniform. (Courtesy Chuck Mamula)

Me taking a rest between scenes and giving my nose a break from wearing those heavy Coke-bottle glasses—the Hanson Brothers' trademark. (Courtesy Chuck Mamula)

In 1977–78, WHA Birmingham Bulls maverick owner John Bassett gives another colorful locker-room speech as my teammate Bob Stephenson looks on and I sit with my eyes closed as if saying, "Here we go again."

My 1979–80 Minnesota North Stars media guide photo.

My 1978–79 Detroit Red Wings media guide photo before being traded to the WHA Birmingham Bulls.

A 2002 photo of Jeff Carlson (left), Steve Carlson (middle), and me (right) posing outside of the Hockey Hall of Fame in Toronto before being honored in the hall of our heroes.

All in the family: My son, Christian, and me "puttin' on the foil." I am extremely proud to say that he has grown up to be a wonderful person and a fantastic hockey player.

Twenty-five years after the making of Slap Shot, *the Hanson Brothers were back in front of the movie cameras in the 2002 release of* Slap Shot 2—Breaking the Ice. *We won the "Best Supporting Actor" award for a DVD Premiere for our roles in this one.*

would go on to play five seasons in the NHL before a fatal car crash in 1986 took his life.

With all of the games being played in front of capacity crowds, it turned out to be a fantastic series. After splitting Games 1 and 2, we were leading the series two games to one heading into Game 4. Maine came out smoking and annihilated us by the score of 10–1 to tie it up at two games apiece. We then headed up to Maine determined to redeem the previous game's debacle. We ended up beating them in front of their capacity crowd, 6–4, and sent the sixth game back to Glens Falls. With the chance that the Glens Falls region could see their first championship in their team's second year of existence, the Adirondack fans packed the Civic Center beyond its capacity. Ned Harkness even showed the game on closed-circuit TV in the Civic Center's banquet hall and sold tickets to it. There were around 7,000 people in the building to see if they could watch history being made. Sure enough, by the end of the game the Detroit Red Wings' misfits, who were cast aside to a small town in upstate New York, had completed their mission.

On May 20, 1981, the Adirondack Red Wings beat the Maine Mariners, 5–2, to capture its first AHL Calder Cup championship. Ned Harkness, Tom Webster, and J.P. LeBlanc led a group of disgruntled "old" and "useless" hockey players, and watched them skate around the Glens Falls Civic Center in celebration with their adoring fans as their captain, Bill Hogaboam, held the Calder Cup high above his head.

I felt on top of the world. I ended the year with 12 goals, 25 assists, and 297 penalty minutes in 98 games. I not only fell in love with a community that fell in love with me, but I made a precious lifelong friend in Ned Harkness, a man who helped me find my confidence again. I felt I really helped this team all year long achieve its ultimate goal and was later shocked by my teammates when they voted me as the team's MVP. Just like in Johnstown when we won the playoff championship, Glens Falls also had a massive downtown parade for us that was packed with fans lining the streets. The partying went on for days. It was insane.

One other exciting addition to this season's story was the arrival of my second daughter. Sarah Elizabeth was born in the Glens Falls Hospital on January 26, 1981, just before I went on a road trip. We were able to schedule an induction for her birth so that the baby was born while I was there to see it.

After dropping off Gram and Pap in Nanty Glo, the Hanson family drove back to Birmingham for a summer of sun and fun. I was anxious for a break after the long season in Glens Falls. I continued to work out all summer at the gym that I was part owner in, and also tried to start to learn the business end of the operation. The summer flew by quickly and before I knew it we were packing up the van again to head back to New York for the 1981–82 season. But, as was my past experience, nothing is ever the same as when you left it. The Adirondack Red Wings would be no exception.

My second year in upstate New York would prove to be a tumultuous one, to say the least. While the excitement in the town was still at a fever pitch, a power-play feud had emerged between Detroit and Adirondack. Detroit's general manager had released most of the players from last year's team and gotten rid of the coaching duo of Tom Webster and J.P. LeBlanc. Detroit then promoted the coach of their IHL farm team in Kalamazoo, Doug McKay, to take over and the fireworks began. He and Ned butted heads from day one and it got uglier and uglier as the season progressed. Both were headstrong personalities with their own ways of doing things and it quickly became an uncomfortable environment for everyone. The distraction that this caused ultimately brought down our team morale and we ended up losing in the first round of the playoffs to the New Brunswick Hawks, four games to two.

As for me, I finished the year by playing in 80 games, scoring 38 points, including my first and only professional hat trick, and racked up 229 penalty minutes. One of the highlights, or lowlights, of the year came early in the season against rival Hershey, when I got into another brawl with my penalty box buddy from the year before. The little brouhaha led to setting a league record for penalty minutes in one game, 520, plus a record 264 penalty minutes by one team, the Red Wings, in a game. I also set a single game Red Wings record for penalty minutes by one player in one game. Since then, there have been rule changes that make it impossible for a team to rack up as many penalty minutes again. That would be it for me in Adirondack, but those were good times spent up there. They were great fans and I was proud to be a Red Wing.

My time under contract in the Red Wings organization took me through some exciting, turbulent, and interesting times. I really felt that the last two years I spent wearing the Red Wing on my chest had allowed the Detroit management to get to know me and like me better. General Manager Jimmy Skinner called me shortly after the end of the season to tell me that he wanted to sign me again and send me back to Adirondack. He felt that I was a good influence for the younger players and that he wanted to have me with the team in the role of a player-coach.

I was really excited about the idea and spent the summer in Birmingham waiting for the contract to arrive. I finally got an envelope in the mail with the Red Wing logo on it, but when I opened it, I didn't get what I was expecting. Instead, I got a letter from Jim Devellano stating that the Red Wings would no longer be seeking my services.

Mike Ilitch, the owner of Little Caesar's Pizza, had bought the Red Wings from the Norris family and hired Jim Devellano as the general manager. Devellano had been with the New York Islanders as their chief scout and general manager of their minor league team, but now he had replaced Jim Skinner and was going through the roster with a big broom. I was unfortunately one of the dust bunnies that got caught up in the house cleaning.

I was devastated and really didn't know what to do. I was 28 years old with a mortgage, a wife, and two children, and I wasn't ready to retire from playing.

I was also struggling with some back problems that were the result of a slew foot I got during the last game of the New Brunswick series. A Hawk player had unexpectedly kicked my feet out from under me and I fell extremely hard to the ice on my back. As the summer went along, I continued to have spasms come and go in my back, but I was able to manage and function through the pain.

Later in the summer, I got a call from my former teammate Frank "Never" Beaton. Frank had played the year before for the Indianapolis Checkers, the minor league team for the New York Islanders, and told me that the Minnesota North Stars were putting their farm team in Birmingham. He was going to try to hook up with the new team, the South Stars, and suggested I do the same. After repeated unanswered calls to Lou Nanne, the North Stars general manager, I tried to get in touch with the local owners of the South Stars franchise, who were a couple of former teammates of mine when we played for the WHA Bulls together. I was hoping to talk to them and inquire about getting signed. However, their hands were tied because every player that was going to be on the team had to first be signed by the North Stars. Lou never returned my calls and it became obvious that he did not want me.

As training camp got closer, I got a call from Fred Creighton, the new general manager of the CHL's Indianapolis Checkers— the New York Islanders' minor league team. Fred was the coach of the Atlanta Flames when I went to their training camp back in 1976, and he asked me if I would be interested in joining his new club. Talk about good timing.

I packed up to head off to Rye, New York, home of the Islanders training camp. The Islanders, who were coming off their third consecutive Stanley Cup championship and about to win a fourth, were amazing—a true dynasty. What a thrill it was to skate with such a cast of future NHL Hall of Famers. What a huge difference in organizations, attitudes, and atmosphere between what I was experiencing at the Islanders camp and what I had experienced with the Red Wings. To top it off, the Islanders' trainers even spent a lot of quality time with me working on getting my back into pain-free and mobile shape, so by the time we broke camp I was skating without pain or spasms.

When I arrived in Indianapolis with Sue, Erin, Sarah, and Caesar, for the first time in a long time Sue's mom and dad did not accompany us. We went from living in the beautiful

Adirondacks and in a fairly large house to living in a city apartment complex.

Don Nedercorn, the equipment manager from my days with the Saints, was the Checkers' equipment manager, so I had at least one familiar face on the team at the start of the season. After battling hard in the American Hockey League and riding buses everywhere we went, the Central Hockey League was a nice break. Instead of going to faraway, desolate, snowbound places like Nova Scotia, Moncton, and Erie, we were flying to Salt Lake City, Birmingham, Denver, Tulsa, and Wichita. Indy didn't have the same flavor and overwhelming community interest in the team as I experienced in Adirondack, but it was a nice setup in a comfortable rink with a good fan base. They had won the CHL Adams Cup championship the season before and had an excellent team.

I really liked Fred as a coach. He was a gruff kind of guy with a no-nonsense attitude, but at the same time had a good sense of humor. The team was a good mix of reputable veterans and promising youngsters. The Islanders knew how to develop their players by having a reserve in the minors should they have to reach down to pull someone up on an interim or permanent basis.

I brought my physical game with me to Indy and went through the league like I usually did, trying to establish myself immediately in every city. The Indy arena had an Olympic-sized sheet of ice, which is larger than the standard NHL ones. At first I was intimidated about playing on such a large ice surface, but after I got used to it and realized that my speed would be an asset, I really enjoyed it. It gave us a bit of an advantage against other teams who were used to playing on the smaller rinks.

We had a really strong team that was led by future Los Angeles Kings MVP goalie Kelly Hrudey. Fred had me play forward most of the time and often hooked me up with Red Lawrence. Red was an outstanding goal scorer and playmaker, and I loved playing with him, especially since I had a clause in my contract that said if I scored 20 goals I received a $5,000 bonus. Up to that time, the closest I ever got to 20 goals in a regular season was during the last two seasons with Adirondack where I scored 11 goals each year. I got very close, but I ended the season with 18 goals in 80 games, while still totaling 285 minutes in penalties.

We clinched the franchise's first regular-season championship and then went on to win the Adams Cup playoff championship by first defeating the Salt Lake City Golden Eagles, and then the Birmingham South Stars, five games to two. The highlight of that series was playing against my old "brother," Steve Carlson, who was playing with Birmingham at the time.

The playoffs were bittersweet for me, though. I had been nursing a bad knee and then got hurt during a fight with Dave Richter, a towering defenseman who went on to play over 350 games in the NHL. I challenged him and when the gloves dropped, I accidentally stepped on a hockey stick and lost my balance just as I was throwing a punch. The stick made me drop my guard and head just as he was delivering an uppercut. He nailed me flush in the nose, breaking it instantly. Immediately my eyes watered up and my nose poured blood like a sieve. I had trouble breathing and I clung on to Richter for dear life. Luckily Dave and I were friends and he could see I was hurt, so not another punch got thrown.

My effort at fighting this big lug was so bad that instead of receiving a fighting major, the referee gave me two minutes for roughing. I really should've gotten two minutes for receiving. I had to leave the ice and couldn't return. The next day I tried to wear a half shield to protect my nose, but it just didn't work out. I ended up having to sit out the final game of the playoffs, but was able to enjoy the celebration with the team when we won the Adams Cup.

With the season over in Indianapolis, Fred told me that he wanted me back the next season and would be in touch with me over the summer. I was 29 years old, and despite the broken nose and the bad knee, I felt I was in pretty good shape. My back held out for the year with the help of regular therapy and daily doses of Naproxen. Now all I had to do was get my nose fixed so I could breathe through it again.

When we got back to Birmingham, I immediately sought a doctor to fix my nose. That turned out to be an interesting experience. I had never really had my nose broken before, at least that I knew of, and when I made arrangements for my rhino-plasty, I had no idea what I was in for. After I got admitted and was put to sleep so the doctor could do his thing, I woke up with my nose stuffed with gauze. Looking like some sort of wild platypus, I felt like I had a pair of socks jammed up my nostrils. When I came back to the doctor a few days later, he told me it was time to remove the gauze from my nose, something I was anxiously longing for. He started to pull the end of the gauze and it was like a magician who pulls an endless supply of scarves from his sleeve. The stuff keep coming and coming. Suddenly, it felt like my testicles were attached to the end of the gauze and he was pulling them through my stomach and out my nose. By the time he was done, I had a pile of bloody rags sitting on the floor that I found hard to believe were all packed in my nose just a few minutes before. It was crazy, but at least I could breathe through my schnozzola again.

As the 1983–84 training camp season approached, I started to get a little concerned because I hadn't heard from Fred. When he finally called me, he said he was having problems getting Bill Torrey, the general manager of the Islanders, to agree to sign me to another year with the Checkers. He said Torrey had signed a bunch of young kids who he wanted to send to Indianapolis to develop. As a result, there was not a place on the team for me.

Fred said he still wanted me to come to training camp with the Islanders though and to see what happened. I appeared at training camp and went through the two-week session, but when the time came to break, Fred told me that Torrey hadn't changed his mind. Fred said to go back to Birmingham, stay in shape, and be ready, because he was convinced that I would get called up early in the season.

I went back to Birmingham feeling dejected, but when I returned, I was contacted by Mike McClure. I had known Mike from my Bulls days in Birmingham. He was the new owner of an ACHL (Atlantic Coast Hockey League) franchise that was going to play at the Birmingham–Jefferson Civic Center and he wanted me to be the coach. Since I wasn't playing, I really liked the idea of getting into coaching and I accepted his offer. The Birmingham South Stars, which I helped beat for the CHL championship just a few months earlier, had folded. I was excited to start coaching and even more excited about being able to sleep in my own bed at night.

I immediately started recruiting my old teammates to see who I could get for my new team. I called anybody and everybody I could through my network of friends and agents to see who might be able to help build the team. Gilles Bilodeau was working for his wife's dad and agreed to come back; Jim Turkiewicz was going to school in Birmingham, but agreed to play at least the home games and travel whenever he could; and Paul O'Neil, a lanky center I played with in Hampton, agreed to join the team. I was off to the races. After about two weeks of tryouts and training camp, I had a team. While I was doing my work in getting players together, Mike McClure was working behind the scenes trying to secure a lease with the Civic Center. He also needed to find other investors to raise the necessary capital needed to operate the team. Little did I know at the time, however, that McClure was running into serious financial problems.

After playing a couple of preseason games, we opened the regular season on the road with a loss to the Nashville South Stars. When the team got back, McClure called to tell me that we were in dire straits financially and on the verge of folding. The next day I met with Mike and he laid it all out on the table for me. It was ugly. He owed the Civic Center a $50,000 rental fee; the ACHL a $20,000 performance bond, and a $5,000 franchise fee. Meanwhile, we were scheduled to have our home opener in just two days against the Mohawk Valley Stars, we didn't have an arena to play in.

Mike then dropped a bomb on me by telling me that he didn't have a financial backer anymore. Undeterred, I suggested we contact the mayor's office to see if he could help us out. Richard Arrington, Birmingham's first African American mayor, was a very nice man and extremely sympathetic to our needs. He told us that he would try to help and he put us in touch with another man who was a well-to-do owner of a local janitorial service. The mayor spoke to him on our behalf and convinced him that it was a good civic thing to do by investing in the team to keep it in Birmingham. The man agreed and we set everything in motion to lock up the deal.

With that, we went ahead and swept the Mohawk Valley Stars in our home opener by the decisive scores of 8–0 and 7–3. The next day, the Birmingham newspaper wrote a scathing story about the new phantom owner of the team. After the new backer, who wanted to remain anonymous, read the article, he recalled all of his investment because he felt he was being made to look like a fool in the article. Coincidentally, ACHL Commissioner Ray Miron was in town and tried to convince the owner to stay in the picture, but he had no luck. The league said they would give us a few more days to obtain our financing or else they would be forced to shut the Bulls down. Over the next couple of days I tried to call Paul Newman to see if he would have an interest in buying the team, but before I ever heard back from him, on October 28, 1983, the ACHL officially suspended the franchise's operations and we had to close up shop. The players dispersed to other teams and I was once again unemployed.

I got on the phone to Fred Creighton to see if he finally had a roster spot for me. It was late October by this point and the Checkers' season was already underway. When I spoke to Fred, he said that while it was obvious to him that there were some young kids on his team that didn't belong there, Bill Torrey hadn't made any decisions yet. I told Fred that I needed to play somewhere so I was in playing shape when something opened up. He suggested that I contact Bill Inglis, who was coaching their farm team, the Toledo Goaldiggers, to see if I could go there on a temporary basis.

I contacted Bill and he was happy to have me join the team. The team played in the IHL (International Hockey League) and had won the Turner Cup playoff championship the past two seasons. I'd never been to Toledo or played in the IHL, but I felt that since they had won a couple of recent championships, it would be a good place to play, at least temporarily, until I got the call to Indy.

Once again I packed up the family and headed to Toledo. When I got there, I met with the team's general manager, Bill

Beagan, and told him my plan to play in Toledo until I got called up to Indianapolis. He said he understood and had a good relationship with Indy, but that I needed to sign a contract by league rules in order to play for the Goaldiggers.

I signed it and went to look for a place to move my family into. We had a hard time finding a place and when we did, it was a very small house in a crummy neighborhood, but it would do, in our mind, for the short term. When I reported to the rink for my first practice, it was a bit of a shock. They played in an old rink with a tiny locker room that was very unaccommodating for the players. When I played my first game there, I thought the jerseys were the ugliest things I'd ever seen—cheesy bright green and yellow, and they were sized for youth hockey players, not grown men. The one I wore hardly covered my forearms and waist.

The players bench was awful. It had two tiered rows so if you just came off the ice, you would have to climb to the back row and then move up to the front row as your next shift got closer. There were times when I would be sitting in the back row and beer or soda would get spilled down my back because the fans sat with their knees stuck in my back. There was no formal separation between the fans and the players on the bench. Sometimes I had to shake peanut shells out of my jersey that fell down my neck from a peanut-eating fan sitting right behind me. There was often a low-hanging ceiling of cigarette smoke over the ice rink from all of the smokers in the arena. One game my wife was walking through the corridor with my kids and a puck came flying through the stairs and nailed her in the arm, narrowly missing my daughter's head.

After about two months of living in our crappy rental house, Sue decided to head back to Nanty Glo with the kids. I didn't blame her and figured it was all right since I really didn't plan to be there too much longer myself.

Our first game was in Milwaukee against the Admirals and during my first shift I got challenged by their tough guy, Derek "Boxcar" Davis. He was a player after my own heart, racking up close to 300 PIMs each year, but I just wasn't in fighting shape yet. We went at it and my experience pulled me through after

I nailed him a couple of times and then threw him down to the ice.

I quickly had a taste of what it was going to be like in this league and I wasn't really psyched up for it. We had a good group of guys on the team, but I was not excited about going on the bus for every road game or playing in the Toledo Sports Arena. However, my motivation was to work hard, get into top shape, and be ready when I got called from Indy. Time crawled by and I wasn't hearing anything from Fred. I was playing, but not with my usual fire and that really bothered me.

Then, to make matters worse, I got the injury bug. I hurt my shoulder one game and had to go to the hospital to get X-rayed. When the doctor looked at the film, he pointed to a vertebra in my spine and asked, "When did you break your neck?" I told him I had never broken my neck and he said, "Yes you did, look right there." Utterly perplexed as to when I would have broken my neck, I searched the caverns of my mind and realized that it must've happened when I was playing B-Squad football for Humboldt High School. Then my back started acting up because I wasn't getting the same care as I got the year before in Indy, and the bus rides were killing me. The whole ordeal really sucked.

I finally got called up to Indy to play in a game because they were short on players. Fred said he would contact Bill Beagan to release me so I could go to Indy the rest of the season. I went back to Toledo all fired up about finally leaving, but got a call a few days later from Fred to tell me that Beagan wouldn't release me. He said Beagan wanted cash for me or other players in return. Otherwise, he was not going to release me from my IHL contract. I went to Beagan to let him know how I felt about it. Bill stood his ground and said he had money invested in me and that he was not going to allow me to just leave without appropriate compensation. I was stuck.

My bad situation just got worse and I became more miserable. I tried to get over my disappointment and take pride in my play, but my bubble had burst. My family was over 300 miles away, I was banged up, and I had to keep wearing an undersized ugly lime and yellow hockey jersey for the rest of the year.

We finished the season in fourth place and made a run to the Turner Cup playoff finals, ultimately getting swept by the Flint Generals. For the first time in my entire hockey career, I was actually glad that the season was over. My stay in Toledo was nothing short of horrible. There were some good times and, as always was the case, the guys on the team were great. But the overall Toledo experience was extremely disheartening. I was so discouraged with how the year went and where I was at that when it came time to clear out my locker and get ready to head home, I grabbed my skates, left the arena, and walked out to the middle of the Martin Luther King Jr. Bridge, which was right next to the arena. There, I said a little prayer and tossed my skates into the murky waters of the Maumee River. Right then and there I made the hard decision that if this is where my hockey career had gone, then it was time to quit. It was one of the saddest moments of my life, but after 10 hard years of playing professional hockey I was ready to move on.

Chapter **11**

Now What?

WHEN I TOLD SUE ABOUT MY EPIPHANY, THE FIRST WORDS
out of her mouth were "Now what?" I told her I didn't
know, but it would be something. I left Toledo and headed to
Nanty Glo so we could pack up again and make the 800-mile
trek to Birmingham. I now needed to figure out just what the
hell I wanted to be when I grew up.

For starters, coaching was something that I was certainly
interested in and I wanted to pursue. One of my best leads out
of the gates was back at my old alma mater, the University of
Minnesota, where my old teammate with the Gophers, Brad
Buetow, had been serving as the team's head coach. He needed
an assistant and my name had gotten thrown into the hat.

Another ally I had up in the Twin Cities was Charlie Hallman,
my old newspaper-reporter buddy. With both of those guys
going to bat for me, I started to get excited about the possibility
of living back home near my friends and family—not to mention
the fact that I would have loved to have been able to go back to
school to finish my degree as well.

Another opportunity that came up was with my old friend Ned
Harkness, who was my general manager with the Adirondack
Red Wings. Shortly after I left Adirondack, Ned left Glens Falls to
become the president of ORDA (Olympic Regional Development
Authority), which managed the Lake Placid Olympic facilities.
Ned told me everything that he was involved in up there and

explained to me that the state's governor, Mario Cuomo, was going to turn over the Gore Mountain Ski Area, which was close to Lake George and Glens Falls, to ORDA to operate. He then asked me if I wanted to come work for him running the ski area. He wanted someone who he could completely trust, which meant a great deal to me. It was a tempting offer, to be sure, but the only catch was the fact that I knew very little about skiing.

I had only skied once in my life, which was at West Mountain in Glens Falls. After nearly killing myself when I ran into a ski lift tower, I promised myself that I would never try that crazy sport again. I asked Ned what exactly I would be doing out there and he said I could serve as their public relations agent. Now, I didn't know exactly what that meant, but I told Ned that I appreciated the offer and that I would think about it.

Ned's offer threw me for a loop. I had to weigh my options. On one hand, we loved living in the North Country of New York and I really liked Ned. But I was strongly drawn to the idea of going back home and being with the Gophers. We also really liked it in Birmingham, but the health club/gym business that I had invested in wasn't prosperous enough for me to make a living at and there really wasn't much else to consider for work there.

I called Ned and asked for his advice, telling him that my heart was leaning toward coaching. He supported me, but told me, "Getting hired to coach is a guarantee you'll get fired from coaching." One thing that Sue and I both wanted at this stage of our lives together was some stability. We had moved so many times over the past decade, we simply wanted to stay in one place.

Ned said coming to work for him may not have the same thrill as coaching, but it definitely offered more security and an opportunity to learn about business. Sue said it sure would be nice to be settled in one place for 12 months out of the year and be able to plan a future with the kids. However, she knew how much of my heart I poured into hockey and how much I wanted to stay in it, so she left the decision up to me. I struggled with it.

After we got back to Birmingham, I waited to hear from Charlie about the Minnesota job while I knew Ned was anxiously waiting to hear from me. Finally, Charlie called to say that Brad would like to bring me on. With that, I knew I had to make a decision. After talking it over with Sue some more, the next day I called Ned to tell him I was going to take him up on his offer.

Erin was going to start kindergarten in the fall and Sarah was only a couple of years behind her. As much as I wanted to coach my beloved Gophers, I also wanted to provide a quality life for my family. To me that meant job security and me being around to spend quality time raising my family. Sue had made so many sacrifices for me over the years, it was time for me to do the same for her.

Ned didn't give me much time, he wanted me on the job in two weeks. So I flew to Albany and then drove to Lake Placid to get all my new-hire paperwork in order. Ned then took me to Gore Mountain, where he had me stay in an old beat-up trailer in the back parking lot of the ski area. The trailer was sitting on the edge of a gravel-covered parking lot that was a short walk to the mountain's base lodge where the administrative offices were located. Ned told me I could stay in the trailer until Sue and the kids arrived.

The trailer was pretty dilapidated with little running water that I did not dare drink, but only used to flush the rusted toilet with. There was no heat or a stove, but there was electricity so I could use a microwave. Ants and mice were frequent visitors, especially at night when I was sleeping on the small foldout couch. Also, the bears would walk down from the woods, past the trailer, and over the hill during the night on the way to the town dump. After about two days in this backwoods retreat, I started wondering what the hell I had gotten myself into.

After a few weeks of living in these conditions, Sue and the girls finally arrived. I couldn't wait to see them; what a sight for sore eyes. Ned decided to fire the general manager and promoted me to the position. I was suddenly thrust into managing a major New York ski area, something I'd never done before.

We moved into a small, brown, hog-slab-sided house that was a stone's throw away from where I was staying in the trailer. It was a cozy little place that worked fine for us as we started a new phase of our lives.

From 1984–91 I managed Gore Mountain, which was considered the "Best Kept Secret in the East." When Ned and I arrived, his promotional skills soon transformed it to one of the "Most Popular Ski Areas in the East." I literally had crash courses in how to ski and understand the business. Immediately I became responsible for the management of a unionized labor force of up to 300 people and oversaw hundreds of thousands of visitors who came to Gore each year to enjoy the alpine and cross-country skiing. Fortunately for me, and for ORDA, Ned put me under the tutelage of a very smart and cordial man named Bob Paron who was managing Whiteface Mountain. Bob was a wonderful man who patiently taught me much about the ski business and about how to deal with employees and customers.

I remember my first winter during the Christmas holiday, which is one of the busiest times during the ski season. The ski area got bombarded with bus tours that came from New York City to ski the mountain and enjoy the après parties. I will never forget the day this loudmouth from Manhattan walked in my office and started complaining to me about how he and his friends couldn't ski because there was too much snow on the trails. Keep in mind that about eight months earlier I was being paid to punch people in the face for much less. Just as I was about to fly across my desk, my reasonably minded secretary walked in to settle me down and defuse the situation.

After that, she schooled me on ways to effectively deal with "tourons" (tourists and morons). She said I needed to find a way to deal with them firmly but cordially or I would find myself dealing with a New York City attorney and quickly be without a job. She was so right. That was really a tough thing to do because it was totally against my nature, but change I did, again, for the sake of my family.

While we were there, Sue got pregnant with our third child. Around midnight on March 10, 1986, Sue woke me up to tell me that it was time to get to the hospital. Knowing that she was two weeks past due, I knew I was going to be up against the clock. Not wanting to plunge the car over a ravine, I tried to stay calm and collected. We made it to the hospital, but the delivery came so fast that Sue didn't even have time to get her socks off before the baby poked his head out. It was an enormous 11-pound, 6-ounce baby boy that looked like a fat little Buddha. The hospital later confirmed that he was, in fact, the largest baby ever born in the history of the Glens Falls Hospital. Sue and I squabbled over what we were going to name him. She liked Caleb and I liked Cody, but our decision was made when our daughter Erin told us to just name him Christian. Christian it was. I was thrilled. I finally had my little hockey player, and he was just like his old man—big and tough.

Two years after Christian was born, I got him on skis. He took to skiing like he was born with them on and quickly progressed from the bunny hill to the intermediate trails. Gore had a vertical drop of 2,100 feet with some fairly steep and long runs that Christian would fearlessly race his sisters on.

When he was three years old I got him on ice skates. I bundled Christian up, put an old hockey helmet on him, and along with his sister, Sarah, we went skating. From that point on, he was hooked and hasn't stopped since. By this time, both girls were in the Johnsburg School in North Creek and were on the New York State ski team. Sarah was also taking horseback riding lessons, Erin was taking saxophone lessons, and Christian was chasing kildeers (birds) in the parking lot. We were really happy and thoroughly enjoyed everything about our lives.

Then one day, out of the blue, Ned asked me if I wanted to get back into hockey.

Chapter 12

Rats...

THE CAPITAL DISTRICT ISLANDERS (CDI) HOCKEY TEAM was the AHL farm team for the New York Islanders and played in Troy, New York. The team had just finished its opening season and had a very difficult year at the box office. The owners were familiar with Ned's background and success in starting and operating the Adirondack Red Wings franchise located about 45 minutes up the road in Glens Falls. The owner wanted Ned to take over the operations of CDI and turn it into a successful franchise. Ned told them he was committed to ORDA, but that he had someone in mind who might have an interest and would do a great job for them. Although I saw Gore as a career job, I was still interested in hearing more.

So, he and I met with the owner of CDI and the mayor of Troy. By the time we left, we had negotiated a multi-year contract that would pay me more than twice the amount of money I was making at Gore. I didn't commit to anything before I left the Troy office because I needed to talk it all over with Sue, but a negotiated contract was waiting for my signature. It was a gut-wrenching conversation and decision for Sue and me. We really liked where we were and what we were doing.

Ultimately, the thought of more money, of getting back into pro hockey, and a chance to move to Glens Falls, where we could get a nicer home and into a better school district, finally swayed our decision for me to leave ORDA and become the general man-

175

ager of the Capital District Islanders. I was excited about getting back into something that I had almost forgotten how much I missed since I retired from playing seven years earlier.

There would be many things we would miss about our home in North Creek. Among the things we would not be missing, however, were wild bears poking their heads into our bedroom window; finding snakes in our washing machine; the countless blood-sucking black flies; and picking porcupine quills out of our dog's nose. So we packed up yet again and moved to a rental house in Queensbury, New York, an extension of Glens Falls that was only about 45 minutes away.

My new job was a big adjustment, to say the least, starting with my commute to Troy every day. With CDI, however, I was spending a lot of time on the road wearing a suit and tie, trying to get companies and individuals to buy advertising and season tickets. It got old fast, but I needed to get out there and make things happen for CDI.

Once the season started, things didn't settle down. We played out of the RPI Houston Field House, which was an old navy warehouse in Rhode Island during World War II that got designated by the U.S. government as war surplus. The president of RPI got the government to donate, tear down, transport, and erect the massive building on the school's campus. It was a great college coliseum, but not a very nice facility for a professional hockey club. It was a real struggle to sell tickets and corporate sponsorships but we made the best of it.

In spite of playing in an old barn, our product on the ice was exciting to watch. The team played a fast brand of hockey with former Islander star Butch Goring as the head coach. The first year that the team existed it did not make the playoffs. The next two years, though, while I was managing the operation, we made the playoffs. It was a great turnaround. Both years while I was there, we increased ticket sales and sponsorship dollars. But as the season went on during the 1992–93 season, the owner of the team started making it known that he was not going to operate the team for another season. I couldn't believe what was happening. I left the great life and job security at Gore to get back into hockey with another franchise that was going defunct. It was like deja vu all over again.

Ned and I had stayed in touch constantly. When I told him of the latest developments, he approached a guy he knew in Schenectady about buying the team. One thing led to another and sure enough, we were back in business. The guy was Albert Lawrence, the king of insurance in the Capital District region, and he was hailed by many as a generous man who donated much of his time and money to various nonprofit organizations. When he bought CDI, I felt relieved and hopeful that I could continue to move the franchise in the right direction by making it profitable and popular like its upstate rival. But I soon discovered that there was a dark side to this man and despite the decisions I made to improve his investment, his ego did not allow anyone but him to be in total control.

At the end of the season, the New York Islanders decided to move their minor league team from Troy to Salt Lake City. Our three-year affiliation agreement expired and the Islanders did not want to stay in Troy any longer. That left the CDI franchise without an NHL affiliate, so I needed to secure a replacement for the vacancy the Islanders left. I contacted Lou Lamoriello, the GM of the New Jersey Devils, to see if I could stir up interest in him to move his farm club from Utica to Albany.

Lou and I had some very good discussions and he became extremely interested in partnering with us. As I was negotiating our new agreement and making good progress, Al Lawrence decided he wanted to handle the deal. He took over and came to terms on an agreement with the Devils to have them put their farm team in Albany as our affiliate. The agreement that Al negotiated and signed was much more expensive than the one that I was working out with Mr. Lamoriello. But, I thought, "Hey, it's his money. He can do what he wants with it."

I convinced Al that it was time to move out of the RPI Field House and upgrade our image by moving across the Hudson River to the Albany Knickerbocker Arena. The Knick was a $68 million major league arena built in Albany in 1990. Al liked that idea and had me proceed, but first we had to get the permission from the Red Wings, who owned the franchise territory rights. Detroit refused to grant us permission so Al filed a lawsuit against the Red Wings and won the right to move our club to the Knick. I negotiated a very favorable lease agreement with the arena's management and by the end of May we had a new home and a new NHL affiliate.

I decided that the next thing to do was to create a new identity for the team, which would generate additional revenue for the organization. I wanted to come up with a new name and logo for the team that would allow us to sell unique merchandise and advertising. Mr. Lamoriello wanted his players dressed in the New Jersey colors and wanted them to be called the Devils, just like the parent club. Al was not against this and it took considerable effort from me to convince him of the merits of having our own identity and uniforms. After Al agreed to create a new identity, he told me he wanted to call the team the Albany Dalmatians. He wanted the uniforms to be white with black spots on them. He also wanted helmets with dog ears on the sides and a dog snout on the front. Al had a couple of Dalmatian dogs for pets and felt that his Dalmatian-looking hockey team would be great. When I realized that he was serious, I told him that his design would definitely be unique, but never in a million years would the players or New Jersey agree with this plan. I suggested that we come up with a colorful name relating to something indigenous to the area and then create a logo to complement the name.

After much deliberation, he decided to have a poll taken in the local newspaper of an assortment of names and then see what came back as the popular choice.

I immediately went to my public relations director, Geoff Knapp, and my director of media relations, Jeremy Duncan, to brainstorm new name ideas. After a few beers, we came up with "River Rats." With the Hudson River in our backyard, River Rats could refer to local kids who frequently skated on the river, similar to the term *rink rats*, or it could simply be a furry rodent from the banks of the river. Either way, we liked it and submitted it on the contest list.

Al Lawrence and Lou Lamoriello hated the name, but sure enough, it won by a three-to-one margin. Lawrence was still not totally convinced that we should use this name, but I went ahead by hiring a local advertising agency to come up with a logo. I gave the company my idea of a rat with a smirking attitude splashing out of the water with a hockey stick in its hand and a wink in its eye. After a bit of tweaking, I had our first game jersey made with the new logo and called a press conference to unveil "Rowdy the Rat," of the new Albany River Rats. It was a huge hit. The media ate it up and even *USA Today* ran a feature about it. Soon after that, the *Hockey News,* considered the bible for all hockey information, named it the best logo in minor league hockey.

I thought I had hit a series of home runs with my bold moves over the summer, but by mid-September 1993, before our first game, Al Lawrence called me into his office and told me that I was fired. I was floored. When I asked why, he said that I had lied to him. In reality, he couldn't stand the fact that I had come up with a good idea that wasn't his own. When I strongly protested his false accusation and asked him to give me a specific example, he refused and simply told me that he was terminating my employment. He did not give me any severance pay or say anything about my employment contract that came with the franchise when he bought it, either. As a result of his refusal to honor our agreement, I had to take legal action against him.

It took nearly a year from the day that I got fired to get awarded a judgment against Lawrence. During that time, I tirelessly sought employment with other hockey teams and other places, but had no luck. With no money coming in, bills needing to be paid, and the cost of daily life, I exhausted all of our savings and had to rely on relatives' contributions, mostly from Gram and Pap, in order to keep from filing bankruptcy or having my mortgage go to foreclosure. Once I was awarded my settlement, I was able to pay back all of my dear relatives who helped me through that awful time. I guess it's true what they say about realizing who your true friends are when you are at your lowest. I can't thank them enough. I learned a lot of valuable lessons about life that year and am a much stronger person as a result.

Chapter 13

The Boys Are Back in Town

URING THE LAST YEAR OF CDI, I GOT A CALL ONE DAY FROM my old friend Steve Carlson. He was serving as the head coach of the Memphis River Kings in the Central Hockey League at the time, and asked me if I would be willing to come to Memphis to do a reunion of the Hanson Brothers at one of his games. We had only gotten together as the Hanson Brothers just one other time since the premiere of the movie in 1977, and that was for a TV special called "Hockey Night in Hollywood," which was co-hosted by Wayne Gretzky and Alan Thicke and celebrated the history of Canada's national sport in Hollywood movies. I was excited to see the guys, so I hopped on a plane for Memphis.

Jeff and I were glad to help out Steve, but figured the event wasn't going to be a very big deal, especially considering there was a college basketball playoff game going on close by. All we had to do was drop the puck at a ceremonial center-ice face-off and after the game sign a few autographs if any fans were waiting around. Jeff, Steve, and I all had short hair at the time and appeared in just our regular clothes. When we went out to drop the puck, we realized that they had sold about 8,000 seats at the Pyramid Arena that night, their largest crowd of the year. Our introduction was greeted by a standing ovation and after the game we sat for close to four hours signing autographs. We were shocked by the response and I thought, if this can happen in a nontraditional hockey market like Memphis, maybe it will happen in Troy, New York, where I was struggling to fill half of the 5,000-seat building for the Capital District Islanders.

On April 3, 1993, I took the reunion of the Hanson Brothers a step further by having us put on our Chiefs jerseys along with the black-rimmed glasses. We then skated in the team's pregame warm-ups, and also had a special guest appearance by Gordie Howe. "Mr. Hockey" was on his "65th Birthday Tour" and he and his wife Colleen agreed to stop by for this special night. Gordie also put on a pair of Hanson Brothers glasses and skated in warm-ups with us and the team. He was later described in the newspaper as, "Poetry in slow motion as he skated in on a breakaway against the CDI goalie and beat him with a perfect shot that rang off the post and into the goal."

When he and the Hanson Brothers left warm-ups, we got a standing ovation. The RPI Houston Field House sold out and together we signed autographs well after the game had ended. Earlier in the day we attended a "Legends of Hockey" luncheon that I put together with the help of my friend Dr. Bill Cromie, who was instrumental in starting the Ronald McDonald House in Albany. This was the first time the Hanson Brothers used their popularity to help raise money for a needy cause. The entire day was fun and successful and became international news when my PR director put the story out on the AP wire the next day.

My phone rang off the hook with calls from radio stations and newspapers from throughout Canada and the United States asking about the Hanson Brothers. One of the calls I got was from a promoter and agent in Detroit who had seen the story. It occurred to him that the bespectacled Hanson Brothers would be perfect spokesmen for an optometry company. He called me and offered to become our manager and we said, "Go for it." Even though we had a couple of fun experiences getting together again, we certainly did not think it was anything worth quitting our day jobs for. So we just continued on with our normal daily lives.

In August of 1993, Luc Robitaille, an NHL star player for the Los Angeles Kings, was coordinating an effort to host a celebrity charity hockey game at the Great Western Forum to raise money for the TJ Martell Foundation and the Neil Bogart Memorial Fund at Children's Hospital in Los Angeles. About a week before the event was scheduled to take place, ticket sales were running extremely low. So Luc placed a call into the Hanson Brothers and asked if we would play in the game and hopefully help boost a few more ticket sales. We agreed, and two days after the press release went out announcing that we were coming, the Great Western Forum sold out. When we heard the news, we figured that we were on to something.

Figuring that we had better start to look the part, we immediately took steps to go back in time in order to look more like the Hanson Brothers of old. With that, I found a wig shop in Los Angeles on the corner of Hollywood and Vine that had every style of wig imaginable. When we showed the shop attendant a picture of the Hanson Brothers from *Slap Shot* and expressed a desire to get me to look like Jack Hanson again, the stylist pulled out a wig, sat me in front of a full-length mirror, and proceeded to cover my head. Here I was, a macho former hockey player sitting sheepishly while a wig-maiden was adjusting a long-haired wig on my head, trying to comb it all pretty to match my 1976 picture. When she got done, I looked in the mirror and blurted out loud, "I look like a freakin' drag queen!"

When we arrived at the Forum to get ready to play, we were amazed at how many TV cameras, radio stations, and newspaper people were waiting to talk to the movie and hockey stars. We were even more surprised at how many of them wanted to talk to us. What really blew us away was how many of the stars wanted to get their pictures taken with us. I had my seven-year-old son Christian along with me and he wanted to just hang out with the NHL players like Chris Chelios, Pavel Bure, and Marty Brodeur, while Steve, Jeff, and I went from one person to the next to get interviewed about the return of the Hanson Brothers. When we finally hit the ice, we stole the show and had the fans and the players loving every minute of our on-ice antics.

After the game, when we finally got through all of the autographs and picture-taking in the locker rooms with everyone, we went to a postgame party where the Red Hot Chili Peppers were playing. During one of their breaks we auctioned off a game-worn Chiefs jersey and one of the Russian NHL players bought it for $5,000. With his new jersey on he ran around the room yelling in broken English, "I'm a Hanson Brother, I'm a Hanson Brother!" The event was a resounding success and the second time we contributed significantly to raising money for a needy cause. When it was all said and done, the "Rock'n the Puck Celebrity Hockey Game" raised over half a million dollars for the charity.

Even though we realized that the Hanson Brothers were extremely popular and worth a lot of money for charities, it wasn't anything that we were taking seriously because it wasn't making us any money. We saw it as just a fun way to occasionally get away from our daily grind. Therefore, we did not shave our mustaches or grow our hair out or quit our jobs— although shortly after the Forum appearance, I got fired from the River Rats. However, word was spreading like wildfire about what we were doing and calls were pouring in from all over the continent with appearance requests. In November we played in Providence, Rhode Island, at a Big Brothers and Big Sisters charity game that included the Boston Bruins Alumni and the Providence College Alumni.

After another appearance in Fraser, Michigan, where we were mobbed at a youth tournament for two days by hundreds of kids, we got a call from the Anaheim Mighty Ducks of the NHL about having us appear at a special exhibition celebrity game at the Arrowhead Pond Arena in Anaheim between the Ducks and the L.A. Kings. The purpose for this unusual NHL-sanctioned charity game between two NHL rival teams during the regular season was to help raise money to benefit the Southern California fire victims through the local Red Cross chapters. We sold the building out with over 17,000 fans and had a ball with the Mighty Ducks mascot.

The highlight came when we hit the NHL's director of hockey operations, Brian Burke, in the face with a shaving cream pie. We set the routine up with him ahead of time, but wound up catching him off guard. When I smashed him with the pie, he didn't close his mouth and eyes and the shaving cream not only went up his nose, in his ears, and down his throat, it also went in his eyes. As he was gagging uncontrollably, we helped him off the ice because he couldn't breathe, hear, or see anything. I later apologized, but my fellow Minnesotan just laughed it off. After helping to raise another $300,000 for the needy fire victims, we started to think that maybe this Hanson Brothers thing was for real.

Meanwhile, back at home, another opportunity had come my way. Jack Kelly was the president of the NHL's Pittsburgh Penguins and a close friend of Ned Harkness. Prior to joining the Penguins, Jack was the president of the New England Whalers when I played in the WHA. The Penguins were building a practice facility in Pittsburgh and Jack asked me if I was interested in becoming the general manager of it. After being out of work for over a year and surviving on the kindness of my relatives, I immediately jumped at the offer.

Early in 1995 I packed up yet again and moved to Pittsburgh, leaving Sue and the kids behind to sell the house. When I got there, I did not have a place to stay and moved in with my skating school director. That lasted a couple of months until her new boyfriend, who was the Penguins owner's son, got jealous and made her kick me out. By that time, I had hired my nephew to be the assistant operations director and ended up moving in with him for about a month. After that I moved into the basement of my wife's cousin's home for about another month before I finally found a house of our own to move into. What an ordeal! When Sue and the kids came and we were all back together again under one roof, it was like a huge weight had been lifted off of my shoulders.

During that time, besides starting up and managing the Penguins' practice facility, I was also making appearances with the Hanson Brothers. One of those appearances was at a Red Wings game in Detroit. Before the game, we went over to a bar across from the Joe Louis arena to have a beer and hang out. While we were there, the Bud Ice brand manager for Anheuser-Busch saw the reaction we got from the patrons in the bar. He was even more blown away when he saw the reaction we got later on that night at the Red Wings game. Budweiser had just come out with a new beer called Bud Ice, only it was not selling very well. Bud Ice was set to become the official beer sponsor of the NHL and the brand manager saw the Hanson Brothers as a great marketing and promotional tool for the new beer. He then contacted our manager and made a pitch to have us become the promotional spokesmen for Bud Ice. We were floored.

I had been working at the Penguins practice rink for about six months when the Bud Ice proposal was made. I still had my short hair and mustache and wig because I was not convinced that the Hanson Brothers appearances could amount to anything but fun. About the same time that the Budweiser proposal was made, the arena complex owner's son decided that he and his skating director girlfriend wanted to manage the facility. As a result, Jack Kelly was forced to fire me. I was shocked. It was really a tough pill to swallow, especially for the reasons I was provided, but it happened and there was nothing I could do about it. However, the firing made my decision really easy to accept the Bud Ice proposal to get paid to drink and promote beer.

Almost immediately, we made a nationally aired TV commercial and recorded seven national radio commercials. The Budweiser people were great to work with, but they really worked us hard. For almost two years, we'd leave our homes on Thursday and return on Sunday almost every week from September through May. We estimated that we visited at least 100 different cities over the course of the winter, and in each city we made appearances at bars, restaurants, conventions, and hockey games. I will never forget St. Patrick's Day in Boston. We spent from 7:00 AM to around 2:00 AM the next morning driving around in the Bud Bus alongside the sexy Bud Babes, under a motorcycle police escort, no less, going into a different bar every hour. It was fun, but exhausting. When we first started the Bud Tour we always had a bottle of Bud Ice in one hand and another to our lips. After about a week of trying to keep up at that torrential pace, we realized that if we didn't significantly slow down that there was no way we were going to make it through the tour without needing a liver transplant.

We went back to Boston for the 1996 NHL All-Star Game and spent the night visiting most of the bars around the Fleet Center.

Every spot we stopped at was phenomenal and created such a buzz that many people decided not to go watch the game, but to instead hang out with us. Whether we were Zamboni skiing at Madison Square Garden or hitting a back-street bar in Baltimore, the reaction was always the same. We were mobbed, applauded, hugged, and adored—and it didn't matter what age, gender, or race—they all loved seeing us. We had our act down cold. I was always the first one to walk through the door, followed by Steve and then Jeff, all wearing our jerseys: Nos. 16, 17, and 18, and then I'd yell, *"Okay, everybody, it's time to play old-time hockey!"* Then Steve and Jeff would follow with their banter as we went around shaking hands and passing out bottles of Bud Ice.

One night we were visiting pubs in Washington DC for the local Bud Ice rep before appearing at a Washington Capitals game. He had us stop at one small place, but not before he explained that it was really a tough bar that he'd had no luck getting Bud Ice into. Up to the challenge, I grabbed a couple bottles of Bud Ice and bolted through the front door with my battle cry. Before I got half of the words out of my mouth, I stopped dead in my tracks as I stared into the silent and angry-looking eyes of about 100 African American men. Behind me were Steve and Jeff, who were pushing their way forward because they couldn't see past me and had no idea why I stopped. When they arrived they, too, were stunned at what they saw. Feeling a bit fearful for our lives, we quickly and nervously just started handing out cold bottles of Bud Ice. Five minutes later we were high-fiving everyone in the bar and taking pictures with our newfound friends. It was awesome. And, needless to say, our rep got the account.

After a year of nonstop traveling and promoting, Bud Ice had gone from No. 4 to No. 1 in the market share of ice beer. However, the NHL did not like that one of their major sponsors was having the Hanson Brothers play such a large and visible role in the NHL markets. Budweiser had plans for us to appear in San Jose for the 1997 NHL All-Star Game, but were told that the NHL wanted to keep us away. The NHL apparently felt that the Hanson Brothers did not represent the kind of image that they wanted to project to their fans. This seriously hurt our feelings and gave us a bad taste in our mouths. Here we were, touring the country as spokesmen for Budweiser and acting as colorful ambassadors for a game we love. We were meeting millions of hockey fans and the NHL did not see the value of that. Although *Slap Shot* showed a violent side of minor league hockey, it also was a satire and a comedy. In reality, the Hanson Brothers were lovable guys and great promoters of hockey.

We had some great times during our tour. I will never forget the time we were in the bowels of the St. Louis Blues Arena before a Blues game one night. As we were walking through the corridor heading toward the elevator, coming in the other direction was a big guy who suddenly shouted out, "I don't believe it! I just don't f*cking believe it! It's the f*cking Hanson Brothers, my heroes!" We thought, oh no, here we go. As we got closer, though, we realized it was the actor, John Goodman. He gave us all a big hug and as we rode up the elevator together, he just kept saying, "I don't f*cking believe it. I'm with the f*cking Hanson Brothers." He asked us for our autographs and asked us to send him a Chiefs jersey, which he later even wore on an episode of his show *Roseanne*.

It was not uncommon for us to be at an autograph-signing expo or a convention with other big-time celebrities and have our line be much longer than theirs. Stuff like that always blew me away. We were at a national Budweiser convention with the "Bud Light Ladies Night Out Guys," who were extremely popular then, plus we were right next to the beautiful supermodel Rachel Hunter. At all three locations, people could get a free picture taken with or an autograph from the person of their choice. The line for the Hanson Brothers dwarfed the "Ladies Night Out Guys" and made Rachel Hunter's line look anemic. We ran into Loraine Newman one day in L.A. while we were getting ready to do a radio interview. She said she couldn't believe her eyes and that she and everyone else at *Saturday Night Live* loved us. Who knew?

It was also common for NHL players to want to meet us before or after we appeared at their games. One night at Madison Square Garden, Wayne Gretzky and Mark Messier asked us to come to the locker room to talk and take pictures with the guys.

Another time Ted Nolan, coach of the Buffalo Sabres, had us come into the locker room before the team went out to start the game and had us give the team a pregame speech. While in St. Louis one time, Chris Pronger and Al McInnis, both All-Star defensemen for the Blues, snuck out of their pregame warm-ups and into the back room where we were waiting so they could get their pictures taken with us. It wasn't only hockey players or movie stars or typical hockey fans that enjoyed us. We seemed to be known by and connect with all different people.

We were asked to make an appearance in Florida at a national Days Inn convention one time. When we got to the hotel ball-room where it was being held, the vast majority of the people in the room were from India. Men with turbans on their heads and ladies with dots on their foreheads dominated the large crowd of hotel owners and operators. When we announced our arrival in typical Hanson Brothers fashion, they lined up for hours for pictures, autographs, and laughs. But as much fun as it was, as great as the Budweiser people were to work with, and as good as the money was, being on the road for about two years straight was wearing me down. I was missing much of my home life with my wife and growing children. I decided it was time to cut back on the Hanson Brothers road trips and try to stay home more. Luckily, Jeff and Steve agreed. However, this created another problem. Now I had to find another way to make a living and the last thing we wanted to do was move again.

As luck would have it, I heard about a sports complex that was being built on an island in the Allegheny River not far from my home. Rumor was that it was being constructed on a toxic waste site and it was supposed to be large facility with several ice rinks. I tracked down the person who was responsible for the project and had an opportunity to meet with him face to face. I was nervous about going in for my interview, because I had grown out my hair while I was out on tour. I didn't want him to think I was a hippie rock star or anything, but it turned out the guy was totally cool with it. He was a fan of the movie and had no problem with me continuing to make Hanson Brothers appearances on my own time. He hired me and in the fall of

1998, together we opened the Island Sports Center on Neville Island.

One of the benefits of working at the "Island" was that I could also coach my son, who started playing hockey when we lived in Queensbury, and continued when we moved to Pittsburgh. He was playing AAA hockey at that point and I was lucky enough to be able to coach him up to the age of 16. Because we often had to travel out of state to play, we spent a lot of time together, which to this day is one of the reasons we are best friends. Sometimes it got tough coaching kids, managing the sports center, and being a Hanson Brother. We decided to cut back the number of appearances we were doing, but the demand was still extremely high. Shortly after we stopped touring with Bud Ice we severed ties with our manager from Detroit and at that point, Steve and his wife started handling all of our bookings. We were now free to pick and choose where we wanted to appear. Things had settled down and I was finally in a good place, both personally and professionally.

Chapter 14

Slap Shot II—
Breaking the Ice

AS WE CONTINUED TO DO WHAT WE COULD FOR CHARITABLE causes as the Hansons, in 2001 we unknowingly piqued the interest of some executives at Universal Studios. One day Steve got a call asking if we were interested in being in *Slap Shot II*. Who'da thunk it? Nearly 25 years after the release of *Slap Shot*, Universal was going to do a sequel. We were all really excited. That March we found ourselves on a plane to Vancouver to film another movie that we literally knew nothing about. We didn't know what it was about, who was in it, or what our roles would be. We heard rumors that Kiefer Sutherland and Denis Leary were among the A-list actors who were going to star in the film. We all sat back, speculated, and pondered the future.

When we got there, we signed the contract and were handed a script. Talk about a leap of faith. After going through the wardrobe routine and a few other formalities, we briefly met the director, Steve Boyum, and some of the actors. We also met Stephen Baldwin, who was signed as the marquee star of the film. We had first met Stephen a couple of years before in Ann Arbor, Michigan, at a celebrity golf tournament hosted by Jim Harbaugh, then quarterback of the Indianapolis Colts. When we met Stephen out on the golf course, he immediately got on his cell phone to call his agent. While we were standing next to him, he told his agent to get him in a movie with the Hanson Brothers. We thought he was just trying to impress us. But to our surprise, when we got to the set, there he was with a big smile on his face, pointing his finger at us saying, "I told you guys."

We hit it off with Steve Boyum right away. He was an athlete and a big fan of ours, plus he had a great sense of humor. He immediately told us that we had free rein to be ourselves and play our roles as we saw fit. He was there to guide us and help us along. I don't know if he really knew what he was in for, but right off the bat we gave him a taste of what we could do. Our first scene was in a restaurant when we were supposed to tell Baldwin that we are being sent home. We had our scripted lines, but felt they weren't right. When Boyum yelled "Action," we came out to do the scene with Baldwin and rattled off, "Old-time hockey, like Eddie Shore, Dit Clapper, Toe Blake, and Gordie Howe... *Gordie*!" All three of us put our elbows in the air in a Gordie Howe salute. The entire set cracked up and from that point on, we knew we had control.

When we finally got to do our first on-ice scene, it called for Baldwin to tell us to get on the ice. While we were setting up for the scene, I noticed Baldwin standing against the boards with his helmet propped up on top of his head. He looked like a Conehead the way he had his helmet on. I asked one of the other players if he always wore his helmet like that and he said yes. Everyone was afraid to tell him how goofy he looked because he was a star. I said to the guy, "There is no way I'm going to be in a hockey movie with someone looking like that." So I went over to Baldwin and started to talk to him, asking him random questions. I then asked him if he was ready to go and he said yes. I asked him again if he was sure he was ready, and with a questioning expression he said yes one more time. I said, "No, you're not," and I smashed him on top of his helmet with my fist—properly jamming it down onto his head the way it was supposed to be. I then smiled and said, "Now you're ready!"

Gary Busey was the co-star that we were really looking forward to meeting. When we did, he was nothing like we expected. He was calm and controlled and said he was a big fan of ours. When we got around to shooting our first scene with him, he was to come to the players bench during a game and the Hansons were to grab him and forcibly drag him away through the players hallway. The first time we did it, he complained to us that we were too gentle with him. The next time he made the same complaint again. So the third time we violently grabbed him and drug him away while we pounded on his chest and head. I thought we were going to kill the guy, but he liked it, and fortunately, so did the director. Gary was an interesting guy, to say the least. I remember sitting with him on several occasions, listening while he told us about his views on spirituality and on life. Old Gary has some issues, that is for sure, but what a great actor.

The movie set was really subdued compared to when we shot the original Slap Shot, and the main reason for that was because of the Hanson Brothers. Being in our 40s, I guess we just didn't have the same carefree attitude or desire to pull the childish pranks we did back in 1976. We still made a lot of friends and laughed a lot, but this was a five-week shoot for us, whereas the original was three months. Plus, I think the weather had something to do with keeping our moods more somber than usual, too. The entire time we were in Vancouver it rained with the exception of one day. On that day, we all planned to go golfing, but I didn't get to go. During the entire day before we shot a scene with the Hansons sitting in the back of the team bus. While Steve and I played with our video games, Jeff ate beef jerky. I started nibbling on the jerky between takes and as the day went on, I must've ended up eating a whole bag of the stuff. Through the night my stomach rumbled and by morning I came down with an extreme case of beef jerky diarrhea. While the guys played golf on the only day of sunshine in Vancouver, I spent the day in my apartment hanging close to the toilet. It seemed like a bad flashback from the 1970s.

We had fun, though, and had a good time being together again, nearly a quarter of a century later. It was hard to believe it had been that long, and yet it seemed like a lifetime ago. Wives, kids, careers, and just plain old life in general had crept up on all of us.

Just before the release of the movie, Universal held a few "big screen" tests of it in theaters. The results came back with mixed reviews, but the overwhelming remarks from the viewers were that the Hanson Brothers were great and they wanted to see more of them in the movie. Universal knew they had a sure bet to make money by going direct to DVD with the movie, so instead of taking the financial risk of distributing the movie to theaters, they decided to take the safe route and just put it on disc to be sold in stores and video rentals.

On March 26, 2002, *Slap Shot II—Breaking the Ice* was released and it exceeded all of Universal's revenue expectations. Just prior to its official release, Universal put the Hanson Brothers on a promotional tour and everywhere we went—TV talk shows, radio shows, newspapers, or personal appearances—the excitement was the same. The Hockey Hall of Fame in Toronto even held a special ceremony for us by showcasing *Slap Shot* and *Slap Shot II* in their front display case. There was also a well attended press conference there for us, where some of the Hall's dignitaries and past inductees spoke about the legacy of the movie. After all the accolades, we spoke and mentioned how honored we were to be recognized by such a prestigious organization.

After the movie came out, we got invited to attend the DVD Premiere Awards in Hollywood, the DVD industry's Oscars, where we received Best Supporting Actor nominations. We attended the gala decked out in white-tail tuxedoes with fluorescent cummerbunds, pastel ruffled shirts, and colored Converse high-top sneakers. When we arrived by limo, it appeared to us to be just like the Academy Awards. There was a crowd of screaming spectators, the traditional red carpet for celebrity interviews, the cocktail party, and the awards show. The room was filled with movie stars, directors, and producers, all dressed in their black tuxedoes and designer gowns with gaudy jewelry. Here we were in our 1970s prom attire, but we didn't care, we were having a blast just being there.

As the show progressed with people accepting their awards and making their speeches, Jeff decided to head to the bathroom. A few minutes after he left the table, our category came up and actor Bruce Boxleitner announced, "And the winner is…the Hanson Brothers!" Steve and I looked at each other and then around for Jeff. He was nowhere to be seen, so we walked up on stage and I said, "This is a great surprise and honor, but we have to wait until my brother Jeff gets back from the bathroom to accept. While we wait, we would like to announce that after many years of looking all over the world for our long-lost father, who abandoned us when we were little kids in Bear Butt, Minnesota, we've finally found him and, in front of this grand audience here tonight, we'd like to announce to the world that [actor] Ben Stein is our dad."

Ben was the evening's master of ceremonies and I called him out on to the stage from behind the curtain. Steve and I gave him a big hug and Steve pulled out his Instamatic camera to take a picture of me with my arm around Ben. Then we switched and I took a picture of them. I said to the audience, who was just howling with laughter at that point, "Is there any question? Look at his glasses and his nose. Look at his shoes." (He was wearing high-top sneakers also.) "Look at his tie," which was a bright color that coordinated with the colors we had on. Right then, Jeff burst through the doors and ran down the aisle, leaped up onto the stage, and said in the mic, "Sorry, folks, I had to go feed the dogs." We gave our acceptance speech and closed by saying we were going to have to leave soon to go bail Gary Busey out of jail. It was classic, truly classic.

Later in the evening, we were presenters for an award, and while we were waiting backstage to go on, Jeff was talking to David Carradine. He told him that if he wore Converse sneakers like we had on, then he would have been able to travel across the desert much faster as Qui Chang in the TV series *Kung Fu*. Meanwhile, I was talking to big Bo Svenson and told him that had he used a hockey stick instead of a two-by-four in *Walking Tall* we could've been there to help. As for Steve, he was just trying to talk shop with some hip-hop artist. Talk about a fish out of water. When the show was over, Quentin Tarantino ran up to us asking if he could get a picture with us. He said he grew up watching *Slap Shot* and was a huge fan of ours. Then, just as we were ready to leave, we realized that we were only given one award, so I went back up on stage, walked over to the table where some extra awards were sitting, and I took two more. Just as I did, the lady who brings the awards out to the winners on stage said that I was not allowed to take them. I said, "Sorry, honey, but there are three of us and you gave us only one award. If you want to stop me, call Ogie Oglethorpe," and I walked away with them.

Shortly after the awards, Universal Studios wanted to sign us to a movie contract for at least two more films. We negotiated a contract and just before they were ready to make Part III, Universal went through a sale and a restructuring of the company that put everything on hold. The Universal people who were instrumental in getting Part II made either were let go or reassigned. We were bummed out, but figured it was out of our control. A few years later, I contacted one of the producers who had worked on *Slap Shot II*. When I spoke to her, she informed me that her division dealt strictly with making movies that were rated no higher than PG-13, that she could not make another *Slap Shot* movie—because Parts I and II were both rated R. I told her that whenever the Hansons made appearances, our fans ranged in age from "ankle-biters to old-timers," and that it might be a great idea to make Part III geared toward kids and families. She was so intrigued with the idea that she went out and acquired the rights for it from another division within Universal. As a result, the Hanson Brothers are starring in a *Junior Slap Shot* film that is geared towards the family audience. Needless to say, Jeff, Steve, and I are thrilled. We can't wait to entertain the next generation of hockey fans who want to play some "old-time hockey"!

Chapter 15

Thoughts on Dave Hanson

Frank Beaton

"I remember one time we were playing against each other a few years after we were teammates together down in Alabama. I was still with Birmingham at this point and he was with Indianapolis. Anyway, I was skating up the ice and the next thing I knew my hockey stick was missing. Dave had skated up beside me and just grabbed it out of my hand. He then skated over to his bench and then sat down, where he proceeded to start laughing like hell at me. I am out there looking over at the sonofabitch and damn it all if I don't start laughing too. He was a real character, he really was."

Brian Burke, GM, Anaheim Ducks

"When I was playing in Springfield, John Paddock, the coach of the Ottawa Senators, was on our team. He was a tough guy and was trying to get to 250 penalty minutes or some crazy thing and needed to get into some fights. Well, we played against Dave's team one night and John asked me if Dave was very tough. Paddock wanted to know if he fought fair or not, and how he should approach him. I told him he was really tough and that he had better be careful because Dave was quick. Sure enough, he went after him and Dave just popped him right away, boom-boom, square in the nose before he could even square up. Well, Paddock thought that he sucker-punched him and was pissed. I saw it, and Dave didn't sucker him, he just got to him really fast. Meanwhile, I am on the end of the bench while Paddock and Hanson were both in the penalty box. We are all looking at each other and Paddock starts yelling. I thought that he was yelling at Dave, taunting him for a rematch, but instead I realized that he was yelling at me, blaming me for not giving him a better scouting report. I just had to put my head down and laugh at that one, it was a classic."

• • •

"I first met Dave back in 1973 when we played together on a summer league team for college kids back in Minnesota. He was an excellent teammate, just a great guy. He always backed everybody up and really took care of us. We later played against each other in the minor leagues as well. We have always kept in touch over the years and I couldn't be happier for all of his success."

Jack Carlson

"As a player, Dave was a hard-nosed kind of a guy who came to play every night. We played together for one season in Johnstown before I got called up to the WHA's St. Paul Fighting Saints. He was a great teammate and always gave you an honest effort. He was tough, too, and always stood up for what he thought was right. Whenever things got sticky out on the ice he was never afraid to stick his nose in there and get dirty. He would never back down and would do whatever he thought was necessary to help his team win. He was a smart player too and knew when to pick his spots out there so that he wouldn't hurt his team. He just knew his role and he did it very effectively, that is why his teammates respected him.

"Dave was a valuable player to the organizations that he played for. Did he score a lot of goals? No. But in my opinion you don't measure someone's worth to their team by that. You have to look at all of the intangibles and see what his role was. A guy like Dave did a lot of the dirty work so that his teammates could bask in the glory. I tell you what, though, those teammates wouldn't have been scoring goals and getting all of the glory had it not been for Dave. Guys like that, myself included, didn't need or want the glory, we just wanted to do whatever we could in order to help our teams win. Our contributions couldn't be measured by goals and assists. No way."

Frank Beaton

"Dave was just a class guy all the way around, a real salt-of-the-earth kind of person. You know, Dave's nickname as a player was 'Killer,' which he got from the movie. In reality, however, his true-life persona couldn't have been further from that. Dave was the nicest guy and was a great teammate. Everybody loved him. He was a real gentleman who cared deeply about his friends and family. Dave was actually very calm, level headed, and quite intelligent. In addition to being a gentle giant, he was actually a real fine family man. The nickname was a total contrast to the real-life person, it really was. Now, the role that he played out on the ice, that was the real deal. Dave was one of the toughest guys ever to lace 'em up. He was an extremely tough guy and always stood up for his teammates. He played hard but he also played fair. He wasn't dirty, like his character in the movie. He had a role to do and he did it very honorably. I just am proud to call him my friend."

John Brophy

"I coached Dave when he was with us in Birmingham. Dave was one of the best teammates an organization could have. He was just a great presence in the dressing room. As a coach, he was one of my favorites. He was a no-nonsense kind of a guy who went about his business as a true professional. He would come in and get ready and he would get his teammates ready to play, too. He knew what he had to do out there and was always ready to do whatever he felt was necessary to help his team win. He could play defense or forward and was very versatile as a player. He was extremely physical and was one of the toughest guys I have ever known. He wasn't the biggest guy, but man was he tough. His fights didn't last too long because he usually took care of business pretty quickly. He wasn't one of those guys who ran his mouth out there either. He just very quietly went about his business, even if that meant dropping the gloves and taking care of somebody. He just played the game clean, with respect, and was treated with respect as such. It was a pleasure to know Dave and a pleasure to coach him. He is a good man and I couldn't be happier for his success."

Paul D'Amato (aka "Tim 'Dr. Hook' McCracken")

"Dave is just a great guy. He is a family man and just a real down-to-earth kind of guy. He was also a very good hockey player. For a big guy, he was actually very good with the puck. He was also extremely tough, and maybe one of the most feared guys of his era."

Roy Mlakar, President of the NHL's Ottawa Senators

"I got to know Dave when we were both with Providence, of the old AHL. Off the ice, Dave was the complete opposite of what he was like on the ice. Off the ice he was soft-spoken, charitable, and an unbelievable family man. On the ice, however, he was one of the toughest guys around. He could have been vicious, but he played the game with respect. Players feared going into the corners with him because they never knew if he was going to finish his check or really nail them. Every opposing player would be wondering if he was going to get a stick in the ribs, in the groin, or across the back. He was an intimidating player, very unpredictable. He was a quick learner and always did what he was asked to do. He was a true professional and was always one of the hardest working guys on the team. As a person, he was an absolute joy to be around. He is just a great guy. I tell you what, with his combination of skill and toughness—if he played today he would be a $2 million a year hockey player. No doubt about it. He was that good."

Guido Tenissi (aka "Billy Charlesbois")

"Dave and I had a lot of fun rooming together. We got along well and had some good times. Being in the movie together was a lot of fun for all of us. The Carlson brothers lived in the room below us, so we all used to hang out together quite a bit on our off time. I remember one time Jeff and I went up to the local mall and started looking around inside a toy store. There were a bunch of race car sets in there and we thought that might be kind of fun. So we bought a couple sets and set them up back in our apartments. From there it just escalated. Guys would come over and drink beer while we all played with the cars. It was hilarious. It was a great way for us to pass the time and to stay out of trouble. Before long, guys would customize their cars by painting them and doing different things. It was a lot of fun. I was glad that they included that scene in the movie, because it was really what we did a lot of the time to stay busy. The movie was about 80 percent true in that regard. I mean, most of that crazy stuff really happened."

Paul Holmgren, GM of the Philadelphia Flyers

"I have had the pleasure of knowing Dave for a number of years. We played hockey and football against each other in high school back in St. Paul, when he was at Humboldt and I was at Harding. So we go way back. We later played junior hockey together as teammates with the St. Paul Vulcans. We both turned pro around the same time and wound up as roommates with the Johnstown Jets. I just can't say enough great things about Dave. He was a great teammate and just a great guy. I certainly respected the way he played the game, he was one of the toughest players I ever played with or against in my career. He was just a great competitor and had a real passion for the game. I will tell you one thing, though, if Dave would have decided to play football, there is a very good chance that he would have gone on to star in the NFL. He obviously made the right career choice in playing hockey, but he was an animal on the football field as well. He was just a vicious hitter, both on the ice and on the gridiron. On the ice he was one of the best open-ice hitters around, and he was clean, too. He laid out a lot of guys over the years. He didn't play dirty or anything like that, he played the game the right way. If somebody was going to take liberties with him or one of his teammates, though, watch out, because he was just as vicious as a fighter. Guys didn't want to mess with him, that was for sure. I am just proud to be his friend and couldn't be happier for all of his success in life. He is a great family guy and has done very well for himself in the business world. So I take my hat off to him."

Barry Melrose, ESPN Hockey Analyst

"The 'Killer' was tough, no question about it. He played hard every night and was a great competitor. Coming from Canada,

I never knew that there were any tough guys from the United States until I met Dave and the Carlson brothers. When I first saw them play it was shocking, because they were just that tough. They could really intimidate guys out there, and in hockey that is half the battle. The third Carlson brother, however, Jack—who was an NHL enforcer for many years—was tougher than all three of them put together. Jack was one of the toughest heavyweights of all time; he was scary. I can't even imagine the fights those three brothers must have had in the basement growing up on the Iron Range in Northern Minnesota. They must have been epic.

"I played against Dave many, many times over the years. I was a right-handed defenseman and he was a left-handed winger, so we lined up together every time we played. It wasn't very fun, that was for sure. It was no treat lining up against that big lug, either. He played hard and was really physical. He was for sure one of the toughest guys of my era, no question."

Ron Docken (aka "Yvon Lebrun")

"I first met Dave when we were teammates with the Johnstown Jets. As a player he was very well respected. As an enforcer, he was one of the toughest guys around during that era. In fact, I never saw him lose a fight. He was quiet off the ice, but on it he was all business. As I got to know him, though, I learned that there was a lot more to him than the fact that he could fight. He is a great guy and very well liked. Dave is a very articulate person and very talented. He was even an accomplished artist and caricaturist. So there was a lot more to Dave once you scratched the surface. He is just a very humble, quiet guy. He came from a modest background in St. Paul and never tried to be too flashy. He sort of flew under the radar, that was how he liked it, I think. He didn't care much for the limelight off the ice, but on it he would do whatever he felt was necessary to protect his teammates. He truly was 'Killer' Hanson."

Gilles Leger

"I had Dave when I was coaching the Birmingham Bulls back in the old WHA. We made a big trade with the Detroit Red

Wings to get him. In fact, it was historic in that it was the first ever trade between the rival WHA and NHL. Dave was tough, though, and we wanted him, so we pulled the trigger to get him. Boy, we had some tough guys on those teams, that was for sure. We even set a professional hockey record for the most penalty minutes ever accumulated in a single season, if that is any indication. The players would almost have to call out which guys they wanted to fight ahead of time because so many of them wanted to drop the gloves. Those were some wild times. Overall, Dave was a good player and he knew his role. He was tough, but he left that toughness on the ice. He was a real gentleman off the ice and was very respected by both his teammates as well as his opponents. He is a great family man and an overall great guy. I am just proud to call him my friend."

Charley Hallman, St. Paul Hockey Writer

"When I was a cub reporter for the St. Paul Pioneer Press, my sports editor used to send me to high school hockey games night after night. I wound up covering the St. Paul City Conference kids during an era where they didn't get a lot of coverage compared to the suburban kids. After many, many years of covering hockey from high school to college to professional, I got to be a pretty good judge of talent. Before long I started scouting for some local junior teams. I eventually came upon a kid from Humboldt High School, Dave Hanson, who was just an outstanding athlete. He was this big, strong, blond-haired, blue-eyed kid who was just tougher than nails. He didn't score a lot of goals but he played a solid wing, he finished his checks, and he liked to get back on defense. I really liked him right from the get-go. I told my good friend Herb Brooks that he should take a look at this kid. Herbie was coaching in the junior ranks at the time and was just about to take over as the coach at the University of Minnesota. Well, Dave wound up graduating from high school and then going on to play for a year with the St. Paul Vulcans, a local junior team. They were really, really good. I mean, I think all 18 kids went on to play college hockey, that was how good those kids were.

"Off the ice, Dave was one of the nicest guys you would ever meet. On the ice, though, he was one of the toughest suckers out there. I mean he could fight, he was just extraordinary. He was also a great, great skater. He struggled early on, though. In fact, the first new pair of hockey skates he ever got were purchased for him by Herbie Brooks and given to him by me. We gave them to him under the table so that he could have some new skates and be able to keep up with the other kids. He came from a good family but didn't come from a lot of money. It meant a great deal to him. We wanted him to learn how to skate the proper way and his old beat-up skates were preventing him from doing certain things out on the ice. So we just did it. We got him some sticks too. We wanted to help him out; he was a great kid with a lot of potential.

"Before long, the pro scouts were telling Dave that he was good enough to make the jump to play pro hockey. He and I had hit it off and he would come to me for advice. Well, I really liked the kid so I wound up breaking the bond of journalistic ethics, I suppose, and represented him as his agent. I never took a dime on the deal, I just did it to help him out. He was a great kid and I wanted him to succeed at the next level. I was really rooting for him. He came from a very modest upbringing and didn't get recruited like a lot of the suburban kids, and I wanted this kid to get his shot. Now, Glen Sonmor was the coach of the WHA's St. Paul Fighting Saints at the time and he and I had been friends for years. Glen loved the kid and wanted to sign him. So we sat down for about an hour and hammered out a three-year contract for him. It was for good money, too—it was a really nice deal for him.

"Dave signed with the team and was sent down to get some seasoning with the team's top farm club, the Johnstown Jets of the old Eastern League. Glen's father-in-law was the team's general manager at the time and we knew that he would take good care of him. Dave thrived down there and really honed his skills as not only an enforcer, but also a very skilled two-way player. He, along with the Carlson brothers, terrorized that league en route to making quite a name for themselves. That would be the beginning of his professional career, and I was really proud to have played a small part in his success.

"I remember sitting with him early on when he was just a kid and having lunch together. He would tell me his dreams of one day being able to make his living from hockey. He wanted to be the best player he could be and he was willing to do whatever it took to make that dream a reality. I tell you what, I am so proud of him. To see all of the success he had as a player and then as a coach and manager, it is just wonderful. And he did it the right way, never taking any shortcuts. I am truly proud to have been a small part of his life because he is a good man. I couldn't be happier for all of his success, both as a career man and also from all of the notoriety he gained from the movie. He is just a classy guy. I had my favorites over the years and Dave was definitely at the very top of the list."

Doug Woog

"David played for me back in the early '70s when I was coaching the St. Paul Vulcans junior team. I first met him when he was at Humboldt High School in St. Paul. Not a lot of kids came out of West St. Paul in those days, so he was special. He was one of the top city kids at the time and had already established himself as one of the toughest kids around. He was raw, though, and we didn't know how good he really was because he didn't have a lot of coaching and didn't play against a lot of the top talent from the area. So we brought him in and he played really well for us. He was a big, rugged guy who liked to play physical hockey. He didn't go out looking for trouble out on the ice, but he never shied away from it. If anybody was interested in testing him, he would oblige and usually make them pay for it. If there was ever an altercation out there, he would be their first guy to step in and would make sure none of his teammates got taken advantage of. Man, he was a tough kid, one of the toughest I ever coached in my career. He wasn't cheap, though, he played it straight. This was back in an era where there were no facemasks and the kids could fight whenever they wanted to. So Dave made the most of that opportunity and used that time to better himself as a player.

"David is just a guy who came from very modest means and really made something of himself. He did it his own way, too, which you really have to respect. He was just a tough competitor and never gave up. I am very proud of all that he has accomplished in life. He has always been an extremely loyal person and is just a great guy. We have stayed in touch over the years and it is neat to see how far he has come. He gives back by teaching kids now, too, which is really neat. I have a lot of respect for him, I really do. I just love the guy, he is one of my all-time favorites."

Rob Ramage, Former Teammate

"I first met Dave back in 1978 when I was just an 18-year-old kid and got signed by the Birmingham Bulls of the old WHA. They had terrorized the league the year before and had even set some sort of record for the most penalty minutes ever for a professional hockey team. Well, the team got into some financial troubles and wound up dealing away all of their top guys after that season and decided to go with a bunch of young kids instead. In addition to myself, they brought in Craig Hartsburg, Pat Riggin, Rick Vaive, and Michel Goulet, among others, and we were known as the 'Baby Bulls.'

"Now, because all of the top guys were gone from the season before, including all of the enforcers—Frank Beaton, Steve Durbano, Gilles Bilodeau, and Dave Hanson—the other teams in the league really went after us. They wanted to intimidate us and make us pay for what they had just gone through the season prior when we were the 'Brawling Bulls.' Well, we were a bunch of 18- and 19-year-old kids and had no chance against some of these guys. They wanted to kill us. So management brought back in Dave Hanson early in the season to protect us. He had been with the Detroit Red Wings, but they dealt for him to bring him back. He rode shotgun for us and gave us all a little breathing room out there. We were thrilled, let me tell you.

"The only thing I had known about Dave prior to that was that he was 'Killer Hanson' from *Slap Shot*. We were thrilled to get someone of his stature and toughness on our team, though, and he really made a huge difference for us that year. His reputation alone was enough for other teams to leave us kids alone.

It was amazing. He was a very respected guy and made us all feel a little bit braver out on the ice. Whenever there was a bench-clearer, I made sure to hang out by Dave. That was a good place to be during those situations, that was for sure.

"We just got to know each other that year and became good friends. So our friendship started all those years ago and is still going strong today. He put me under his wing and was almost like a big brother to me. He taught me how to lift weights after practices and helped me out a great deal. He was really big into off-ice training and using Nautilus machines, stuff that was unheard of at the time. He had been training with some football players from the University of Alabama and was just a specimen. He told me that I was now playing with grown men and that if I wanted to have a long career in professional hockey that I needed to get a lot stronger. So every day after practice we would head over to campus to train together and work out with these guys. I didn't know what I was doing at first, but Dave worked with me and really helped me out. After a while it really started to make a difference and the results were amazing. I started to gain a lot more confidence and it translated into more scoring for me. It was, for sure, a huge catalyst in jump-starting my career.

"The next year all of us Baby Bulls went on to get drafted in the NHL, and I had the good fortune of being selected No. 1 overall by the Colorado Rockies. I wound up playing in the NHL for a total of 14 seasons and I owe a lot of that to Dave Hanson. No question. He is a great guy and someone I am proud to call my friend. I was in awe of him back in those days and really admired him. He was a great leader and just a decent, honest guy who I really respected a great deal. He taught me about toughness, about having a work ethic, and about what it takes to be successful at this level. I can't thank him enough and tell him how much I appreciated that guidance and wisdom all those years ago. He is just a solid guy and one of my all-time favorite people."

Jerry Houser (aka "Dave 'Killer' Carlson")

"As a player, Dave was this hugely intimidating presence. But when you got to know him off the ice, he was the nicest, sweetest guy. He was this quiet, artistic, sensitive guy who was very intellectual. It was like Jekyll and Hyde. Dave is just a real person, a great guy. He was all about having fun and I really admired that about him. I was proud to play him as "Killer Carlson" in the movie, and I am proud to call him my friend today. He is a great person. He really taught me a lot about hockey and about how to approach different situations out on the ice too. I mean he would watch my fights and my on-ice stuff and really coach me on what to do in order to make it look authentic. So I appreciated that a lot too. You know, it was just such a thrill to work with Dave and the Carlson brothers. These guys were so much fun to be around. They were a big part of why the movie turned out the way it did because they kept it real. They lightened up the mood and got everybody to relax. I have been on a lot of movie sets in my day and this one was by far the most laid back. That element of sincere, relaxed fun comes out in the movie, too, which is really neat. Just being together with all of the guys on the set was like being on a team. We all hung out together, drank together, and pulled pranks on each other. It was like a fraternity, we genuinely liked each other. Viewers are attracted to that feeling, that raw emotion. Sure, the content of the movie was fantastic, but the actors really liked each other and wanted to be around each other. That genuine camaraderie was conveyed in the movie and played a part in its success, too."

Bud Hanson, Dave's Dad

"Dave is a very fine person. He has never changed from the kid I always knew him as. He had goals in his life and he accomplished them. He is just a great guy. He was a very good athlete, too, just outstanding. Sports just came naturally to him, it was his passion. Hockey and football were his best sports, but as a kid he played them all. In football, as an All-State running back, his coach just ran him and ran him, but he never tired out. He loved to hit guys and I think he loved to get hit, too. He was like that in all sports. Whether he was going over water ski jumps or racing his bicycle, he was fearless. Hockey would prove to be his favorite and he would prove to be a diamond in the rough. He was a good skater and he was tough. He was a strong leader and did whatever he felt was necessary to help his team to win. He was just naturally strong and tough. Lord knows he didn't get it from me! He always fought fair, though, and did it with respect. He did live by the honor code, that was very important to him. Overall, I just couldn't be prouder of Dave. He is a great dad and a great husband. They have a great family and that has always come first in his life. Yes, Dave is a real stand-up guy. He has certainly made our family very proud. I love him very much."

Yvon Barrette (aka "Denis Lemieux")

"The Hanson Brothers were very different in real life than that of the characters they played in the movie. On the ice they were goons, but off the ice they were real gentlemen. They were such nice guys, all of them. We had so much fun together. We partied a lot and just had fun hanging out with each other. Those were great times. As an actor, however, I will say this: I studied the Hansons very much because I wanted to learn from them what it was like to be a real hockey player in that type of environment. They got to be themselves in the movie, very carefree, and just have fun. As actors, we had to learn how to be hockey players. It was tough, but they made it easier for all of us."

Paul Stewart

"I will never forget the first game I played against Dave, it was back in 1975. I was with Binghamton and he was with Johnstown. I had heard about the Carlson boys, and about how tough they were, but wasn't familiar with Dave. Needless to say, we became very familiar with each other on our first shift. We went at it a few times and, yeah, he was pretty tough. You know, going into Johnstown reminds me of the old Tennyson poem 'The Charge of the Light Brigade,' which starts out: 'Into the valley of death we went...' You see, this was around the same time when the 'Philly Flu' had come about, where guys got mysteriously ill right before they would have to play the Broad Street Bullies. It was the same thing with Johnstown, nobody wanted to face those guys. They had some really tough players on those teams, I mean really tough. Those guys were known for all of their bench-clearing brawls and intimidating tactics. I held my own, though, and did all right against those boys. You know, I have always maintained that if it weren't for guys like Dave Hanson, the Carlson brothers, Terry O'Reilly, and Stan Jonathon, I wouldn't have a reputation. Those guys were tough and you had to earn their respect, no doubt about it. That was the way hockey was back in those days—tough. If you couldn't hack it, then you weren't going to stick around for very long. So I embraced it and did whatever I had to do in order to help my teammates win.

"Dave was the same way and he was very good at his job. He wasn't dirty or anything, either. He was a very respected player and I appreciated that about him. Whenever I fought Dave I knew it was going to be rough, but clean and honest. You have to respect that. He played hard and he hit you straight. He wasn't vicious or dirty or anything like that. He was just hard-boiled tough. He was also a solid hockey player. He could play the game and was very versatile. It was unfortunate that he sort of got labeled as a fighter, because, had a coach really used him properly, he could have been an All-Star. He could pass and shoot and skate, but was only really utilized in certain situations—which was too bad in my opinion.

"As far as *Slap Shot* went, being a part of the movie was a lot of fun. I was a player for the Long Island Ducks in the movie and I had a great time. My big scene came when Paul Newman was antagonizing our goalie, Handrahan. When he said 'Hey, Handrahan, your wife is a dyke. She sucks pussy,' I was standing right beside him. It was pretty funny.

"You know, I had played against Dave and the Carlson brothers a year prior to the movie, but really got to know them once we started filming it. They were a riot. We all used to hang out and drink during the filming and it was a blast. The movie was so realistic, it really was. The bus scenes especially, that was exactly how it was in those days. That part of the movie was no parody, they nailed it. The fight scenes were pretty accurate, too. I mean that stuff really went on in those days. Those were crazy times.

"Then, once the movie wrapped, we all went back to playing hockey and back to beating the hell out of each other. We all wound up playing against each other over the ensuing years in the WHA and throughout the minor leagues. We were all pals, but we fought each other like cats and dogs, too. Hey, that was just what we did. It wasn't personal, it was just hockey.

"You know, even though we fought each other a lot, Dave and I became good friends after hockey and I think the world of him. I once told him that one of my only regrets in hockey is that I was never a teammate of his, because we could have really terrorized the league together. He got a kick out of that.

"Dave and I went up against each other a lot over our careers. The next time we squared off was in the WHA, when he was with Birmingham and I was with Cincinnati. The Birmingham Bulls, those guys were animals, they loved to fight and mix it up. They were nuts. Well, the reason I got called up to Cincinnati was because of the 'Thanksgiving Night Massacre,' where the 'Bullies' wreaked havoc on the Stingers. It was brutal. Because of that I got called up from their AHL farm team in Binghamton back in 1977. So I guess I sort of owe Dave a thanks for indirectly getting me called up to the WHA!"

Jim Boo, Former Teammate

"Dave is just a great guy. If you were ever going to have to pick teams from scratch, he would be the first guy I would take. He is a guy you want to go to war with. He is just a great teammate and a great friend. Dave and I were teammates together back in junior hockey when we played with the Vulcans. He was a really good player and man, he was tough. We wound up winning a national championship together that year, which was a lot of fun. I couldn't be happier for all his success in life, it couldn't have happened to a finer guy. He is always there for people when they need a hand and is just a good person.

"Dave and I even studied martial arts together, which was something we did competitively for about four or five years. He was a great athlete and he was really into it. I tell you what, luckily for both of us, those karate moves came in handy on more than one occasion when we would wind up out in the parking lot of a bar after some drunk idiot would want to see how tough we really were. Needless to say, those brawls never lasted too long. We would take care of business and then head back inside for more beers. We even worked as bouncers together at the Blue Chip bar in St. Paul. Half the time Dave and I would have to finish the fights that the owner would start, but we didn't care. We were having fun and didn't mind mopping up his messes. It was good practice for us as far as we were concerned. And hey, those were the days when you could fight a guy and not have to worry about getting stabbed or shot, unlike today where you never know what would happen. Those were great times, they really were. Old-time hockey, that was what it was all about."

Glen Sonmor, Former Coach

"I first met Dave back in 1973 when he was playing junior hockey with the St. Paul Vulcans. I was the coach of the St. Paul Fighting Saints, of the WHA, and saw that he had a lot of potential. He was a big, strong kid who had a lot of raw talent and was tough as hell. He was very rugged and we liked him a lot. So we went ahead and drafted him and then sent him down to get some seasoning at our minor league affiliate, which was the Johnstown Jets. He tore it up down there, racking up a whole bunch of penalty minutes in just two seasons. We finally called him up in 1977, after they shot the movie, but he only wound up playing a handful of games with the Saints that year before the team folded due to financial problems. Dave wound up going on to finish that season with the New England Whalers, but I was able to reacquire him two years later when I took over as the head coach with the Birmingham Bulls.

"There, he wound up racking up a whopping 241 penalty minutes in just 42 games, which was an ungodly amount. What is even more amazing about that statistic, though, is that he finished ranked fourth in penalty minutes on the team that year. We had four guys who were just tougher than hell: Dave 'Killer' Hanson, Frankie 'Never' Beaton, Gilles 'Bad News' Billodeau, and Steve Durbano. People always wondered why Durbano, maybe the toughest of the bunch, didn't have a nickname—to which I would respond, 'He didn't need one, all of the opposing players knew he was f*cking crazy.' We terrorized opposing teams through toughness and intimidation that year. It was a tactic and it worked. We even set a major league hockey record for penalty minutes, breaking the old mark that was established by Philadelphia's infamous 'Broad Street Bullies.'

"Hockey down there was a tough sell and we had to find a way to fill up the seats in our arena. Say what you want, but the fans loved it. Hey, it's like the old saying goes: 'If we don't stop all this fighting in hockey, we're going to have to build bigger rinks.' Sure, some of the fans didn't care for our style of play, but that was what the management demanded. So I did my job and gave them what they wanted. I tell you what, there was never a dull moment with those guys. Those were some wild times, let me tell you. Dave also scored 16 and 22 points in those seasons, too, which proved that he was a good hockey player and had a lot of talent.

"I wound up going on to coach the North Stars in 1978 and I was able to get Dave one last time in 1979–80 back up in Minnesota. He only wound up playing a couple dozen games for us, but it was great to have him on the team. Unfortunately, I couldn't convince Louie Nanne, the GM at the time, to keep him around after that. He wanted to go with quicker guys who could score more goals and that was that. Dave was an energy player who could go out there and agitate and just stir things up by wreaking havoc. You know, a big hit or a big punch were sometimes just as good as a big goal. They can all swing the momentum and Dave was a spark plug that way.

"I just always appreciated guys like Dave, who were willing to get their hands dirty for the good of the team. He is one of the best fighters I have ever seen, and I have been playing hockey for about 70 years—so that says a lot. Besides being big and strong, he was decisive. What I mean by that is that sometimes guys can be tentative when they get into a fight. So when they square off they might be thinking and plotting about what they were going to do. Well, Dave didn't hesitate. As soon as he made up his mind to drop the gloves, he was swinging. That usually meant a quick and decisive ending for the other guy. While the other guy was thinking about and deciding what he wanted to do or whether or not he wanted to be there, Dave might have already smacked him four or five times in the chops. Odds were pretty slim that a guy could recover from that. He was just a devastating puncher.

"As long as I was coaching, Dave was always welcome on my teams. He was a hard-working guy who always stood up for his teammates. He was intense and could really intimidate the opposition. He took guys out with authority and was very tough for opposing players to play against. He loved to finish his checks and could just hit like hell. He was just a ferocious hitter. He would just do whatever was asked of him and was never afraid to sacrifice his body for the good of the team. He was a throwback, he really was. I mean, if there was ever any trouble or if any opposing player was taking liberties with one of our star players, then he was always the first guy to step in and straighten things out. He was a very valuable commodity. You don't win without guys like Dave Hanson. On top of that, he was a great presence in the locker room and was just a very likeable person. I had a great deal of respect for him back then and I still do to this day."

Will "Woody" Espey, Johnstown Jets and Charlestown Chiefs Stick Boy

"I was the stick boy for the visiting team before becoming the stick boy for the Jets and used to love listening to the tough guys from opposing teams posturing in the locker room about what they were going to do if they were forced to tangle with Dave Hanson. The body checks he threw were of the variety that had players slow to get to their feet and even slower to get back to their benches. Hanson would widen his stance, line up the skater, and God forbid if that guy had his head down. Yes, Mr. Dave 'Killer' Hanson certainly did illustrate the heart and soul of hockey in those days."

Chapter **16**

Looking Through Hanson Brothers Glasses into the Future

AS I WRAP UP MY LIFE STORY, I'M AMAZED AT JUST HOW FORTUNATE I've been ever since the good Lord brought me into this world. Sure, there have been some setbacks and disappointments along the way—my mom, Marilyn, died of liver cancer at 57; my only brother, Baby Durk, died unexpectedly from a heart attack at 49; Gram and Pap passed away at the golden age of 97 and 93, respectively—but overwhelmingly I've had more than my share of wonderful blessings. The quality people who have touched my life have been countless, and the jerks have been few. Some have made more of a significant and positive impact on developing my character than others, but all have played an important role in who I am and what I stand for. I still have many of my loved ones in my life, with the most treasured being my wife and children. Sue and I have watched our children grow up to be incredible people. Our daughters are still close by and I still get to watch my son play hockey while he pursues his dream at the University of Notre Dame.

My life continues to be filled with fun and much of it still comes from my get-togethers with Jeff and Steve as we continue to put on the glasses, the foil, and the Chiefs jerseys, traveling around the world all these years later. It has been great meeting millions of fans of all ages, genders, and nationalities and helping to raise millions of dollars for many needy causes.

I also coach young aspiring hockey players today and try to pass on some of the knowledge I've learned over the years to them. I want to be a positive influence to them like so many have been to me. I really believe that team sports, and hockey in particular, are not only something that can help kids stay mentally active and physically fit, but they are a great avenue to help kids develop many of life's skills. We—as parents, teachers, and coaches—need to work with our kids to show them how to play the game the right way, through hard work and with respect.

I remember asking Doug Woog, while he was coaching at the University of Minnesota, what he thought was the biggest difference in hockey today from when I played for him with the Vulcans. Doug said without hesitation that it's the parents. He said when he played the parents would just be supportive spectators and nothing more. Too many parents think that their child needs to get a full-ride college scholarship and play in the NHL. They just won't let the kid play for his own enjoyment and for what he might get out of it long term, even if he isn't the superstar his mom and dad think he is. In spite of this, whenever I have parents making my life miserable with their fanatical behavior, I reflect on the people who have touched my life through sports and think about what they meant to me. I patiently push through the parental muck to hang in there for the benefit of the kids and, so far, I've been able to do that. Some of my personal rewards have come from that one boy thanking me years later for taking the time to be his coach. Those are the things that keep me going.

While this book certainly doesn't have every detail of what has happened in my life, I've tried to write about some of the things that I really felt were important, interesting, funny, entertaining, and that have contributed to building my life. I'm hopeful that what I wrote will put a smile on the face of my family and friends, many of whom were important parts of my life. I also hope it will provide a reason to chuckle for the millions of avid hockey, *Slap Shot*, and Hanson Brothers fans throughout the world. Just maybe there are some who might like to know a little more about how a kid from the country dirt roads of Wisconsin would grow up in a tough city neighborhood and one day become a cultlike figure known around the world to men, women, and children of all ages for a movie role he shared with his two fictitious brothers and the legendary Paul Newman.

As for my own legacy? I am sure I will always be linked to the movie, and that is fine by me. I first want to be known as a good father and husband, that is what has always been most important in my life. As a hockey player, I want to be remembered as a guy who lived by the honor code. The code was about one thing, respect, and that was absolutely earned as an enforcer. If you played honest, fought clean, and didn't try to embarrass your opponent, you could expect the same treatment in return. But if you were a guy who ran around and picked his spots, or fought guys when they were injured, or grabbed them at the end of their shifts, then you would be dealt with accordingly in this business. Those guys did not have the respect of their peers. Everybody knew who the legitimate tough guys were out there.

What can I say? I loved to play hockey and I loved to fight. I certainly wasn't a goal scorer, but I just loved dropping the gloves out there. It was such a rush. To know that you beat a guy and to hear the crowd roar, it was instant gratification. And then to go over to your bench and see your guys all cheering for you in appreciation, it didn't get any better than that. As much as I loved to score a goal, I also loved connecting on a perfect punch or landing a body check. I had no reservations on who I would fight and I just really enjoyed that sort of primal challenge. I didn't win 'em all, that was for sure, but I won the majority of them. And if I did lose, it certainly didn't deter me from fighting again. In fact, it probably drove me even harder. Standing up for my teammates and just being there for them really motivated me.

I feel that I have been incredibly blessed and extremely lucky beyond anything I could have ever imagined. So much of my life has been fun and exciting, and *Slap Shot* and the Hanson Brothers are responsible for much of that. Even after 30 years since the original *Slap Shot* was released, the Hanson Brothers continue to grow in popularity and keep hitting the ice rinks with the same hair, flair, and enthusiasm for life. It was that youthful exuberance, innocence, and unabashed love of the game of hockey that got them thrown into jail all those years ago; and it was their coach who prophetically declared to the police sergeant: "They're not criminals, they're folk heroes." I couldn't agree more.

Yep, from a shy little boy who used to take his bath in a metal washtub to a middle-aged man who wears his hair like he's still in the '70s, I've traveled through life collecting friends, loved ones, experiences, and memories. I thank God for creating the man, the foil, and the legend.

Afterword

It's April 12, 2008, and I'm sitting in the Denver Pepsi Center ready to watch my son, Christian, and his Notre Dame teammates take on the Boston College Eagles in the NCCA Frozen Four Championship. I'm caught up in the fervor being transmitted throughout this packed house of college hockey fans. What an awesome way to spend my birthday!

Christian has battled over the last three years to become a regular member of the Fighting Irish and now he is playing as a top center on a team that had beaten all the odds to get to college hockey's biggest showcase. His underdog team became the first No. 4 seed to knock off a No. 1 seed when they beat the New Hampshire Wildcats, 7–3, in the West Regional playoffs at Colorado Springs on March 28. They went on to beat the Michigan State Spartans the next night in the Regional finals, 3–1. The real shocker came on Thursday, April 10 when Notre Dame, in their first Frozen Four appearance, beat the Michigan Wolverines—the tournament's overall top seed—in overtime by a score of 5–4. Besides the gut-wrenching battle that went on between the teams, there were two very scary moments when Christian went down to injury during that incredible game.

On his initial shift in the first period, Christian got hit behind the Michigan net and slowly skated himself off the ice on one leg. He did not play during the rest of the first period. His mother and I sat in stunned silence, full of parental concern. At the end of the first period he skated off the ice to the locker room looking all right, but we still were extremely nervous and had no idea what was wrong.

Christian came out for the second period and played the rest of the game. Although he looked fine in everyone else's eyes, I could tell that everything was not right—he was not skating as well as he had been earlier in the game. When the overtime period started, he took the opening faceoff and went down like he had been shot by a sniper in the rafters. As he lay on the ice and attempted to get up, I could tell something was seriously wrong with his leg because he could not bend it. The referee stopped the game and Christian was assisted off the ice. My heart was in my throat. He disappeared from my sight and went into the hallway next to the player's bench. A few minutes later, he was back on the bench and then on the ice. After the team won the game on a quick wrist shot from one of the rookies, I met Christian in the parking lot on his way to the bus. He told me that the team doctors suspected that he had torn his meniscus. Twice they had to manipulate his leg to pop and unlock his knee so he could continue to play. He then said there was no way he was not playing in the Frozen Four Championship Game and my heart exploded with fear and pride at the same time.

As I stood for the playing of the national anthem at the Frozen Four Championship game, I reflected (as tears welled up in my eyes) on how incredibly fortunate I am to have an outstanding young man for a son. Christian had set goals for himself as a young boy to be a good citizen, be a good student, and someday earn a scholarship to play college hockey, and he had achieved those goals. I was overwhelmed with emotion while I stood there with my hand over my heart listening to the "Star Spangled Banner" and looking down on my boy standing at attention with his gold helmet tucked under his arm, ready to play the game of his life. My mind flashed back to the first time he put on skates and I quickly ran through the years to now. A huge lump swelled up in my throat.

Although Notre Dame lost the game, it was still an awesome birthday for me. There is no greater reward than to play a positive role in a child's development and to have that child grow up to be a wonderful person. In my 50-plus years in this world, I could not remember a more proud moment than this. Yet I won't be surprised if there are more moments like this to come.